Oracle Application Server
10*g* Essentials

Other Oracle resources from O'Reilly

Related titles

Java Programming with Oracle JDBC	Oracle in a Nutshell
Learning Oracle PL/SQL	Oracle PL/SQL Language Pocket Reference
Mastering Oracle SQL	Oracle PL/SQL Programming
Optimizing Oracle Performance	Oracle SQL Tuning Pocket Reference
Oracle Essentials	Oracle SQL*Plus Pocket Reference

Oracle Books Resource Center

oracle.oreilly.com is a complete catalog of O'Reilly's books on Oracle and related technologies, including sample chapters and code examples.

oreillynet.com is the essential portal for developers interested in open and emerging technologies, including new platforms, programming languages, and operating systems.

Conferences

O'Reilly brings diverse innovators together to nurture the ideas that spark revolutionary industries. We specialize in documenting the latest tools and systems, translating the innovator's knowledge into useful skills for those in the trenches. Visit *conferences.oreilly.com* for our upcoming events.

Safari Bookshelf (*safari.oreilly.com*) is the premier online reference library for programmers and IT professionals. Conduct searches across more than 1,000 books. Subscribers can zero in on answers to time-critical questions in a matter of seconds. Read the books on your Bookshelf from cover to cover or simply flip to the page you need. Try it today with a free trial.

Oracle Application Server
10*g* Essentials

Rick Greenwald, Robert Stackowiak,
and Donald Bales

O'REILLY®

Beijing · Cambridge · Farnham · Köln · Paris · Sebastopol · Taipei · Tokyo

Oracle Application Server 10g Essentials
by Rick Greenwald, Robert Stackowiak, Donald Bales

Published by O'Reilly Media, Inc., 1005 Gravenstein Highway North, Sebastopol, CA 95472.

O'Reilly books may be purchased for educational, business, or sales promotional use. Online editions are also available for most titles (*safari.oreilly.com*). For more information, contact our corporate/institutional sales department: (800) 998-9938 or *corporate@oreilly.com*.

Editor:	Deborah Russell
Production Editor:	Mary Anne Weeks Mayo
Cover Designer:	Ellie Volckhausen
Interior Designer:	Melanie Wang

Printing History:

August 2004:	First Edition.

RepKover™ This book uses RepKover,™ a durable and flexible lay-flat binding.

ISBN: 0-596-00621-7
[M]

For my family, LuAnn, Elinor, Josephine, and Robin, who have granted me a life more wonderful than I could have imagined.

—Rick Greenwald

To Jodie, my love, in our 25th year of marriage, and to my boys Nick and Mike, who are passing through their teenage years almost "like everyone else" their age.

—Robert Stackowiak

For my wife Diane and daughter Kristyn, who sacrifice their time and my presence so that I may write.

—Donald Bales

Table of Contents

Preface

For more than 15 years, Oracle® Corporation has been one of the world's leading technology companies. Much of the company's reputation is built on its enterprise database product—the leading database for online transaction processing and enterprise applications for more than a decade. In recent years, however, Oracle has enhanced its product offerings to encompass a complete technology stack, including the E-Business Suite (providing applications), the Collaboration Suite (providing communication throughout an organization), and Oracle Application Server, which is the focus of this book.

Oracle Application Server is a middle-tier application platform suite offering a variety of capabilities. Although Oracle Application Server has grown in popularity and functionality in recent years, there has been a dearth of third-party books about the product. Our goal is to remedy this situation.

 In this book, we use the term *Oracle Application Server* to refer mainly to Oracle Application Server 10g, the latest release of Oracle's product. Where necessary, we also describe features in the previous product releases, particularly in Oracle9i Application Server. Many features are identical across versions. Note, however, that because some readers may be using older releases, when we describe a new feature that was first made available in a particular release, we indicate that fact to help avoid confusion.

About This Book

Five years ago, two of us were the principal coauthors of *Oracle Essentials*, a new kind of book that attempted to describe all the underlying principles that shape the Oracle database, one written concisely for an intelligent audience. *Oracle Essentials* was not a large book—there were fewer than 350 pages in that first edition (we have since written two more editions)—but it covered a lot of ground. It did not attempt to describe detailed syntax; instead, it focused on broad architectural concepts and important features.

The more we thought about it, the more we realized that Oracle Application Server was, in some ways, even more in need of this type of treatment. Oracle Application Server contains many different types of functionality, from its basic web server features to its support of business intelligence. Many people who consider using the product are familiar with only a portion of the entire range of capabilities or are overwhelmed by the choices provided. Few people have a grasp of how larger issues, such as the interplay between components or the various architectural choices for deploying Oracle Application Server.

Hence this book. The goals of *Oracle Application Server 10g Essentials*, summarized in the next section, are similar to the goals we tried to achieve in our earlier book that many people have found very helpful. We hope we have met our objectives for this book as well.

Goals of This Book

Our main goal is to give you a foundation for understanding and using Oracle Application Server effectively and efficiently. Therefore, we wrote with these principles in mind:

Focus
> We've tried to concentrate on the most important Oracle Application Server issues and components. Each chapter aims to provide a comprehensive but concise discussion of how Oracle handles an area and the repercussions of that treatment.

Brevity
> One of the first decisions we made was to concentrate on principles rather than syntax and to keep the book short and well-focused on underlying concepts. Including myriad syntax diagrams and examples would defeat this purpose. Moreover, such material is readily available in the product documentation.

Acceleration
> We've tried to make this an ideal first Oracle Application Server book for a wide spectrum of Oracle users—but not the last! You will very likely have to refer to Oracle documentation or other, more specific books for more details about using Oracle Application Server and its components. However, we hope this book will act as an accelerator for you. With this book's solid foundation, you will be able to take detailed information from other sources and put it to the best use.

Among us, the authors have more than 40 years of experience with Oracle. We've tried to apply that experience here as best we can.

Audience for This Book

We wrote this book for people at all levels of Oracle expertise, as well as for those with varying degrees of familiarity with the different areas of capabilities within Oracle Application Server. There are many types of readers:

- Those concerned with using and managing web servers
- Those who do Java™ development and deployment
- Those who use Oracle's own tools, such as Oracle Forms and Oracle Reports
- Those who use and develop for Oracle Application Server Portal
- Those who use and administer business intelligence, mobile, or integration software

And these are only a few of the "typical" Oracle Application Server users.

Chances are that some of the items in this brief list apply to you, and some don't. However, because Oracle Application Server comes with all this functionality, we believe you can use the product more effectively if you have background that helps you understand the varied capabilities of Oracle Application Server.

Our guiding principle has been to present this information compactly without making it overly tutorial. We figure that the most important ratio in a book such as this is the amount of useful information you get balanced against the time it takes you to get it. We sincerely hope this volume provides a terrific bang for the buck.

Structure of This Book

This book is divided into 15 chapters and 1 appendix, as follows.

Chapter 1, *Introducing Oracle Application Server*, describes the range of Oracle Application Server capabilities and some of the options for purchase and installation.

Chapter 2, *Architecture*, describe the basic architecture of Oracle Application Server and optional deployment architectures used to provide scalability and availability. This chapter provides the core technical information needed to effectively use the product.

Chapter 3, *Systems Management*, provides a brief overview of the processes and tools used to manage the complete Oracle Application Server environment.

Chapter 4, *Security and Identity Management*, looks at how Oracle Application Server provides security and identity management services that can be used for all the components that make up the Oracle Application Server environment.

Chapter 5, *Oracle HTTP Server*, is the first chapter in a series of chapters examining specific components of Oracle Application Server. The Oracle HTTP Server is the core of the Oracle Application Server environment.

Chapter 6, *Oracle Application Server Containers for J2EE*, covers the OC4J container that runs Java applications. Oracle Application Server, in its most basic state, is used as a Java deployment platform, and OC4J is the target of these deployments.

Chapter 7, *Caching*, looks at the three caches used in Oracle Application Server—the Oracle Application Server Web Cache, which is used for all types of content, and the Java Object Cache and Web Object Cache, which are used with OC4J. Use of these caches can significantly accelerate the performance of Oracle Application Server.

Chapter 8, *Java Development*, covers Java development and deployment with Oracle Application Server.

Chapter 9, *Oracle Development*, looks at three Oracle-specific development technologies—PL/SQL, Oracle Application Server Forms Service, and Oracle Application Server Reports Services—and describes how they are used and deployed with Oracle Application Server.

Chapter 10, *XML Development*, describes the use of Oracle Application Server with XML.

Chapter 11, *Web Services*, explores the use of the Web Services technology with Oracle Application Server and its component development options.

Chapter 12, *Business Intelligence Components*, looks at the issues facing business intelligence users and the ways in which Oracle Application Server Portal, Oracle Reports, and Discoverer address these issues. The chapter also touches on data mining and management of the business intelligence components in Oracle Application Server.

Chapter 13, *Oracle Application Server Portal*, covers the OracleAS Portal product and its range of capabilities.

Chapter 14, *Oracle Application Server Wireless*, describes the use of Oracle Application Server as a platform for mobile computing.

Chapter 15, *Integration Components*, describes the integration software that is included with some editions of Oracle Application Server.

The appendix, *Additional Resources*, lists a variety of additional resources—both online and offline—you can use to learn more about the topics presented in this book.

About the Oracle Application Server Software

The way to get the most out of this book is to actually try out the Oracle Application Server software itself. Oracle Corporation invites you to download the product for free from the Oracle Technology Network (OTN). You can find out how to do that by going to:

> *http://www.oracle.com/appserver/books/*

There you will find documentation, instructions for obtaining the software, and a wealth of information about all aspects of the product.

Conventions Used in This Book

The following typographical conventions are used in this book:

Italic

> Used for file and directory names, URLs, emphasis, and new terms where they are defined.

`Constant width`

> Used for code examples and literals.

`Constant width italic`

> In code examples, indicates an element (e.g., a parameter) that you supply.

UPPERCASE

> Generally indicates Oracle keywords.

lowercase

> In code examples, generally indicates user-defined items such as variables.

> This icon indicates a tip, suggestion, or general note. For example, we'll tell you if you need to use a particular version of Oracle or if an operation requires certain privileges.

> This icon indicates a warning or caution. For example, we'll tell you if Oracle doesn't behave as you'd expect or if a particular operation negatively impacts performance.

How to Contact Us

Please address comments and questions concerning this book to the publisher:

> O'Reilly Media, Inc.
> 1005 Gravenstein Highway North
> Sebastopol, CA 95472
> (800) 998-9938 (in the United States or Canada)
> (707) 829-0515 (international/local)
> (707) 829-0104 (fax)

There is a web page for this book, which lists errata and any additional information. You can access this page at:

> *http://www.oreilly.com/catalog/appserver/*

To comment or ask technical questions about this book, send email to:

> *bookquestions@oreilly.com*

For more information about books, conferences, software, Resource Centers, and the O'Reilly Network, see the O'Reilly web site at:

http://www.oreilly.com

Acknowledgments

Each author has arrived at this collaboration through a different path, but we would all like to thank the many people who made this book both possible and a joy to write.

First of all, we're all grateful to each other. Bob and Rick worked together on *Oracle Essentials*, but Don was new to the mix. What was quite amazing about this process was how well we meshed. Although this particular birthing process included occasional pain and frustration, we sincerely believe the result is far better because all three of us were involved in the gestation. Many times, as one of us wrote a chapter, we would pause to consider a detailed point and then simply pose a question and move on, confident that one of our coauthors would be sure to fill in the blank, egg us on to rewrite, or deliver constructive criticism.

This book would not have been possible without the invaluable assistance of many, many people at Oracle Corporation. This book was the brainchild of Thomas Kurian and Lisa Goldstein, and we would like to give a special thank you to Lisa for her stewardship of this book, from inception to completion—the second most important birthing activity of her recent life. Many thanks to Sheila Cepero as well for her help in getting this book from the drawing board to production.

Pete Farkas provided invaluable tips on Oracle Application Server and did a tremendous job of managing the intricate review process at Oracle (as well as reviewing a number of chapters himself).

Many people helped out with that review process and although we have tried our best to mention everyone here, we may simply be unaware of certain contributions. If we have missed anyone, please let us know so that we can thank you in a subsequent printing of this book. Many thanks to our reviewers: Janga Aliminati, Christine Chan, Jim Clark, Rob Clark, Brian Conneen, Lee Cooper, John Deeb, Lars Ewe, Pete Farkas, Mikael Fransson, Gordon Jackson, Ragu Kodali, John Lang, Bruce Lowenthal, Debu Panda, Blaise Ribet, Ekkehard Rohwedder, Donald Smith, Deepak Thomas, Philipp Weckerle, and Rin Zimmerman. These reviewers did a great job of checking our text, suggesting changes, and finding errors. However, any remaining errors are exclusively our own responsibility.

And thanks as always to the terrific O'Reilly team—our editor, Debby Russell, our production editor, Mary Anne Weeks Mayo, and everyone else who had a hand in this book.

From Rick

Many thanks to Christine Chan who provided a great deal of help in clarifying technical points. Many current and former Oracle employees offered me assistance at various crucial points in the writing and editing process, including Ashesh Parekh, Todd Vender, and Nick Kritikos. A special thanks to Raz Alivarius for his contribution to Chapter 13 and to Judson Althoff for getting the ball rolling.

From Robert

Thanks to:

- The pilots at American Airlines and United Airlines. By avoiding turbulence, I was able to complete much of my portion of the book on dozens of flights while accumulating frequent flyer miles at the same time.

- Doughnut-shop owners in northern Illinois. Without these pastries, the book may have never gotten off the ground. Fortunately(?), we were powered by sugar when we created the outline.

- My management for their continuing support. I'd especially like to thank Susan Cook and Mark Salser. In addition, the guys in Oracle's Enterprise Technology Center, especially Jim Olsen and Geoff Grandstaff, were helpful in providing Grid Control access to a pool of Oracle Application Servers. I'd also like to thank the Oracle Technology Business Unit Application Server specialists and, in the area of business intelligence, Louis Nagode.

- Oracle product managers and developers. They continue to produce excellent documentation that was used in providing the basis for much of what was assembled in this book.

- Oracle's customers. As always, Oracle's customers have a practical understanding of Oracle Application Server and its components.

From Donald

I would like to thank Kathy Bishop from Corporate Communications at Red Hat for supplying me with a copy of Red Hat Enterprise on which to run Oracle Application Server 10g.

CHAPTER 1

Introducing Oracle Application Server

Over the past decade or so, IT environments—particularly those supporting large amounts of data—have been moving toward a different kind of overall architecture. In the past, most IT systems were deployed over two primary tiers: a *client*, which ran the applications, and a *server*, which hosted the database and some other types of generalized logic and services.

For a number of reasons—including scalability, availability, and security—a new tier has been introduced between the client and the server. This *middle tier* hosts a variety of services that function as intermediaries between the client machines (which act as user interfaces) and the data they use. These services include virtual machines that run application logic, specialized server processes that deliver specific functionality (e.g., reporting or integrating information into portals), and infrastructure services (e.g., handling web communications or caching information for improved performance).

Oracle Application Server consists of a set of components that deliver all this functionality, and more. For example, Oracle Application Server can:

- Respond to HTTP requests
- Run application code
- Provide a security infrastructure
- Supply some specific capabilities, such as business intelligence tools, mobile tools and applications, and a messaging system
- Offer improved performance and response time
- Provide the high availability and scalability needed in an enterprise environment

This book is designed to give you a broad overview of the components that make up Oracle Application Server and how they operate. The goal of the book is to provide you with a clear understanding of the concepts and capabilities of Oracle Application Server, particularly those available in the latest release of the product, Oracle Application Server 10*g*. This latest release provides a wide range of functionality, and this book tries to explain what that functionality is, rather than how to implement specific examples. This book isn't merely a description of components, however: it attempts to give you a thorough grounding in the concepts and technology that make up Oracle Application Server 10g. With this framework, you will be able to understand the full range of the product and more rapidly assimilate the details of the product's implementation.

This first chapter sets the stage for the rest of the book. It provides an introduction to a range of topics, most of which are described in greater detail later in the book. A few of the basics, however—for example, a brief history of the evolution of "application servers" and Oracle's packaging—are described only in this chapter, so we encourage you to read it carefully, even if you already have some familiarity with Oracle Application Server.

Before diving into the specific foundations of the product, we'll take a step back to provide some context. We'll discuss why application servers were created and how they evolved, and then we'll move on to introduce the basic features and configurations of Oracle Application Server.

Evolution of the Application Server

The concept of an application server has evolved over the past decade or so, combining several different strands of functionality that we'll explore in this section.

Early Beginnings

Long before Java or application servers existed, there was already a need to service transactions between distributed systems. The *transaction monitor* was originally created to provide a *two-phase commit*, assuring that transactions were made real only when committed on two different platforms. Examples of early transaction monitors that gained popularity include CICS (from IBM) and Tuxedo (originally developed by AT&T and later acquired by BEA). Tuxedo first appeared in 1983 and evolved from simply guaranteeing reliable transactions to also providing a middle tier for offloading the workload from transaction-processing databases. Use of the middle tier enabled the database to support many more transaction-processing users at higher performance levels.

By the mid-1980s, the transaction monitor was sometimes referred to as a *middleware solution* and soon came to be known as an *application server*. Heterogeneous computer and transaction-processing database support, via the X/Open's XA interface, first appeared in 1989. Other functionality soon was added to the middle-tier solutions, including fault tolerance, load balancing, and more security deployment models.

In 1991, Sun Microsystems began developing a new programming tool in anticipation of a coming convergence of computers and digital consumer devices. With few takers for the technology in the early 1990s, Sun's focus turned toward building and enabling applications for the newly popular Internet and to partnerships with companies such as Netscape. Possibly the most important outcome of this research was the emergence of the Java programming language in 1995.

By its nature, the Internet is enabled through a three-tier architecture consisting of the following components, which are shown in Figure 1-1:

- A thin client (browser) on the front end
- An application server in the middle tier
- A database/server on the back end

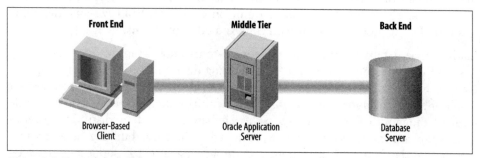

Figure 1-1. Typical three-tier configuration with Oracle Application Server

Thus, the Internet computing model created another market for middleware at the same time that Java gained popularity for Internet programming. The natural evolution of application servers toward serving and supporting Java-based applications began. Several providers of early transaction monitors merged their middleware offerings into new application server packaging.

Another result of the growth of applications deployment over the Internet via a middle tier was widespread adoption of standardized protocols that allowed these applications to communicate with each other. These protocols now include:

XML
eXtensible Markup Language

SOAP
Simple Object Access Protocol* (for messages based on XML)

WSDL
Web Services Description Language

UDDI
Universal Description, Discovery, and Integration

---

* Although this is the original expansion of the acronym, the current SOAP acronym isn't associated with this name; see Chapter 11 for details.

The last three protocols are used in the deployment of Web Services, which are getting increasing attention because they provide a way to combine different functionality from separate application modules to other applications.

Oracle and Application Servers

Oracle Corporation was born in the late 1970s as a company named RSI. Early relational database technology was provided to government agencies through custom consulting, and was then made commercially available as a product in 1979. In 1983, RSI was renamed Oracle Corporation for consistency with the database product name. At this time, the developers made a critical decision to create a portable version of Oracle (Version 3) that ran not only on DEC VAX/VMS systems (the initial platform for the product), but also on Unix and other platforms.

Early Oracle database implementations were commonly deployed on minicomputers, and many customers began to explore using distributed databases utilizing several of these relatively inexpensive platforms. At about the same time that the first application servers appeared to manage these configurations for transactions, Oracle began building distributed features in the database for handling distributed queries and two-phase transactional commits. Although Oracle was building such capabilities in the database, popular transaction-processing monitor support was added through interfaces such as XA to enable greater scalability and ensure the portability of such applications to the Oracle database.

Oracle8i, the "Internet database," added native transaction coordination with the Microsoft Transaction Server (MTS) for Windows platforms. To handle the growing number of connections needed, Oracle also added a Connection Manager feature to the database packaging.

Oracle middleware didn't appear in an application server product as such until 1997–98. Oracle Application Server 4.0 was Oracle's first complete attempt to create a Java-based middle tier in response to the growing Internet deployment model.

In 2000, Oracle redesigned its middle-tier product to enable the following:

- Application services
- Communications services
- Connectivity services
- Integration and commerce services
- Management services
- System services

Components provided in these services and with some specific solutions included industry-standard Web Services, transaction and message handling, Portal technology (including portlets and content management), clustering support, integration components, security and directory support, business intelligence solutions, and wireless support. This redesigned product was known as Oracle9i Application Server or Oracle9iAS and is the basis of the application server described in this book. The "i" was included in the product name, as it was in the Oracle8i and Oracle9i databases, to indicate Oracle's focus on the Internet computing model.

The current version of Oracle's application server product is Oracle Application Server 10g, where "g" stands for "grid," indicating Oracle's view that grid computing will be an increasingly popular model for database deployment. *Grid computing* leverages a large number of systems, also known as *nodes*, on an as-needed basis. Key components in grid computing include the following:

- Nodes
- Network attached storage (NAS) or storage area network (SAN) disk devices
- A database deployable across the nodes (Oracle Database 10g with Real Application Clusters)
- A middle-tier infrastructure for access and load balancing (Oracle Application Server 10g)

Table 1-1 provides a timeline for some key Oracle technology introductions that led to and include the Oracle Application Server family.

Table 1-1. History of Oracle technology introductions

Year	Feature
1979	Oracle Release 2: the first commercially available relational database to use SQL.
1983	Single code base for Oracle across multiple platforms.
1984	Portable toolset.
1986	Client/server and distributed Oracle relational database.
1987	CASE and 4GL toolset.
1993	Oracle7 with cost-based optimizer.
1997	Oracle8 generally available; Oracle previews Oracle Application Server 4.0.
1998	Oracle Application Server 4.0 generally available; Java-based middle tier.
1999	Oracle8i generally available; Java Virtual Machine in the database.
2001	Oracle9i Application Server generally available; Oracle integration in middle tier includes Portal technology; OracleAS Web Cache in Oracle9iAS announced.
2001	Oracle9i generally available.
2003	Oracle Database10g enables grid computing and simplifies and automates key management tasks; Oracle Application Server 10g generally available.

The Oracle Application Server Family

Oracle Application Server 10g is the name of the most recent major version of the Oracle Application Server family of products. These products all share common source code. The family includes the following packages:

Oracle Application Server Java Edition
  A version targeted for Java developers.

Oracle Application Server Standard Edition
  A version targeted for deployment requiring less middle-tier functionality.

Oracle Application Server Enterprise Edition
  A version targeted for more complex deployment. This version offers additional functionality, including business intelligence and integration components and the OracleAS Personalization and OracleAS Wireless features.

 At the time of this writing, these were the only packages available for Oracle Application Server. If additional packages or bundles are offered, we'll provide updates on the web page for this book (see the Preface).

Oracle focuses development around a single source-code model for all its products, including Oracle Application Server. The Oracle Application Server releases are available today on Windows, RedHat and SuSE Linux, and on Unix platforms such as HP Compaq Tru64, HP/UX, IBM AIX, and Sun Solaris. Because features are consistent across platforms for implementations of Oracle Application Server, companies can migrate easily to various hardware vendors and operating systems while leveraging their investments in Oracle technology. This development strategy also enables Oracle to focus on implementing new features only once in its product set, instead of having to add functionality at different times to different implementations.

Oracle Application Server 10g includes a web listener based on the popular Apache Web Server distribution. It also includes support for Java 2 Enterprise Edition (J2EE) containers and a JavaServer Pages (JSP) translator, as well as business logic and data access technologies. Business logic may be enabled through JavaBeans™ and Enterprise JavaBeans (EJBs). Data access technologies may include Java DataBase Connectivity (JDBC), SQLJ, EJBs, and J2EE resource adapters. Finally, Oracle Application Server also provides the infrastructure needed for developing, deploying, and managing Web Services.

Every Oracle Application Server edition also includes Oracle Enterprise Manager 10g Application Server Control, a tool used for configuring and managing each server. Another tool, Oracle Enterprise Manager 10g Grid Control, is used to manage multiple Oracle Application Servers and can provide a single point of access to each

Application Server Control installed with multiple servers. The Grid Control software is installed from a separate Grid Control CD.

The following sections briefly describe each Oracle Application Server edition. At this point, we won't attempt to explain the features mentioned here. You will find more detailed information in the section "Oracle Application Server Components."

Oracle Application Server Java Edition

Oracle Application Server Java Edition is a specific Oracle Application Server package created by Oracle for developers of Java-based software who aren't interested in the deployment features available in other Oracle Application Server editions. The Java Edition bundle includes the following:

• Oracle HTTP Server
• Oracle Application Server Containers for J2EE (OC4J)
• Oracle Business Components for Java (BC4J)
• Oracle Application Server TopLink
• Oracle JDeveloper named user licensing

This edition is the least expensive version of Oracle Application Server.

Oracle Application Server Standard Edition

In terms of functionality and pricing, Oracle Application Server Standard Edition is packaged to compete in the entry-level category for application servers. The Standard Edition adds the following components to features previously noted for the Java Edition:

• Oracle Application Server Portal
• Oracle Application Server Single Sign-On security
• Oracle Application Server Content Management Software Development Kit (SDK)

A restricted-use Oracle Internet Directory is provided in the Standard Edition to enable OracleAS Single Sign-On.

Oracle Application Server Enterprise Edition

Oracle Application Server Enterprise Edition is aimed at larger-scale implementations that require additional features. Enterprise Edition adds the following features to those available in the Java Edition and the Standard Edition:

• OracleAS Forms Services and OracleAS Reports Services
• OracleAS Discoverer

- Oracle Internet Directory
- Oracle Workflow
- Oracle Application Server InterConnect and Oracle Application Server Process-Connect
- OracleAS Personalization
- OracleAS Wireless

Before Oracle Application Server 10g, OracleAS Personalization and OracleAS Wireless, described next, were available only as options.

OracleAS Personalization

This feature provides a means by which a web server can gather data on how a web-site visitor traverses the site. This data is sent to an Oracle database where a taxonomy describing the business and business goals is defined. Analysis of this data occurs periodically using data mining algorithms in the database, and recommendations are created. These recommendations are populated in middle-tier "recommendation engines" that can redirect web-site users to "personalized" web pages of material that are likely to interest them.

OracleAS Wireless

This feature provides an integrated set of capabilities enabling multichannel mobile access, including voice, to applications. At the core of OracleAS Wireless is support of HTTP and XML. OracleAS Wireless enables the building of portlets that can be displayed on wireless devices. It also provides mobile services such as personal information management (PIM) and email, and location-based and two-way messaging services.

Oracle Application Server Components

Up to this point, we've introduced a lot of features available in different versions of Oracle Application Server without providing much explanation of what they do. The following subsections group the main components of Oracle Application Server into three basic categories—core components, application components, and additional components—and describe briefly what these components do.

 Remember that this chapter includes only summary descriptions of the components that make up Oracle Application Server. Subsequent chapters will describe these components in greater detail.

Core Components

The components that make up the core of Oracle Application Server are the Oracle HTTP Server, Oracle Application Server Containers for J2EE, and OracleAS Web Cache.

Oracle HTTP Server

The Oracle HTTP Server, which is based on the Apache Web Server, provides the services needed to handle incoming HTTP requests and can serve as a proxy server. Developers can program in languages such as Perl, C, C++, PL/SQL, and Java, and can leverage libraries and frameworks such as BC4J, the XML Developer's Kit, Java Naming and Directory Interface (JNDI), and JDBC. The Oracle HTTP Server supports Server Side Includes for adding content (such as header or footer information) across all of a web site's pages. Servers can be clustered in high-availability configurations, and Oracle HTTP Server also supports load balancing, which can couple high availability with scalability. Security support includes OracleAS Single Sign-On and encryption with the Secure Sockets Layer (SSL).

Chapter 5 describes the Oracle HTTP Server in greater detail.

Oracle Application Server Containers for J2EE

Oracle Application Server Containers for J2EE (OC4J) is a set of J2EE-certified containers executed using any standard Java Virtual Machine (JVM). OC4J provides a JSP translator, a servlet engine, and an EJB container. It also provides other J2EE services to the containers, such as JNDI, JDBC, Java Message Service (JMS), Java Authentication and Authorization Service (JAAS), and Java Transaction API (JTA). OC4J supports clustering, load balancing, and application state replication for web and EJB applications, thus enabling highly available and scalable configurations. OC4J can use Java Object Cache in the OC4J containers.

Chapter 6 describes OC4J in greater detail.

OracleAS Web Cache

OracleAS Web Cache is a memory cache that speeds the delivery of content to requesters. OracleAS Web Cache can store both static and dynamic pages, as well as parts of pages that are marked with Edge Side Include (ESI) tags. This cache also provides other types of functionality, such as balancing request loads between multiple instances of the Oracle HTTP Server and monitoring the speed at which content is returned to users.

Chapter 7 describes OracleAS Web Cache, as well as the other Oracle Application Server caches (Java Object Cache and Web Object Cache), in greater detail.

Application Components

The components of Oracle Application Server described in the following subsections provide capabilities that can create and deploy applications.

Web Services

Web Services are extensively supported in Oracle Application Server. The product includes support for the following:

- Java classes (either stateful or stateless) as remote procedure call (RPC) or document-style Web Services
- Stateless EJBs as Web Services
- PL/SQL stored procedures as Web Services
- JMS topics and queues as document-style Web Services

Clients can invoke these either dynamically or statically.

Other standards supported include publishing and query with UDDI and typed and untyped SOAP messages with SOAP header access via an application programming interface (API). A dynamic WSDL tester allows you to create web-based clients and simplify the testing of Web Services during development.

Chapter 11 describes Oracle Application Server Web Services in greater detail.

Oracle Application Server TopLink

OracleAS TopLink is an object-relational persistence tool used to store Java objects and EJBs in relational database tables. The visual mapping interface allows developers to define how Java classes are mapped to database schema. Thus, a Java developer using OracleAS TopLink doesn't need to write SQL calls. Using the visual mapping tool, the developer can usually handle database schema changes without needing to recode the Java applications. The mapping tool provides graphical views of relationships, queries, locking, caching, sequencing, and other areas of interest that enable performance tuning.

Chapter 8 describes OracleAS TopLink in greater detail.

Oracle JDeveloper

Oracle JDeveloper is a part of Oracle Developer Suite, rather than of Oracle Application Server itself, but it can create the Java applications that are deployed on an Oracle Application Server platform. Oracle JDeveloper was introduced by Oracle in 1998 to enable the development of basic Java applications without the need to write large amounts of code. At the core of Oracle JDeveloper is an advanced application development framework. Oracle JDeveloper provides numerous wizards that create Java and J2EE objects and project types. Some wizards in Oracle JDeveloper include:

- A Data Form wizard
- A Beans wizard for creating Java Beans and BeanInfo classes
- A Deployment wizard providing "one-click" deployment of J2EE applications to OC4J

Database development features include various Oracle drivers, a Connection Editor to hide the complexity of using the JDBC API to establish connections, database components to bind visual controls, and a SQLJ precompiler for embedding SQL in Java code (which you can then use with the Oracle database).

Oracle Application Server comes with a limited-use license for Oracle JDeveloper. The development tool is packaged in the Oracle Developer Suite.

Chapter 8 describes Oracle JDeveloper in greater detail.

OracleAS Forms Services

Oracle Application Server Forms Services provide data handling, navigation, database access, and database validation for Oracle Forms applications. These services allow Oracle Forms to run in an *N*-tier web environment.

Forms deployed to Oracle Application Server are developed using the Oracle Forms Developer, an interactive development tool that is part of the Oracle Developer Suite. Oracle Developer allows you to define applications by defining values for properties, rather than by writing procedural code. Oracle Developer supports a variety of clients, including traditional client-server PCs and Java-based clients. The Forms Builder includes a built-in JVM for previewing web applications.

Chapter 9 describes Oracle Application Server Forms Services in greater detail.

OracleAS Reports Services

Oracle Application Server Reports Services enable the rapid deployment and publishing of web-based reports. Reports can also leverage the Oracle Application Server Single Sign-On capabilities and can be embedded as portlets in OracleAS Portal.

Reports are created using the Oracle Reports Developer, a part of the Oracle Developer Suite. Data can be formatted in tables, matrixes, group reports, graphs, and combinations. You can achieve high-quality presentation using Cascading Style Sheets (CSS), an HTML extension. Using OracleAS Reports Services, XML-based reports can be exchanged via HTTP, and paper-based layouts can be deployed over the Internet using PDF format.

Chapter 9 describes Oracle Application Server Reports Services in greater detail, and Chapter 12 describes Reports deployed for business intelligence.

Additional Components

The components described in the following subsections provide extended functionality that is an important part of Oracle Application Server. These components relate to specific areas of IT, such as business intelligence and integration, or provide capabilities that can be used by developers, such as OracleAS Portal or the Oracle Internet Directory.

OracleAS Portal

OracleAS Portal, packaged with Oracle Application Server, provides an HTML-based tool for developing web-enabled application interfaces and content-driven web sites. Portal applications can be developed using wizards in a WYSIWYG portal development environment. Using this environment, you can create and deploy static and dynamic portal content. Users can be granted access to the environment to create their own customization. For example, you can grant an OracleAS Portal user permission to choose which content areas and links appear in his portal pages.

Java or PL/SQL developers may wish to leverage the functionality of OracleAS Portal without having to use the Portal Development environment. For such power developers, Oracle also provides a Java and PL/SQL Portal Development Kit for custom portlet development or application integration.

Portals are deployed as an integrated service in Oracle Application Server and can use directory services, the OracleAS Web Cache, J2EE services, and business intelligence services provided by OracleAS Reports Services and OracleAS Discoverer.

 The support of *portlets* enables a single web page to be divided into different areas that can independently display information and interact with the user.

Chapter 13 describes OracleAS Portal in greater detail.

OracleAS Discoverer

OracleAS Discoverer is a business intelligence tool used for ad hoc queries and user-generated reports. OracleAS Discoverer also provides an interface to relational online analytical processing (ROLAP) by leveraging analytic features present in the Oracle database and as of 2004, also provides an interface to the Oracle OLAP Option. Included in Oracle Application Server are:

Discoverer Plus
A Java-based browser client that can be used to generate ad hoc queries, reports, and graphs

Discoverer Viewer
An HTML-based browser client that can execute reports or graphs created in Discoverer Plus or the Desktop version of Discoverer

Discoverer Portlet Provider
A package used for lists of workbooks and worksheets

OracleAS Discoverer can leverage the Oracle Application Server Single Sign-On capabilities and can also export workbooks to Oracle Reports Developer for deployment in OracleAS Reports Services.

OracleAS Discoverer has an End User Layer (EUL) that is metadata-driven, enabling business definitions to hide and map to underlying technical descriptions. The EUL is set up and maintained via Oracle Discoverer Administration Edition, a part of the Oracle Developer Suite. Wizards guide the administrator through the process of building the EUL. In addition to managing the EUL, administrators can put limits on resources available to analysts monitored by the OracleAS Discoverer query governor.

Chapter 12 describes OracleAS Discoverer in greater detail.

Oracle Internet Directory

The Oracle Internet Directory provides users a means of connecting to an Oracle server without requiring a client-side configuration file. The Oracle Internet Directory is a Lightweight Directory Access Protocol (LDAP) directory that supports the Single Sign-On capability of Oracle Application Server.

Chapters 2 and 4 describe the Oracle Internet Directory in greater detail.

Oracle Workflow

Oracle Workflow provides a graphical workflow builder that facilitates the modeling of business processes. A rules-based engine and business event system is stored in an Oracle database. Messages can be transmitted via Advanced Queuing (AQ), Oracle Net, HTTP, or HTTP using SSL (HTTPS). Oracle Workflow provides key capabilities needed to deploy Oracle Application Server InterConnect, described in the next section.

Chapter 15 describes Oracle Workflow in greater detail.

Oracle Application Server InterConnect

Oracle Application Server InterConnect provides a heterogeneous application integration platform through logic and services. Deployed in a "hub-and-spoke" manner, Oracle Application Server leverages Oracle Workflow and Oracle AQ to provide a message broker infrastructure. AQ enables asynchronous messages between Oracle databases with adapters available to extend support to other message types and applications. Content-based publish-and-subscribe solutions can be deployed using a rules engine to determine relevant subscribing applications. As new content is published to a subscriber list, the rules on the list determine which subscribers should receive the content, thus efficiently serving the needs of different subscriber communities.

OracleAS InterConnect includes a design-time Integrated Development Environment (IDE), adapters, a metadata repository, a management infrastructure (used with Oracle Enterprise Manager), and SDKs (for writing custom adapters, transformations, and IDE extensions). Adapters are available for HTTP, HTTPS, AQ, Oracle database, FTP, MQSeries, CICS, SAP, PeopleSoft, Siebel, JDEdwards, and CICS.

Chapter 15 describes OracleAS InterConnect in greater detail.

Oracle Application Server ProcessConnect

Oracle Application Server ProcessConnect is new to Oracle Application Server 10g. Using wizards to create a hub-and-spoke deployment model, it's designed to make business process integration feasible. OracleAS ProcessConnect includes a modeling tool, a metadata repository, and adapters. These adapters are based on the JCA specification and enable connections to technology (such as Web Services), packaged applications (e.g., JD Edwards, PeopleSoft, SAP, and Siebel), and legacy systems.

Chapter 15 describes OracleAS ProcessConnect in greater detail.

Managing Oracle Application Servers

Oracle Application Server includes many features designed to ease the burden of management. One of the focuses of Oracle Application Server 10g is to automate many of the management tasks needed for large-scale grid computing deployment. Management capabilities provided in Oracle Application Server include the following:

- Software provisioning (installation, configuration, cloning, patching, upgrades)
- User provisioning (including security and identity management)
- Application management and monitoring
- Workload management (including dynamic resource allocation and failover notification)
- Systems management and monitoring

Chapter 3 describes each management topic in greater detail.

Oracle Enterprise Manager

Oracle Enterprise Manager, a management tool and framework, is a part of every version of Oracle Application Server and the Oracle database. This product has evolved from a Windows-based database management solution and a browser-based tool built on Java to the current HTML-based version. The Oracle Application Server 10g Grid Control web-based tool can manage multiple Oracle Application Servers and databases and provide access to each Application Server Control tool (installed with each Oracle Application Server). Oracle Enterprise Manager 10g can manage other Oracle software as well, including Oracle Collaboration Suite and E-Business Suite.

 At the time of this writing, most of the functionality in previous non-HTML versions of Oracle Enterprise Manager now appears in the HTML version.

Multiple database and infrastructure administrators can access the Oracle Enterprise Manager repository at the same time to manage multiple Oracle products.

The HTML-based Oracle Enterprise Manager console was first released with Oracle9iAS; that version provided important new application performance management and configuration management features. The HTML version supported in that release supplemented the earlier Java-based Oracle Enterprise Manager. Oracle Enterprise Manager 10g, released with Oracle Database 10g, includes both Java and HTML versions.

The HTML-based version of Oracle Enterprise Manager is used specifically to manage Oracle Application Server. Oracle Enterprise Manager can be deployed in several ways:

- As a central console, monitoring multiple databases and application servers' leveraging agents (e.g., Grid Control)
- As a database "product console" (easily installed with each individual database)
- Through remote access (also known as studio mode)

In this book, we'll focus on the HTML-based console that manages Oracle Application Server. The HTML-based console includes advanced management capabilities for rapid installation, deployment across grids of computers, application service level monitoring and management, provisioning, upgrades, and automated patching. For example, application deployment of OC4J is managed via the Oracle Enterprise Manager HTML version.

Chapter 3 describes Oracle Enterprise Manager in greater detail.

EM2Go

EM2Go is a mobile version of Oracle Enterprise Manager that provides a subset of the functionality available in Oracle Enterprise Manager 10g. EM2Go is accessed through a Pocket PC browser on a PDA device. EM2Go monitors the availability and performance of the various application servers managed by Oracle Application Server.

Chapter 3 describes EM2Go in greater detail.

What's Next?

Most readers of technical books skip around in the text, checking out the chapters that seem most likely to help them solve their particular needs at a particular point in time. However, because Oracle Application Server is such a rich and varied suite of software, we encourage you to read this book sequentially. We want to be sure that you familiarize yourself with the varied capabilities available in the product and described in this book.

In the past, we've encountered a number of Oracle Application Server customers who set out to evaluate new technologies, not realizing that the product they own already provided the very technology solution they were seeking. Usually, such customers had simply focused on only one of Oracle Application Server's many capabilities; for example, those familiar with Oracle Application Server's Java capabilities may be less aware of its business intelligence capabilities.

With this introduction to Oracle Application Server capabilities and packaging behind us, we'll move on:

- Chapters 2, 3, and 4 cover basic information on Oracle Application Server architecture, systems management, and security and identity management.
- Chapters 5, 6, and 7 provide detailed information on core Oracle Application Server components: Oracle HTTP Server, OC4J, and OracleAS Web Cache.
- The remaining chapters cover the building and deployment of functional solutions, including Java, XML, other Oracle development tools, Web Services, business intelligence tools, OracleAS Portal, mobile (OracleAS Wireless) solutions, and integration capabilities.

CHAPTER 2

Architecture

If you understand the architecture of Oracle Application Server, you will have an excellent framework for understanding how the product works. Learning how the various components of Oracle Application Server interact can help you avoid many potential problems as you get the product up and running and provide a foundation that lets you quickly identify the root cause of any problems you do encounter.

Your particular role may determine what you want to learn from this chapter:

Programmer
> As a programmer, you may want to understand how Oracle Application Server handles each incoming request so that you can properly troubleshoot problems.

Designer
> As a designer, you will want to know what features are available so that you can provide the best user interface.

Systems analyst or architect
> As a systems analyst or architect, you may want to know what overall functions can be accomplished using the product.

Manager
> As a manager, you may need a high-level understanding of Oracle Application Server so that you can compare it to similar middleware product offerings.

To best serve all these audiences, this chapter covers the big picture. We identify the major components of Oracle Application Server and explain how they interact. We also examine the product's infrastructure and the management and high-availability options available with it. Our goal here is to give you enough information on each individual component (most of which were introduced very briefly in Chapter 1) so that you can understand how Oracle Application Server works as a whole. You will see that some of Oracle Application Server's functionality is actually implemented by J2EE, by PL/SQL, or by hybrid applications that are implemented using Oracle Application Server's core components. Subsequent chapters provide more detailed discussions on each component introduced here.

Oracle Application Server Core Components

At its core, Oracle Application Server consists of three components:

- Oracle HTTP Server
- Oracle Application Server Containers for J2EE
- OracleAS Web Cache

Each component, described briefly in the following subsections, plays a major role in Oracle Application Server operations; they also provide some supporting functionality to their counterparts in various configurations.

Oracle HTTP Server

The Oracle HTTP Server is the web server for Oracle Application Server. It takes an incoming request in the form of a URI. It then either sends the requested static content—for example, an HTML file—directly to the requestor, or reroutes a request for dynamic content, effectively handing off the request, to an appropriate executable resource.

The Oracle HTTP Server can process a dynamic request using any of the following:

Common Gateway Interface (CGI) environment
> For example, programs written in C, C++, Java, Perl, and other languages

FastCGI
> An optimized CGI environment

mod_perl
> A highly efficient Perl execution environment

mod_OC4J
> A scalable J2EE environment

mod_plsql
> A module that executes PL/SQL stored procedures in an Oracle database

Chapter 5 describes the Oracle HTTP Server in detail.

Oracle Application Server Containers for J2EE

OC4J is a set of J2EE containers and a JavaServer Pages translator that provides a J2EE-certified Java environment that is scalable both horizontally and vertically. You can cluster OC4J instances across hosts; doing so eliminates both hardware and software failure and provides almost unlimited capacity. You can run multiple JVMs in an OC4J instance to leverage the capacity of hardware with multiple CPUs.

Chapter 6 describes OC4J in detail.

OracleAS Web Cache

OracleAS Web Cache is an optional component that can play several important roles:

- It can offload request processing from the Oracle HTTP Server and OC4J by efficiently caching both static and dynamic content. OracleAS Web Cache is highly configurable and programmable, so what it caches can be customized to fit any application's needs.

- It can be used as a front end load balancer to the application server when Oracle Application Server is clustered.

 Because using OracleAS Web Cache so often makes sense in the Oracle Application Server environment, the remainder of this chapter assumes its use.

Chapter 7 describes OracleAS Web Cache, as well as the other caches used by Oracle Application Server, in detail.

Core Component Interaction

Figure 2-1 shows the relationships among the three main components of Oracle Application Server.

As shown in the figure, the interactions among components work as follows:

1. OracleAS Web Cache receives an end-user request and determines whether the requested content is available in its cache. If the content is available, it returns that content. Otherwise, it forwards the request to the Oracle HTTP Server.

2. The Oracle HTTP Server immediately sends static content to the end user through OracleAS Web Cache. If the request is for dynamic content, it forwards the request to the appropriate dynamic content provider.

3. If Java-generated content is requested, OC4J processes the request using a JSP or servlet, and then sends the dynamically generated content to the Oracle HTTP Server. The Oracle HTTP Server then passes it on to OracleAS Web Cache.

4. Finally, OracleAS Web Cache passes the content on to the end user.

As the figure illustrates, there are additional dynamic processing engines, such as FastCGI, mod_perl, and PL/SQL. The architecture also includes a number of shadow processes, shown in gray, that support the use of Oracle Application Server core components. These shadow processes include:

Oracle Process Manager and Notification Server (OPMN)
    Monitors the core components to ensure that they continue running

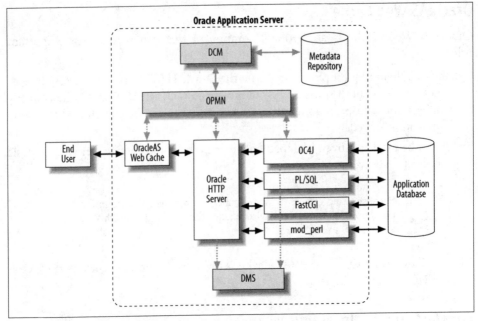

Figure 2-1. Interactions among Oracle Application Server core components

Distributed Configuration Management (DCM)
> Marshals Oracle Application Server's configuration data between OPMN and the core components

Dynamic Monitoring Service (DMS)
> Gathers performance statistics

See the later "Shadow Processes" section for more detailed information on these processes.

The configuration data itself is kept in a repository, which is part of the Oracle Application Server infrastructure, described in the next section.

Oracle Application Server Infrastructure

Shadow processes such as OPMN, DCM, and DMS, and configuration management tools such as Oracle Enterprise Manager, depend on a repository of configuration data. This repository is part of what is known as the *Oracle Application Server Infrastructure*. The OracleAS Infrastructure may consist of a simple file-based repository, or may be as complex as a database repository with an LDAP server.

OracleAS Infrastructure Components

The OracleAS Infrastructure is divided into two parts:

OracleAS Metadata Repository
Holds Oracle Application Server configuration information and other component information in a collection of schemas

Oracle Identity Management
Contains several subcomponents that work together to provide a seamless Single Sign-on facility

In addition, the Application Server Control tool and a group of shadow processes can be considered a part of the overall OracleAS Infrastructure.

OracleAS Metadata Repository

The OracleAS Metadata Repository is either operating system file-based or an Oracle database. The Java Edition of Oracle Application Server uses a file-based repository for DCM. The Portal/Wireless Edition and the BI/Forms Edition always use an OracleAS Metadata Repository in an Oracle database.

If Oracle Application Server is clustered (a topic described later in this chapter) and a file-based repository is being used, one of the clustered Oracle Application Server instances is designated as a *central repository*. This designation isn't necessary if a database repository is being used.

The OracleAS Infrastructure installation normally clones a new Oracle database to use as a database repository. During the installation process, it is possible to use an existing database instance for the OracleAS Metadata Repository, instead of creating a new one. However, specifying an existing instance has an impact on the use of the OracleAS Backup and Recovery Tool, described in Chapter 3.

Oracle Identity Management

Oracle Identity Management is a term used with Oracle Application Server 10g that encompasses all the components used to support enterprise-style security in Oracle Application Server. All these components depend on the OracleAS Metadata Repository:

Oracle Internet Directory
Provides an LDAP directory for security principals (login information)

Oracle Directory Provisioning Integration Service
Allows the LDAP directory to import and replicate data between homogeneous or heterogeneous types of LDAP servers

Oracle Delegated Administration Services
Allows regional administrators and users to update directory information in the Oracle Internet Directory

OracleAS Single Sign-On
Supports the Single Sign-on capability for all Oracle Application Server applications

OracleAS Certificate Authority
Provides an infrastructure for creating and maintaining SSL certificates

Chapter 4 describes Oracle Application Server security in greater detail.

Application Server Control

The web-based Oracle Enterprise Manager 10g tool used to monitor and control Oracle Application Server is known as *Application Server Control*. Application Server Control is actually an Oracle Application Server application that is installed with the OracleAS Infrastructure and with each individual application server home. The tool has a graphical user interface and is used to manage individual instances of Oracle Application Server. Other portions of the overall Oracle Enterprise Manager 10g product handle management of the database and a grid of computing resources.

Oracle Enterprise Manager stores component configuration data in the Metadata Repository. Doing so simplifies the management for multiple Oracle Application Server instances when Oracle Application Server clusters are being used.

Chapter 3 describes Oracle Enterprise Manager 10g, Application Server Control, and Grid Control, as well as other Oracle Application Server management tools, in more detail.

Shadow Processes

Oracle Application Server has many different components, and some deployment architectures may have more than one instance of any one of these components. To keep the burden of monitoring, managing, and coordinating the interaction between these components from being too overwhelming, Oracle Application Server includes three shadow processes, shown earlier in Figure 2-1:

- Oracle Process Manager and Notification Server
- Distributed Configuration Management
- Dynamic Monitoring Service

These shadow processes also use the OracleAS Metadata Repository. DCM updates component configuration files so that they will match the values in the repository. OPMN uses the repository to identify what components should be started and monitored. DMS stores runtime statistics in the repository.

Oracle Process Manager and Notification Server

The Oracle Process Management and Notification Server monitors the health of the individual components in an Oracle Application Server architecture. OPMN monitors and manages all Oracle Application Server components, with the exception of the following:

- The repository database, if used
- The listener for the database
- The Application Server Console

If a particular component becomes unavailable, OPMN automatically restarts it. OPMN also informs any dependent component that a component isn't available. For example, suppose that a request for a Java application comes into an Oracle HTTP Server. It is passed to the mod_oc4j module, which passes the request to an OC4J process. If the OC4J process goes down, OPMN lets the mod_oc4J process know that it should prevent any additional requests from being routed to the failed process. In this way, OPMN simplifies management while making the entire set of Oracle Application Server components highly available.

Distributed Configuration Management

For high availability and scalability, you can create *clusters* of Oracle Application Server components (Oracle HTTP Server and OC4J) and OracleAS Web Cache. The Distributed Configuration Management service coordinates configuration information across all members of a cluster.

DCM automatically replicates base configuration information to a new member of a cluster. It also propagates changes to any of this information to all members of a cluster. In addition to this base information, each cluster member also has some individual configuration parameters of its own, such as port numbers for the instance.

You can also use DCM to make a backup of your configuration files that can be used to restore these crucial files in the event of corruption.

DCM is invoked through the Application Server Control tool or via the dcmctl command-line tool.

Dynamic Monitoring Service

Oracle Application Server uses the Dynamic Monitoring Service to collect information about the performance of some of its components. DMS uses sensors to measure various types of durations or simply the occurrence of different types of events. DMS periodically collects the information from these sensors and compiles it into metrics. You can access these metrics using a variety of different tools. The most commonly used is dmstool, a command-line tool for presenting DMS metrics. The metrics may also be accessed in different portions of the Application Server Control tool.

DMS sensors are built into Oracle Application Server Containers for J2EE, so metrics are automatically provided for all applications that run in an OC4J container. You can add sensors to any application you deploy on Oracle Application Server through a DMS API, so the use of DMS is completely extensible. You can also turn off DMS to save the small amount of overhead incurred.

Installation Types

The complexity of the Oracle Application Server infrastructure depends on the type of product installation. There are three Oracle Application Server installation types:

- J2EE and Web Cache
- Portal and Wireless
- Business Intelligence and Forms

Each installation type builds on its predecessor's functionality; consequently, each requires a more complex infrastructure.

J2EE and Web Cache

The J2EE and Web Cache installation provides a high-performing and very scalable J2EE application server. In the Enterprise Edition version of the Oracle Application Server product, it consists of the following:

- Oracle HTTP Server
- Oracle Application Server Containers for J2EE
- OracleAS Web Cache

Note, however, that OracleAS Web Cache isn't included in the Java and Standard Editions.

This installation requires a DCM repository in which Oracle Application Server configuration data can be stored. The repository for this version can be either file-based or stored in an Oracle database.

Portal and Wireless

The Portal and Wireless installation contains all the components of the J2EE and OracleAS Web Cache installation. It also contains:

- OracleAS Portal, a complete, out-of-the-box, user-configurable portal solution
- OracleAS Wireless, which allows you to use web-based applications on mobile devices

Although this edition doesn't contain the following components, it uses them at runtime, so the infrastructure has to exist before you install this edition:

Identity Management

This infrastructure must exist in the form of Oracle Application Server Single Sign-On product support; this product allows your users to use one set of login credentials for all applications running on the application server.

Oracle Internet Directory

This infrastructure is added to the Identity Management infrastructure because Oracle Application Server Single Sign-On requires an LDAP server.

Note that OracleAS Portal and OracleAS Wireless store their own application data in the infrastructure's OracleAS Metadata Repository.

Business Intelligence and Forms

The Business Intelligence and Forms installation contains all the components available in the OracleAS Portal and OracleAS Wireless installation, as well as the following additional components:

- OracleAS Discoverer
- OracleAS Forms Services
- OracleAS Reports Services
- OracleAS Personalization

This installation doesn't add any more complexity to the infrastructure because no additional infrastructure components are required, but it does add more metadata. Like the Portal and Wireless edition, the Business Intelligence and Forms edition uses a preexisting infrastructure. However, there is also a standalone installation for the Forms Server and Reports Server that doesn't require an infrastructure.

Scalability Architectures

Oracle Application Server is highly scalable as a J2EE application server. As demand for a particular J2EE web application grows, so too can the application server's capacity grow, both vertically and horizontally. The following subsections describe the various types of scaling supported by the product.

Vertical Scaling with OC4J

Oracle Application Server can scale its capacity vertically by running more than one instance of OC4J on a given host, or by running more than one Java Virtual Machine in a given instance of OC4J.

Multiple OC4J instances per host

An Oracle Application Server instance can be configured to run one or more instances of OC4J. In such a configuration, each OC4J instance runs with its own

JVM. However, running multiple instances of OC4J on the same host is more of a configuration convenience than it is a means of scalability because multiple OC4J instances on a single machine share the same configuration files.

It isn't uncommon for several applications to share an application server. By running multiple OC4J instances, each heterogeneous application can run in its own OC4J instance. This reduces the risk that the deployment of an application may affect other applications (or appear that it has). It also makes it possible to do resource consumption accounting by application, which is a necessary evil in many business environments.

Multiple JVM processes per OC4J instance

Vertical scaling is better achieved by running more than one JVM process in an OC4J instance. Doing so leverages the processing power of a host that has multiple CPUs.

When more than one JVM process is running, HTTP session objects and EJB states are replicated among the JVMs. In addition to the server's offering increased capacity to process incoming requests in such a configuration, the server is also better equipped to recover from JVM process failures. In case of such a failure, it can redirect a request to one of the other JVMs running in the same OC4J instance.

Replicating HTTP session objects can become a resource-intensive task. To better manage this state replication, Oracle Application Server provides a mechanism that provides a finer level of control. Each JVM is assigned to an island. An *island* logically groups JVMs together for the purpose of HTTP session object replication. If two or more JVMs have the same island name (even in clustered Oracle Application Server instances on different hosts), HTTP session objects are replicated among them. This capability means that you can control which JVMs replicate state with each other.

For example, if you have an OC4J instance that has four JVM processes running, you can have two JVMs assigned to default_island, and the other two assigned to island_two. With this configuration, HTTP session objects are replicated between the two JVMs that are part of the same island. This reduces the overhead of replicating each HTTP session object because each JVM has only one replication site, rather than three.

In contrast, no refined replication control exists for EJB state. EJB state replication doesn't use the island replication facility. The state of any stateful EJB is replicated among all JVMs in an OC4J instance (or in clustered Oracle Application Server instances).

Horizontal Scaling with Oracle Application Server

Horizontal scaling is accomplished using clusters. A *cluster* groups two or more Oracle Application Server instances so that they appear as one application server.

Clustered Oracle Application Server instances utilize only the Oracle HTTP Server and OC4J components.

Figure 2-2 shows two Oracle Application Server instances in a cluster. In this figure, a load balancer receives a user request. The load balancer forwards the request to an Oracle Application Server instance, where it is processed. Looking at the figure, you can see that both instances of Oracle Application Server use the same metadata repository, as well as any other resource, such as an application database.

Oracle Application Server farm

To be clustered, Oracle Application Server instances must be part of the same farm. A *farm* is a group of one or more Oracle Application Server instances (clustered or not) that share the same OracleAS Infrastructure or that use the same Oracle Application Server instance for their file-based OracleAS Metadata Repository.

Oracle Application Server instances automatically become part of a farm during installation. The farm assignment is based on which OracleAS Infrastructure or Oracle Application Server instance (for a file-based repository) they use for their OracleAS Metadata Repository. This assignment can be changed at a later date using Oracle Enterprise Manager.

Oracle Application Server cluster definition

An Oracle Application Server cluster definition is created within a farm using Oracle Enterprise Manager. After a cluster is defined, the first Oracle Application Server instance added to the cluster defines the cluster-wide configuration. Thereafter, each server that is added to the cluster gets its configuration and any deployed applications from the cluster-wide configuration. The only configuration properties that aren't part of the cluster-wide configuration are the OC4J-specific properties: the number of JVM processes per OC4J instance and the ports an OC4J instance uses to communicate with the Oracle HTTP Server.

Cluster management

Clustered Oracle Application Server instances appear as one application server not only to the end user but also to the Oracle Application Server administrator. If changes are made to any Oracle Application Server instance in a cluster, the DCM process automatically replicates the changes to all the other instances in the cluster. This process significantly reduces the amount of work an administrator has to do to deploy applications in a clustered environment.

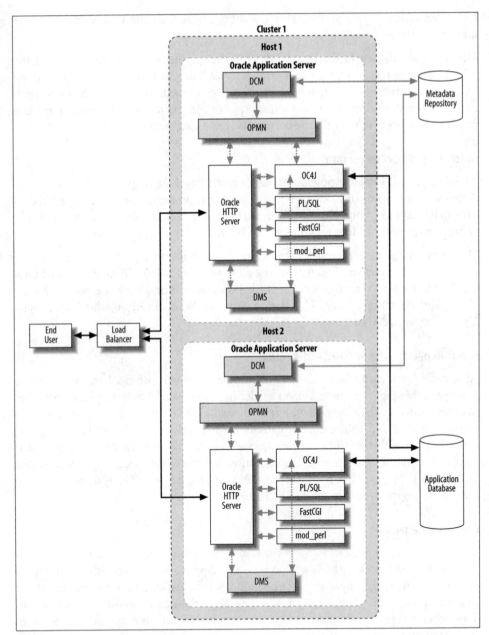

Figure 2-2. Clustered Oracle Application Server instances

Load Balancing

As mentioned earlier, a load balancer is required when Oracle Application Server instances are being clustered together. There are three traditional choices for load balancing:

- Hardware
- Operating system
- OracleAS Web Cache

Of the three, Oracle recommends using a hardware-based load balancer. The following subsections describe these three approaches, along with a brief discussion of load balancing with the Oracle HTTP Server.

Hardware load balancer

A hardware load balancer works by receiving a request from an end user and then forwarding the request to a clustered Oracle Application Server instance. Hardware load balancers support various forwarding algorithms, including the following:

Fastest Response
> Forwards a request to the application server that responds the most quickly

Round Robin
> Forwards a request to the next application server in a predetermined list of servers

Least Connections
> Forwards a request to the application server with the fewest number of connections

Calculated Ratio
> Forwards a request to the application server with the best calculated ratio based on predetermined statistics

Geographic Location
> Forwards a request to the application server located closest to the requestor

Hardware load balancers are preferred because they are faster and have redundant components that eliminate downtime caused by mechanical or electrical failure. Figure 2-3 shows a typical hardware load balancer configuration. In this figure, an end user sends a request to a hardware load balancer. The hardware load balancer forwards the request to a clustered instance of OracleAS Web Cache. OracleAS Web Cache returns cached content, if available. If cached content isn't available, it forwards the request on to a clustered instance of Oracle Application Server.

Examples of hardware load balancers include the following products:

F5 Networks' BIG-IP
> See *http://www.f5.com/f5products/bigip/*

Nortel Network's Alteon
> See *http://www.nortelnetworks.com/products/01/alteon/*

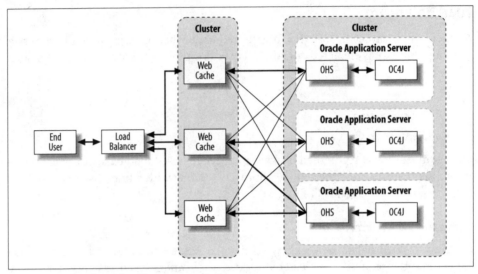

Figure 2-3. A hardware load balancer example

Operating system load balancer

Some operating systems provide a built-in load-balancing mechanism. In particular, Microsoft Windows Advanced Server allows you to forward requests to different machines that share the same IP or MAC level address. In addition, load-balancing software applications are available for almost all operating systems.

OracleAS Web Cache load balancer

OracleAS Web Cache can be used as a load balancer for clustered Oracle Application Server instances. When OracleAS Web Cache acts as a load balancer, it uses a Weighted Available Capacity algorithm to determine the particular Oracle Application Server instance to which it will forward the request. This algorithm uses a weight, assigned by an administrator, to distribute the load unequally among instances. If the weighted available capacity is the same, OracleAS Web Cache uses a Round Robin algorithm.

If an Oracle Application Server instance fails, OracleAS Web Cache redistributes requests to the remaining instances. Meanwhile, OracleAS Web Cache intermittently polls the failed server until it is once again available to process requests. At that time, the failed server is included in the load-balancing algorithm.

For more information about this capability of OracleAS Web Cache, see the detailed discussion in Chapter 7.

Oracle HTTP Server load balancer

While our discussion so far has focused on load-balancing requests to clustered Oracle Application Server instances, another type of load balancing may also be taking place. Oracle HTTP Server's mod_oc4j load-balances requests among multiple JVM processes in an OC4J instance or among OC4J instances in a cluster.

If an OC4J instance is configured to use two or more JVM processes or is part of a cluster, mod_oc4j routes a stateful request to the JVM that last processed the stateful request. If the JVM that last processed a stateful request has failed, the request is rerouted using a predetermined algorithm to another OC4J instance's JVM process that is part of the same island as the failed JVM.

Three algorithms are available for rerouting a request to a failed OC4J instance:

Round Robin
> As usual with a Round Robin algorithm, mod_oc4j uses the next OC4J instance (and the next JVM process in the same island), remote and local to the Oracle Application Server instance, on a predetermined list.

Random
> With the Random algorithm, an OC4J instance is picked randomly from the predetermined list.

Metric-Based
> This algorithm uses OC4J performance metrics to determine where to route a request.

All these algorithms can be configured with local affinity, so a local OC4J process is used in favor of a remote process. Similarly, the Round Robin and Random algorithms can employ a weighting factor to determine which OC4J process is chosen.

Stateless requests are always processed using one of these predetermined algorithms. You can configure the desired algorithm, along with all the other settings, using Oracle Enterprise Manager.

High Availability

The availability of an application server can be measured by comparing the actual amount of time it is operational against the total time it could possibly be available. Highly available systems may need to operate 100% of the time. To accomplish that level of availability, you must address every possible single point of failure. In addition to hardware and software failures, you must have a way to continue operations while both the hardware and software are being upgraded or replaced.

Oracle Application Server solves these high-availability problems with clusters and with two different failover solutions for the OracleAS Infrastructure.

Oracle Application Server Clusters

We introduced the concept of clusters earlier in this chapter. Although both a farm and a cluster are made up of multiple instances of Oracle Application Server components, a cluster is a more integrated grouping than a farm.

In a cluster, the individual instances of a component are aware of each other, and they cooperate to provide service. The OPMN server keeps the members of a cluster informed as to the status of other members in that cluster, so if one member fails, the others pick up its load. The members of a cluster are designed to be interchangeable, providing a higher level of availability than an individual instance or a group of instances in a farm.

You can create clusters of OracleAS Web Cache instances or Oracle Application Servers. As mentioned earlier, a cluster requires some type of load balancer in front of the cluster to distribute the load. The redundant nature of an individual instance within a cluster makes clustering a way to provide a high-availability solution.

Oracle Application Server can also run on hardware clusters. These clusters provide an underlying redundancy and transparency for anything running on them, including Oracle Application Server.

Infrastructure Failover

Oracle Application Server clusters deliver high availability with their own software. However, these clusters don't provide high availability for the OracleAS Infrastructure. Because all Oracle Application Server components need to access the infrastructure and because the availability of an entire system is dependent on every part of the system, this deficiency can imperil the availability of your application server.

To address this risk, you can implement Oracle Application Server 10g with either of two types of failover solutions:

Oracle Application Server Cold Failover Clusters
> This approach uses hardware clustering to provide some measure of availability protection.

Oracle Application Server Active Failover Clusters
> This approach provides a higher level of availability and combines it with increased scalability for your infrastructure.

OracleAS Cold Failover Clusters

The OPMN server manages most Oracle Application Server components and services, and this server can automatically restart any failed processes. This capability protects against the failure of individual components of Oracle Application Server. However, larger problems, such as server failure, are beyond the scope of OPMN.

Thus, Oracle Application Server provides an availability solution, OracleAS Cold Failover Clusters, that guards against these larger-scale failures.

OracleAS Cold Failover Clusters are built on capabilities inherent in a hardware cluster. A hardware cluster facilitates the sharing of resources between nodes, provides a health-monitoring heartbeat, and supports failover from one node to another without impacting users. Hardware clusters provide a "virtual IP" address, which it can associate with either node in the cluster. Users don't know which physical node is servicing requests for the virtual IP address.

If you are familiar with database availability concepts, you will recognize the term *cold failover*. With Oracle Application Server, the term has the same meaning it does for a database: one identical set of resources stands by, waiting for a failure in the primary system. If that system fails, the cluster starts to use the standby system. Figure 2-4 shows the architecture of a typical OracleAS Cold Failover Clusters implementation before a failure has occurred.

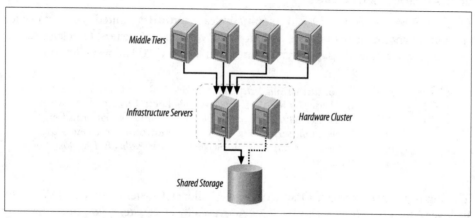

Figure 2-4. OracleAS Cold Failover Clusters prefailure

Because many Oracle Application Server components depend on the infrastructure for continuous operation, OracleAS Cold Failover Clusters are designed to protect the components of the OracleAS Infrastructure. If an active node in an OracleAS Cold Failover Cluster configuration fails, the IP address is switched to the failover node, and the infrastructure processes are started on that node. Once these processes are available, middle-tier components can access the new infrastructure, as shown in Figure 2-5. Because the storage for both infrastructure nodes is shared, there is no need to recreate or migrate the information in the database.

You can have instances of other Oracle Application Server and OracleAS Web Cache coexisting on either node in the OracleAS Cold Failover Cluster. However, no failover for these instances is supported. You can group the instances in their own cluster, but the operation of these clusters is separate from the operation of the OracleAS Cold Failover Cluster.

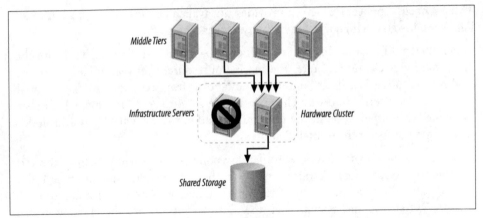

Figure 2-5. *OracleAS Cold Failover Clusters post-failure*

OracleAS Active Failover Clusters

Oracle Application Server 10*g*, in its initial release, provides limited (i.e., beta-style) support for another type of failover solution: Active Failover Clusters. OracleAS Active Failover Clusters uses the same architecture as OracleAS Cold Failover Clusters.

> At the time of this writing, OracleAS Active Failover Clusters is still in limited release. By the time you read this book, OracleAS Active Failover Clusters is likely to be available for a number of platforms for Oracle Application Server. For up-to-date information on certified platforms, please see *http://otn.oracle.com/products/ias/hi_av/10g_904_ HA_Certification.html*.

The big difference between OracleAS Active Failover Clusters and OracleAS Cold Failover Clusters is that with OracleAS Active Failover Clusters, you don't have to have one node in the hardware cluster sitting around waiting for a failure. Both infrastructure nodes can service infrastructure requests. Because both nodes in an OracleAS Active Failover Cluster are servicing requests, OracleAS Active Failover Clusters can provide some scalability, in addition to the availability offered by both types of failover clusters.

The architecture for an OracleAS Active Failover Cluster configuration is shown in Figure 2-6.

The major differences between this configuration and a OracleAS Cold Failover Cluster configuration are the following:

- An OracleAS Active Failover Cluster configuration uses a hardware load balancer in front of the active infrastructure nodes.
- The infrastructure uses Real Application Clusters (RAC) for its database.

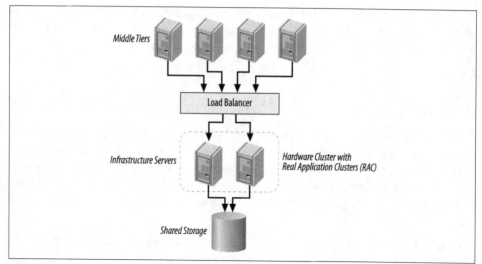

Figure 2-6. OracleAS Active Failover Clusters architecture

Both nodes have the same infrastructure components running at the same time, and the load is split between the infrastructure nodes. If one node fails, the failover is much faster and more transparent than it is for OracleAS Cold Failover Clusters.

OracleAS Active Failover Clusters use a RAC database to provide scalability and availability for the OracleAS Metadata Repository. RAC is Oracle's clustered database solution. It runs on a hardware cluster and allows any application to run against a clustered database without modification. For more information on RAC, please refer to the discussion in our companion database book *Oracle Essentials* (O'Reilly).

In addition to using RAC for the OracleAS Metadata Repository, OracleAS Active Failover Clusters have duplicate infrastructure processes, such as those used for identity management, running on each node in the cluster. All nodes in an OracleAS Active Failover Cluster must have virtually identical configurations, down to the pathnames for Oracle *HOME* directories.

Oracle Application Server Applications

The following sections provide brief descriptions of the applications that are part of the architecture of Oracle Application Server. Each application, or set of applications, is covered in it own chapter; the following sections focus on how they fit into the overall architecture of Oracle Application Server.

OracleAS Portal

OracleAS Portal performs its basic construction of portal pages in the Portal Page Engine, which is a J2EE application. OracleAS Portal also makes extensive use of the

PL/SQL language in the construction of its pages. OracleAS Portal is closely integrated with the OracleAS Single Sign-on capability provided by the Oracle Identity Management infrastructure, so an OracleAS Portal installation requires an infrastructure.

Chapter 13 describes OracleAS Portal in detail.

OracleAS Wireless

OracleAS Wireless is designed to enable wireless devices such as cell phones, messaging devices/pagers, and wireless Internet-connected laptops to connect to an application that provides content. The Oracle Application Server architecture includes a device/network gateway provider, an XML application framework, and an adapter that enables communication to and from the application leveraging a multichannel server.

Chapter 14 describes OracleAS Wireless and its various mobile components in detail.

Business Intelligence

The primary business intelligence (BI) components available in Oracle Application Server are OracleAS Discoverer and OracleAS Reports Services. Oracle Application Server also includes an OracleAS Personalization component that leverages data mining features to present web-site pages based on previously analyzed tendencies of visitors.

OracleAS Discoverer tools enabled for Internet access include Discoverer Plus and Discoverer Viewer:

Discoverer Plus
> This tool is a full-featured ad hoc query and analysis tool. It is initiated using a downloaded Java applet. After the initial applet download, the applet resides in local cache.

Discoverer Viewer
> This tool can view intelligence query results and charts generated by Discoverer Plus in a browser. It is servlet-based and leverages Discoverer Services.

Both tools take advantage of the fact that Oracle Application Server contains a data cache, which enables rapid data manipulation without the need to requery the back-end database. The database tier of the architecture contains Discoverer workbooks, the End User Layer, and, of course, the data.

The OracleAS Reports Services component lets you create high-quality printed and web-based reports. OracleAS Reports Services uses Java servlets (known as *Java servers*) to receive requests and then direct the requests to a runtime engine that provides the requested functionality. You can configure the number of runtime engines for OracleAS Reports Servers initially started, the maximum number of engines that can be running at one time, and the idle time before an engine is shut down. Multiple OracleAS Reports Servers can provide load balancing, although not failover.

Chapter 9 describes OracleAS Reports Services in detail, and Chapter 12 describes OracleAS Discoverer and other business intelligence components.

OracleAS Forms Services

OracleAS Forms Services can build applications that provide an interactive graphical interface for data entry with support for data validation. As with OracleAS Reports Services, OracleAS Forms Services use Java servlets to receive requests and direct them to a runtime engine. Each user has a matching runtime process, which is also a Java servlet. As with OracleAS Reports Servers, you can have multiple OracleAS Forms Servers that can provide load balancing, although not failover.

Chapter 9 describes OracleAS Forms Services in detail.

CHAPTER 3

Systems Management

Many Oracle Application Server users aren't aware of all the management activities that go on around them. But comprehensive and effective systems management is vital to providing a reliable, available, and secure environment. Without this management, even the most highly functional environment may not be optimally implemented or used. In Oracle Application Server, the focus of systems management is Oracle Enterprise Manager 10g.

Oracle Enterprise Manager 10g is the latest version of Oracle Enterprise Manager, a management tool framework with a graphical user interface that can manage a variety of Oracle products, including Oracle Database, Collaboration Suite, E-Business Suite, and, of course, Oracle Application Server. Oracle distributed the first version of Oracle Enterprise Manager with Oracle7 and added a browser-based Oracle Enterprise Manager console (built with Java) with Oracle8i and an HTML console with Oracle9iAS.

Every time a new Oracle product or product version is introduced, the new features and capabilities also introduce new management challenges. In the past, keeping up with this ever-increasing list of features required a fairly steep learning curve for novices. Recently, however, Oracle has simplified management by providing self-managing and self-tuning features in its products and by implementing more automated management facilities in Oracle Enterprise Manager 10g.

Our focus in this chapter is the use of Oracle Enterprise Manager 10g in managing Oracle Application Server. For more general information about Oracle Enterprise Manager 10g, consult the Oracle documentation. See the Appendix for specific references for Oracle Enterprise Manager 10g and other products described in this chapter.

Two basic tools are available through Oracle Enterprise Manager 10g that allow you to manage Oracle Application Server: Oracle Enterprise Manager 10g Application Server Control, which comes as part of Oracle Application Server 10g, and Oracle

Enterprise Manager 10g Grid Control, Oracle's management solution for your entire Oracle environment, including Oracle Application Server. (Throughout this book we refer to these tools simply as Application Server Control and Grid Control.)

Application Server Control

This GUI tool is the standard administrative console for Oracle Application Server. When you install Oracle Application Server, an Application Server Control instance is installed for each individual application server you manage. You can use the console to provide a variety of administrative tasks on that server. For example, you can start and stop an application server, enable and disable Oracle Application Server components, modify server configurations, create Oracle Application Server Containers for J2EE, deploy and monitor J2EE applications, manage ports and clusters, and examine logs.

Grid Control

This GUI console provides additional management capabilities not available in Application Server Control. Grid Control is typically installed on a single location to provide a central console that allows you to monitor and access all the application servers in your environment. In addition to managing multiple application servers, Grid Control also allows you to manage databases, applications, and hosts. Using Grid Control you can link to and launch each Application Server Control. You can also perform historical monitoring, alerting, management of jobs and policies, Application Service Level Management (ASLM) and monitoring, and configuration management.

Both Oracle Application Server 10g and Oracle Database 10g are designed to be deployable on computer grids in which many servers are used and need to be managed. Grid Control allows you to perform a variety of grid management tasks such as resource pooling, provisioning of computer resources, dynamic workload management, and dynamic control of changing grid components. While Grid Control is designed particularly to simplify grid management, it also greatly simplifies the management of more traditional Oracle multitier implementations.

This chapter briefly describes the use of Application Server Control and Grid Control. It also discusses other management functions—backup, recovery, and security—that are the responsibility of the Oracle Application Server administrator. It concludes with a discussion of working with Oracle Support to resolve system management problems that may arise. You will need to understand each area if you are going to design and implement effective management strategies for your own Oracle Application Server environment.

Application Server Control

The Application Server Control tool is the main administrative console for Oracle Application Server. An Application Server Control instance is installed in each application server home and provides a web-based interface for administering that application server. Figure 3-1 shows the Application Server Control home page.

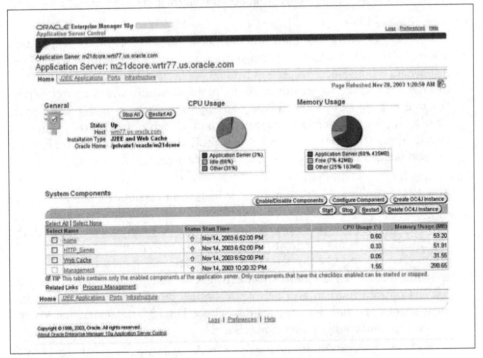

Figure 3-1. Application Server Control home page

From the home page, you can:

- Start, stop, enable, disable, and configure Oracle Application Server components and view their status
- Create additional OC4J components
- Deploy applications
- View pie charts showing CPU and memory usage
- Monitor hosts
- Connect to links to manage J2EE applications, ports, and infrastructure
- View log files, and manage the log repository

For example, you can examine the Log Repository (described later) through a Log Viewer by selecting the Logs link appearing in the upper right on this page.

Application Server Control provides a wide spectrum of capabilities. The following sections look at a few typical administrative functions available through this tool.

Application Server Control Management Stack

The Application Server Control management stack that enables the management functions you can perform with Application Server Control consists of the following services, introduced in Chapter 2:

Distributed Configuration Management
DCM manages configurations tied to a specific OracleAS Metadata Repository and can propagate Oracle Application Server configurations across an entire cluster.

Oracle Process Manager and Notification
OPMN provides process control (e.g., starting and stopping application servers) and process monitoring for application servers.

Dynamic Monitoring Service
DMS collects performance data, including OC4J application and OracleAS Web Cache performance. The data is collected by the Oracle Enterprise Manager 10g Management Agents for use in real-time performance monitoring and for historical monitoring in Grid Control.

Application Server Control uses these facilities in a variety of ways. For example, you can use Application Server Control to configure the two key Oracle Application Server business intelligence components, OracleAS Discoverer and OracleAS Reports Services. You can also monitor OracleAS Reports Services performance, and can view and manage OracleAS Reports Services job queues.

Managing Ports

You can use Application Server Control to reconfigure ports, used by Oracle Application Server components and services, and allocated during installation. You can also view or change these ports. Links to the Oracle Application Server documentation make it easy to prevent conflict with other ports on your system by determining ports that may be affected by your changes.

Viewing and Managing Log Information

During normal operation, various Oracle Application Server components populate logs with information—for example, startup and shutdown information, warnings, and errors. You can use Application Server Control to view this information.

Oracle Application Server components that generate log files include:

Core components
BC4J, OC4J, Oracle HTTP Server, and OracleAS Web Cache

Management and installation components
Oracle Enterprise Manager 10g, DCM, OPMN, and the Universal Installer

Deployable tools and enabling technology components
> OracleAS Portal, OracleAS Discoverer, OracleAS Forms Services, OracleAS Reports Services, and OracleAS Wireless

Using the Logs link in Application Server Control, you can easily search for log files related to any of these components. You can also browse these logs directly from the Application Server Control user interface to help you diagnose problems.

You have the option of consolidating log information into a single repository, and doing so simplifies the diagnostic process when you are analyzing multiple components. The Log Loader, started through Application Server Control, initiates and populates the Log Repository. Warning and error messages that are gathered here are used when you troubleshoot problems that can occur in specific Oracle Application Server components. You'll also find these useful when reporting problems to Oracle Support (described in the last section of this chapter).

Administering J2EE

You can perform a variety of J2EE administration functions by invoking the OC4J home page through Application Server Control. These include:

- Adding OC4J instances (via a wizard)
- Configuring J2EE resources, J2EE application security, Java Messaging Services, and other J2EE services
- Deploying and monitoring J2EE and Web Services applications (via a wizard-based interface)

Administering Clusters

You can also use Application Server Control to manage a group of application servers hosting a common set of OC4J applications as a cluster. Setting up a cluster allows you to modify common configuration settings only once for all cluster members. You can also deploy applications across the cluster in a single step. The architecture of clusters is described in Chapter 2.

Grid Control

The web-based Grid Control tool is a key part of Oracle Enterprise Manager 10g. You can use this tool to manage and monitor multiple application servers through a single interface. This interface provides a single view of all the application servers along with links to each server's Application Server Control. Because other infrastructure components are also monitored, Grid Control gives you a way to measure and assure levels of application service that leverage multiple components.

While Application Server Control is used for administrative tasks on an individual application server or cluster, Grid Control can manage multiple application servers remotely and/or through firewalls.

 As mentioned earlier, you can also use Grid Control to manage databases, Oracle Collaboration Suite, and Oracle E-Business Suite. However, the focus in this section is on its use with Oracle Application Server.

Grid Control Infrastructure

The Grid Control infrastructure includes the following components used to manage Oracle Application Server:

Grid Control Console
> The console, sometimes called the *central console*, allows you to view, monitor, and manage application servers as well as other Oracle components.

Oracle Management Service
> Oracle Management Service, a J2EE application deployed on Oracle Application Server, renders Oracle Enterprise Manager's HTML user interface.

Management Repository
> This central repository of enterprise-wide management data includes many types of data—for example, hardware and software configuration data leveraged in life-cycle, cloning, and patch management. It also stores historic performance and availability data used for trend analysis and reporting.

Oracle Management Agents
> These agents monitor the application servers and communicate the results of this monitoring back to the Oracle Management Service. They also are responsible for running jobs for the Application Server Control tool. You deploy one Management Agent on each host. The agent will then monitor all components on that host, including all installed Oracle software and non-Oracle components using Oracle Enterprise Manager 10g's extensibility.

The Grid Control architecture for managing multiple application server targets is shown in Figure 3-2. The protocol used may be either HTTP or HTTPS.

Management Agents are available for the wide variety of operating systems on which Oracle Application Server runs and are responsible for automatic service discovery, performance monitoring, and job execution. Management Agents can also send Simple Network Management Protocol (SNMP) traps to performance monitors in tools such as CA Unicenter Network and Systems Management, the HP OpenView Operations console, and IBM Tivoli. Agents can also perform any generic response action, such as writing to a log file or another console's API (which allows Oracle Enterprise Manager to integrate well with other management tools and procedures).

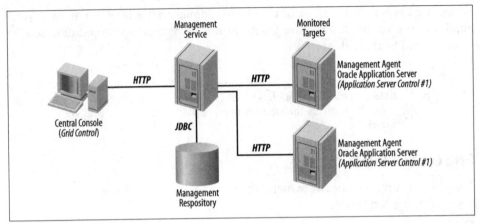

Figure 3-2. Grid Control architecture

Using Grid Control

This section takes a closer look at managing Oracle Application Server through Grid Control. Logging into the console brings you to the console home page. That page shows the status of all components in your environment, as well as rollups of jobs, events, critical patches, and deployments.

Figure 3-3 shows Grid Control's monitoring of an Oracle Application Server infrastructure. The pull-down Deployments Summary selected in this figure lists all the Oracle Application Server instances installed. You can also choose to view only the status of application servers by choosing only Application Servers under the View dropdown list on the upper left.

You can quickly search for all application servers by selecting Application Servers under Target Search. This results in a list of all application server targets, including high-level statistics and status for each. Selecting a link to a particular Oracle Application Server instance brings you to the Grid Control Application Server home page for that instance (see Figure 3-4 for the top portion of how this page typically appears).

The Grid Control home page operates in a different way from the Application Server Control home page, which you can access via the Administer link in the Related Links section.

Four links are shown, enabling you to quickly navigate the interface: Home (your initial location), J2EE Applications, Web Applications, and Performance.

At the top of the console page, you will also find links to Setup (for setting up and managing additional administrators, notification methods, etc.), Preferences (for example, notification schedules), Help, and Logout.

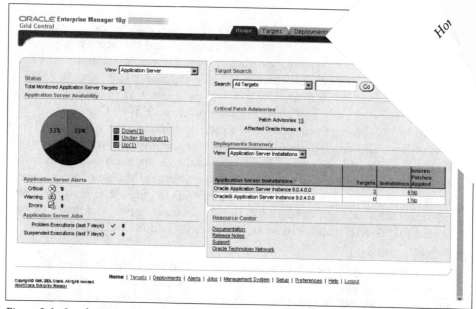

Figure 3-3. *Oracle Enterprise Manager 10g's Grid Control console home page*

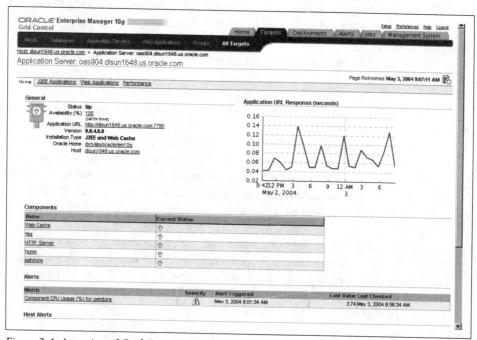

Figure 3-4. *A portion of Grid Control's Application Server Control home page*

...e page

This page is designed to give you a quick view of the status of an application server and is segmented into the following areas: general characteristics (e.g., status, availability, URL, version, installation type, Oracle home, and host links), an application URL response chart, a list of components (e.g., Oracle AS Web Cache, Oracle HTTP Server), a list of current alerts (for parameters such as memory usage), a list of host alerts (for parameters such as CPU utilization), and related links. The Host link takes you to the host home page where you'll find performance and configuration information for the host, as well as a software inventory. Related links allow you to access other areas, such as the patch list, metrics, manage metrics (with thresholds), alert history, blackout history, monitoring configuration (if you have the OPERATOR TARGET privilege), and administration (a login prompt for the Application Server Control tool will appear). Of course, many of these areas also include additional drill-downs.

J2EE Applications page

This page is typically used to determine where J2EE application performance bottlenecks are. It displays a list of J2EE applications, along with their total processing time, average servlet/JSP processing time, number of servlets/JSPs processed, total servlet/JSP processing time, average EJB method execution time, number of EJB methods executed, and total EJB method execution time. Because the screen shows resource usage, you can drill down to find the source of bottlenecks.

Web Applications page

This page provides an overview of all monitored web applications and their status, as well as a summary of all outstanding availability and transaction performance alerts. Drill-downs provide ASLM tools that enable you to ensure high availability and optimal performance of web-based applications, as well as diagnose application performance problems. The availability of web applications is defined by administrator-specified criteria that determine whether your application is up. Application Service Level Management tools also let you monitor application performance through a multidimensional approach: using synthetic transaction performance monitoring, and measuring the actual application response times as experienced by your real end users. Once a performance problem is detected, you can interactively trace transactions from the client through the middle tier down to the SQL statement level, thus enabling you to quickly identify the components that may have contributed to application bottlenecks. Historically, page performance is also traced through the J2EE activity tiers, providing deep diagnostics that identify the processing time consumed at the JSP, servlet, EJB method, and SQL statement levels.

Performance page

This page graphically shows charts of parameters such as CPU usage, memory usage, OracleAS Web Cache hit rate, HTTP response and load, HTTP server process usage, active HTTP connections, servlet response and load, and number of active sessions. Refreshes can be manual or automatic at various intervals. Historical trending of various time lengths can be viewed to trends of up to 31 days. Through various links you can identify top servlets and top JSPs (servlets and JSPs can be ranked by requests processed, average processing time, or total processing time).

EM2Go

Although EM2Go isn't part of Oracle Application Server itself, Oracle Application Server administrators will find this product very helpful in monitoring their targets while on the run. EM2Go is the mobile component of Oracle Enterprise Manager 10g. It facilitates administrator access to a subset of the Oracle Enterprise Manager functionality through a Pocket PC browser on a PDA device.

Because EM2Go leverages the architecture of Oracle Enterprise Manager 10g, no additional infrastructure is required to start using the product. EM2Go includes the following:

- Oracle Management Service, a J2EE web application hosted by Oracle Application Server 10g
- A Management Repository for its persistent data store
- Distributed, lightweight Oracle Agents that monitor all services on the host and execute remote operations on managed services

Communication between EM2Go and Oracle Management Service, and between Oracle Management Service and the Agents, is performed via HTTP or HTTPS.

Oracle Enterprise Manager automatically gathers and evaluates diagnostic information from Oracle Application Server systems distributed across the enterprise. As with all services managed by Oracle Enterprise Manager, an extensive array of Oracle Application Server performance metrics are automatically monitored against predefined thresholds, and alerts are generated when metrics exceed these thresholds. The EM2Go home page displays all the alerts, enabling the administrator to drill down into the alert details to investigate what triggered the problem. Using EM2Go, the administrator can monitor the availability of the application servers. The diagnostic reports for CPU usage and memory usage are also available from your device, providing a graphical view of current or historical data.

Optional Oracle Enterprise Manager Application Server Packs

Two add-on packs, available through Oracle Enterprise Manager 10g, provide you with additional Oracle Application Server management capabilities. They supplement the standard functionality by allowing you access to specific, functional areas within Grid Control.

These packs are particularly useful if you need to monitor multiple Oracle Application Server components. Monitoring multiple components will help you understand such characteristics of your environment as web application availability, end-user performance, transaction performance, on-demand cross-tier transaction performance, and historical cross-tier application performance.

Oracle Enterprise Manager 10g Application Server Diagnostics Pack
> This pack helps you to identify performance bottlenecks and provides tools for resolving problems. It enables ASLM through end-to-end analysis of performance across multiple components. You can measure the performance seen by end users, web server performance, and transaction processing times. By comparing these different measurements, you can quickly diagnose where the source of a performance problem lies. You can also trace transaction paths, identify bottlenecks such as the slowest URLs and problematic EJBs and SQL, and understand performance through other components including servlets, JSPs, and JDBC.

Oracle Enterprise Manager 10g Application Server Configuration Management Pack
> This pack allows you to track current Oracle Application Server hardware, operating systems, patches, and policies, as well as other current software installations and patches. It also enables automated cloning and patching.

Backup, Recovery, and Security Management

The management tasks discussed in previous sections represent only a portion of those that must be performed at a typical site. Many other management tasks are ordinarily the responsibility of your organization's database administrator (DBA). However, backup, recovery, and security management are often the responsibility of the Oracle Application Server administrator, so the following sections will touch upon these tasks. For details, consult the Oracle documentation.

Performing Backup and Recovery

Backing up your configuration and application data in such a way that it can be recovered in the event of a failure or error is an essential maintenance task for any administrator. When you back up Oracle Application Server, make sure that your backup procedures back up both Oracle Application Server itself and the contents of the Oracle Application Server infrastructure (if used); that infrastructure is frequently housed in an Oracle database.

A complete backup of your Oracle Application Server environment includes the following:

- Configuration files for the instance, the Oracle software files, and system files.
- Contents of the OracleAS Metadata Repository (if used); remember that the repository is an integral part of the infrastructure.
- Additional files associated with the Oracle environment, such as log files, configuration files for the database, and other scripts and information used by Oracle Application Server components.

Make sure that your backup plan includes backup steps for all this information.

Types of backup

As with the Oracle database, two basic types of backup are available for Oracle Application Server:

Complete, or cold, backup
> With this type of backup, you back up all Oracle HOME directories in the middle tier, including the Oracle HOME for the Oracle database used for the infrastructure, a complete cold backup of the OracleAS Metadata Repository, and a complete backup of all Oracle system files.

Online, or incremental, backup
> With this type of backup, you back up only the configuration files that have changed since the time of the last backup and perform an online backup of the OracleAS Metadata Repository.

With Oracle Application Server, as with any software, make sure to perform periodic complete backups as well as more frequent incremental backups. If you make a major change to your Oracle Application Server environment, take that opportunity to perform a complete backup to avoid losing the effects of this change.

Oracle Application Server farms and clusters are managed using DCM. You can use DCM directly or invoke it via Application Server Control. The DCM requires a repository, either in the database or as a set of files. If you use file-based DCM, you also have to back up (and subsequently recover) the files used as part of your backup procedure. These files are located on the repository host for the cluster or farm. If you use a database for the configuration information, standard backup procedures will also back up this information.

> DCM lets you create an archive of a particular configuration. You can use this archive as a way to save known "good" configurations. This allows you to restore previous configurations if you need to do so later.

OracleAS Backup and Recovery Tool

The OracleAS Backup and Recovery Tool is a Perl script that backs up configuration files and the Metadata Repository. This tool is included on the OracleAS Application Server Repository Creation Assistant (OracleAS RepCA) CD set that comes with Oracle Application Server. The OracleAS Backup and Recovery Tool automates the process of backing up all the individual entities needed for a complete Oracle Application Server backup, as described in the previous section.

The OracleAS Backup and Recovery Tool has its own set of configuration files that indicate which directories it uses to hold the different portions of the backup. You need to install the tool for each infrastructure and middle-tier server in your environment, and edit the configuration for each instance of the tool. You can add files, directories, or groups of files and directories (using wildcards) to the configuration file.

Backup

You can use the OracleAS Backup and Recovery Tool to perform either complete or incremental backups of configuration files, the OracleAS Metadata Repository, or both. You can specify the level of an incremental backup, where each level backs up the files that have changed since the time of the last backup at the same level.

The OracleAS Backup and Recovery Tool doesn't back up or recover a OracleAS Metadata Repository that was added to an existing database. You have to handle this database through standard Oracle backup and recovery procedures in coordination with the BRT.

Recovery

You can use Oracle Application Server backups to recover your installation, whether or not you have experienced a failure that has corrupted the Metadata Repository.

If the repository has been corrupted, you have to recover it to a point in time just before the corruption occurred. If only configuration files have been lost, you can simply restore them using the OracleAS Backup and Recovery Tool. The Oracle Application Server documentation contains complete instructions for using this tool, as well as information that can help you determine which type of recovery operation you need to perform.

Implementing Secure Access and Management

If you are performing security management, you must have an appropriate username and password to access the Application Server Control or Grid Control tools:

Application Server Control

Use the `ias_admin` username and supply your assigned password to gain access to Application Server Control.

Grid Control

Use your Oracle Enterprise Manager 10g username and password to gain access to Grid Control.

If you plan to use the Oracle Internet Directory, the default for any password that you create must be at least five characters with at least one numeric character.

The OracleAS Metadata Repository and the Grid Control Management Repository are stored in Oracle databases. Oracle database administrators or database security administrators typically uses a DBA username (e.g., SYS) and connect as SYSDBA to start these database instances and perform other operations. Doing so provides the administrator with the necessary *privileges* (the rights to execute certain SQL statements) that have been assigned to the DBA *roles* (named groups of privileges).

Administrators who access Grid Control only for the purpose of monitoring individual application servers may not be provided these extended privileges or given login access to the Application Server Control tool. The details, however, depend on how your organization decides to maintain security and grant access.

Most users of Oracle Application Server simply need user authentication. For large implementations, you may want to configure *global authentication* across these distributed systems for users and Grid Control administrators and their roles. Global authentication allows you to maintain a single authentication list for multiple distributed servers and to implement OracleAS Single Sign-On.

You can use OracleAS Single Sign-On for authentication when logging into Grid Control. You can also secure the communication between agents and Oracle Management Services so that HTTPS is used.

Chapter 4 describes Oracle Application Server user security and identity management in more detail. But for now, be aware that in typical three-tier implementations, Oracle Application Server runs some of the application logic, serves as an interface between the clients and database servers, and provides the Oracle Identity Management infrastructure. The Oracle Internet Directory provides directory services running as applications against an Oracle database. The directory synchronization service, provisioning integrated service, and delegated administrative service are part of the Oracle Internet Directory. Security in middle-tier applications is controlled by applications' privileges and by preserving client identities through all three tiers. You can use the Application Server Control tool to configure and change configurations of the Oracle Internet Directory and OracleAS Single Sign-On.

Working with Oracle Support

No matter how much you know about Oracle Application Server, there are bound to be some issues that you can't resolve without help from Oracle Corporation. Part of the job of the Oracle Application Server administrator (or the DBA serving in that role) is to help resolve those issues. Oracle offers several levels of support:

- Basic product support
- Advanced support
- Incident support

Each support option costs extra, but regardless of your support level, you can get the most from Oracle by understanding how to best work with them.

Resolving problems with the assistance of Worldwide Customer Support Services can initially be frustrating to novices who report problems. You may be required to provide a lot of detailed technical information as part of this process. Oracle's mechanism for responding to a reported Oracle Application Server problem is called a *Service Request* (SR)—formerly known as a *Technical Assistance Request* (TAR). Oracle responds to Service Requests based on the priority or severity level at which problems are reported:

Priority level 2
> If the problem is impacting your ability to complete a project or do business, you should report the problem as priority level 2 to assure a timely response. If the problem is initially assigned a lower level, and the response hasn't been adequate, you should escalate the problem-resolution priority.

Priority level 1
> If business is halted because of the problem, you should report the problem as priority level 1. However, note that if you report a problem at level 1, you must be available for a callback (even after hours). Otherwise, Oracle will assume that the problem isn't as severe as initially reported, and they may lower the priority level for resolution.

You can report problems via phone, via email, or at the MetaLink web site. MetaLink support, which is included with basic product support, has become increasingly popular in recent years. With MetaLink you can quickly get answers to problems similar to your own. You may save time this way or even avoid the need for a physical response. MetaLink provides proactive notifications, customized home pages, technical libraries and forums, product life-cycle information, a bug database, and the ability to log SRs (TARs).

When you contact Oracle Support, you need your Customer Support Identification (CSI) number. Oracle Sales Consultants can also provide advice regarding how to report problems. In addition, Worldwide Customer Support Services offers training regarding effective use of their services.

Oracle Support issues MetaLink Notes whenever software bugs or vulnerabilities are discovered, and issues appropriate patches. Oracle Enterprise Manager 10g's Grid Control tool can automatically connect to MetaLink to provide you with up-to-date patch availability information specific to your installation. You can automatically gather patch-level information about your Oracle Application Servers using the enterprise configuration-management capabilities in Grid Control (viewable by selecting the Deployments tab, shown in Figure 3-5). Here you'll also find a link to lists of critical patch advisory alerts and the patches that should be applied in response to those alerts. You can then select the patches, stage them, and install them through Oracle Enterprise Manager's job system.

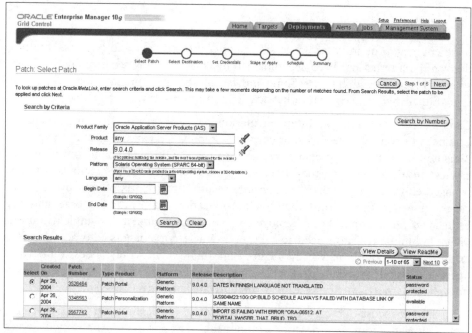

Figure 3-5. Grid Control configuration and patch management

CHAPTER 4

Security and Identity Management

In recent years, the increased accessibility of corporate data and business information via the Internet has been accompanied by corresponding security threats. Every system is vulnerable to hackers. Some of these hackers are criminals; some are pranksters. Either way, they can wreak havoc with corporate software and data.

Careful security planning and implementation is a key part of systems management. You need to control access to your corporate applications and protect both applications and their underlying data from harm caused by both malicious outsiders and careless insiders. Securing the Oracle Application Server environment is a multipronged effort, requiring that you consider security in all parts of your overall Oracle component infrastructure: the Oracle Application Server, the database, and any E-Business Suite applications deployed in your environment. In implementing a secure solution, you also need to take non-Oracle components into account. For example, you should analyze the security of your web browsers, assess underlying operating system vulnerabilities, determine whether your configuration requires a firewall, and investigate the need for virtual private networks (VPNs).

This chapter focuses on how to implement Oracle Application Server as part of a secure infrastructure. We describe components of the Oracle Application Server security framework that provide both the security and the identity management needed for centralized user management and support for complex password management policies. We conclude the chapter by briefly describing approaches and architectures for secure deployment.

Oracle Application Server Security Objectives

Oracle Application Server is designed to provide both basic and advanced security services while adhering to security standards. Oracle Application Server provides the following security services:

Authentication
> Verifies the identity of users and systems requesting applications, resources, and data (see the sidebar, "Identity Management").

Authorization
> Provides system-level determination and granting of the proper level of privileges to users or systems, thus possibly limiting their ability to use applications or resources or to manipulate data.

Access control
> Grants access to applications, data, and other resources consistent with security policies based on the authentication of the user, the authorization she has, and the type of access being requested.

Accountability and intrusion detection
> Ensures that activities contrary to policies are detected and recorded.

Data protection
> Protects data from access by unauthorized users via such mechanisms as encryption and integrity checks.

Identity Management

Identity management is a term used to describe the process of authenticating users and maintaining their identity over time and across multiple applications. The later section, "Oracle Identity Management," describes the framework used for the centralized management of user security in many Oracle Application Server deployments. Some Oracle Application Server components, such as OracleAS Reports Services and OracleAS Forms Services, may be deployed using their own user management and security services. OC4J applications may also be deployed using non-Oracle identity management services, such as Microsoft Active Directory, SunOne (formerly *i*Planet), and Netegrity SiteMinder. These third-party management services can be used with Oracle Identity Management.

In managing Oracle Application Server, your security goal should be to deploy the product in such a way that it can pass an independent security assessment. In such a secure deployment, you also need to consider coding practices, eliminate single points of failure in the security mechanism, set minimal privileges as a default, and enable intrusion detection to limit damage from security breaches. Those are extensive security topics that go well beyond the scope of this chapter. See the Appendix, however, for additional sources of security information.

Oracle Application Server Security Framework

Oracle Application Server provides a security framework that incorporates the following key components:

OracleAS Single Sign-On
> Enables use of a single password for authentication when establishing an initial connection and transparent authentication in subsequent connections. See the discussion of OracleAS Single Sign-On in the "Oracle Identity Management" section.

Oracle Internet Directory
> Used for authorization and user provisioning (e.g., supplying relevant user information needed for authentication by other services). See the "Oracle Internet Directory" section.

Oracle HTTP Server
> Based on Apache and includes its own basic security mechanisms to restrict access to directories or URLs. See Chapter 5.

Java Authentication and Authorization Service
> Enables secure access and execution of J2EE applications. JAAS is described in the later section "Java Authentication and Authorization Service."

Oracle Application Server Certificate Authority
> Used in the authentication process to ensure that entities such as users, databases, and clients are who they say they are. See the "Certificates" section.

The discussion of these components in this chapter only scratches the surface. Consult the Appendix for references to more detailed security-related documentation.

You may also consider using other Oracle Application Server components as you develop secure applications, such as OracleAS Web Cache, OC4J, and OracleAS Portal. For information about OracleAS Web Cache, OC4J, and OracleAS Portal, see Chapters 7, 6, and 13, respectively.

Figure 4-1 shows a typical Oracle Application Server security deployment architecture.

The Oracle HTTP Server shown in this figure relies on authentication methods that can restrict access to files and services such as basic user authentication (and OracleAS Single Sign-On), client-supplied X.509 certificates, and authentication by IP or hostname addresses. (Oracle Identity Management's role in authentication is described in the next section.) The Oracle HTTP Server enables intrusion detection by logging authentication attempts. It also extends the more generic Apache HTTP server through Oracle-specific *mods* such as the one for OracleAS Single Sign-On.

SSL connections are desirable in highly secure environments in which encryption and data integrity are mandated. SSL connections rely on digital certificate authentication

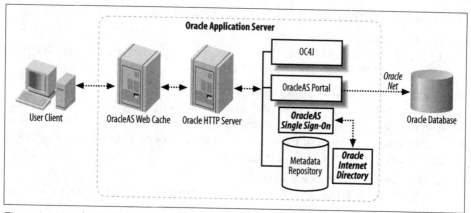

Figure 4-1. Oracle Application Server security deployment architecture

using the Public Key Infrastructure (PKI). (See the later "Certificates" section.) Because OracleAS Web Cache provides a caching front end to the Oracle HTTP Server and proxies requests to Oracle HTTP Server where necessary, OracleAS Web Cache is typically the termination point for SSL connections. However, OracleAS Web Cache can pass the contents of the SSL certificates to the Oracle HTTP Server for further use.

Additional advanced security mechanisms can be implemented with the Oracle HTTP Server. The SSL cryptographic protocol protects data between the Oracle HTTP Server and web clients. Session renegotiation is supported in such a way that different directories can have different degrees of encryption. Because SSL processing can consume a significant portion of CPU resources, Oracle Application Server 10g allows for the use of external dedicated SSL appliances to speed up the encryption process. SSL connections from the Oracle HTTP Server to OC4J are also supported.

The security of J2EE applications using Web Services is usually dependent on the coding of the applications themselves. But such applications can also be integrated as part of a more secure implementation using HTTP authentication, Oracle Wallets (described in a later section), or the UDDI registry. Introduced in Chapter 1, UDDI is essentially a "Yellow Pages" directory in which business entities can register themselves and the services they provide.

Oracle Identity Management

Oracle Identity Management provides user authentication, management, and authorization for Oracle Application Server services. Specific components of Oracle Application Server, such as OracleAS Portal, OracleAS Forms Services, OracleAS Reports Services, and OracleAS Discoverer, are designed to leverage Oracle Identity Management as well.

Oracle Identity Management includes the following services:

Oracle Internet Directory
An LDAP-compliant directory service for centralized user management that provides LDAP APIs for C, Java, and PL/SQL.

Oracle Directory Provisioning Integration Service
A set of bidirectional services and interfaces that can notify applications and non-Oracle LDAP directories of changes to user information. These services enable synchronization of the Oracle Internet Directory with other repositories, non-Oracle directories, and metadirectories.

Oracle Delegated Administration Service
A part of Oracle Internet Directory providing trusted administration of directory information by users and application administrators.

OracleAS Single Sign-On
A service providing OracleAS Single Sign-On access to applications accessed through Oracle Application Server and other web applications.

OracleAS Certificate Authority
A service used for generating and publishing X509v3 certificates used in authentication based on a PKI.

The Oracle Internet Directory enables users to be defined by identity, credentials, profiles, and preferences in a single and central location. All other Oracle Identity Management services rely on the Oracle Internet Directory to provide this information.

As noted earlier, Oracle Identity Management isn't required for all Oracle Application Server deployments. For example, a simple OC4J application might use other identity management services such as Microsoft Active Directory. In other situations, you might choose to use the Oracle Internet Directory preconfigured for directory synchronization with Microsoft Active Directory or other LDAP-compliant directories.

The challenge of managing multiple user accounts in a large organization can be mitigated by using the Oracle Internet Directory for identity management. You can use the Oracle Internet Directory to consolidate separated user definitions to a single location and also synchronize passwords with non-Oracle Internet directories. For example, you can synchronize the orclpassword attribute in the Oracle Internet Directory with the userpassword attribute in SunONE/iPlanet.

Oracle calls this directory-based user management *Enterprise User Security*. It allows passwords to be maintained for application users in a central location. The identity management infrastructure can also manage database roles and security clearances (for use with the Oracle database's Label Security feature).

Oracle Identity Management and OracleAS Single Sign-On

Oracle Identity Management supports a variety of complex password policies. These fall into two categories:

- Value-based policies (including minimum lengths and the presence of a minimum number of special characters)
- State-based policies (e.g., expiration and maximum number of retries)

Many users face a proliferation of passwords as they gain access to more applications and systems. Because it is so easy for users to forget passwords when they have so many to remember, users may end up writing them down in public places, thus creating a security risk. Oracle Identity Management can help lift this burden on users by enabling deployment of single sign-on, allowing a single user and password combination across these applications and systems.

Follow these steps to set up a basic single sign-on system:

1. Install the identity management infrastructure database, database server, and single sign-on servers using the Oracle Universal Installer.
2. Configure the HTTP servers in the single sign-on middle tier.
3. Configure the HTTP hardware load balancer or OracleAS Web Cache.
4. Configure the identity management infrastructure database single sign-on server to accept authentication requests from an externally published address of the OracleAS Single Sign-On server.
5. Reregister the mod_osso (OracleAS Single Sign-On extension) to the OracleAS Single Sign-On middle tier.

Federated identities are supported in OracleAS Single Sign-On; these allow user identities to be authenticated from one or more trusted authentication sources. *Multilevel authentication* is also supported and can grant higher privileges with higher degrees of authentication through the use of certificates, which are described in the next section.

Certificates

Certificates are used in the authentication process to ensure that entities such as users, databases, and clients are who they say they are. An OracleAS Certificate Authority (OCA) can grant a certificate that is signed by the OCA private key and then publish the certificate with the entity's name and a public key. The certificate also usually includes information about rights, uses, and privileges assigned, a serial number, and an expiration date.

Where data is encrypted using an owner's private key, it can be decrypted only with a matching public key. Similarly, data encrypted using a public key (usually data to be shared with another entity) can be decrypted only with that entity's matching private key.

The OracleAS Certificate Authority is critical to creating the public keys. The management of public keys is often said to occur through a PKI.

Oracle wallets

You can use Oracle wallets as part of the enabling infrastructure in highly secure Oracle Application Server implementations. A *wallet* is a password-protected container that stores private keys, certificates, and trusted certificates needed by SSL.

Security managers can use the Oracle Wallet Manager to manage passwords, provide Triple-DES encryption for storing private keys associated with X.509 certificates, store wallets in a Microsoft Windows registry, store X.509 certificates and private keys in the PKCS#12 format, and store multiple certificates for each wallet (SSL, S/MIME signature, S/MIME encryption, code-signing, and certificate authority signing). Wallets can be uploaded and retrieved from LDAP-compliant directories.

Oracle Internet Directory

The Oracle Internet Directory is an LDAP-compliant directory service used for Oracle Application Server user management. The Lightweight Directory Access Protocol is a standard for directories of users and resources. As an LDAP-compliant directory service, the Oracle Internet Directory can interact with other LDAP-compliant directories, mentioned earlier in the description of the Oracle Directory Provisioning and Integration Service.

You may want to configure a highly available Oracle Internet Directory by deploying the Oracle Internet Directory repository across multiple database instances in a RAC configuration. In such a configuration, multiple Oracle database servers appear as a single instance. When you do this, you may also want to use a hardware load balancer as a front end to the multiple Oracle Internet Directory instances. Using RAC and a load balancer can also provide a high-availability OracleAS Single Sign-On service, or you can configure highly available OracleAS Single Sign-On using failover to a standby machine or through Oracle Internet Directory replication.

If you build a RAC configuration, you should consider coordinating the issuing of certificates. For example, keeping private keys in only one location is desirable for security. You can do this by storing the SSL certificate on a hardware accelerator appliance. The SSL session key negotiation and symmetric encryption workload from the Oracle HTTP Server or OracleAS Web Cache would also be handled on the appliance, resulting in better performance.

Java Authentication and Authorization Service

The Java Authentication and Authorization Service can ensure secure access and execution of J2EE applications. The JAAS provider includes a Java standard framework and programming interface supporting user authentication, authorization, and implementation of JAAS policies (permissions).

Two providers store users, roles, and JAAS policies:

XML file user manager
> Supports role-based access control and authentication from XML files

LDAP user manager
> Provides role-based access control and authentication using LDAP and the Oracle Internet Directory

J2EE applications can be integrated in an OracleAS Single Sign-On deployment model.

A J2EE application can use JAAS to restrict access to specific users based on the specific authorization permissions they have been granted. For example, consider usage in a retail firm. A contract administrator determines which product suppliers are allowed to deliver to retail store locations. The contract administrator user is given permission to use the application to add suppliers and products to the database. JAAS enables authentication of the contract administrator's login identification and the authorization needed to update supplier and product information. A store manager might use the same application to monitor shipments from these suppliers to determine when to expect the arrival of inventory. However, if that manager isn't permitted to negotiate contracts, he would not be given authorization to add suppliers or products to the database.

For more information on JAAS and its use with OC4J, see the "Java Authentication and Authorization Service" section in Chapter 6.

Secure Deployment

To ensure security throughout your IT environment, you have to decide how you are going to deploy the components of the overall environment. This section covers some of the considerations you need to keep in mind when implementing a secure deployment of Oracle Application Server 10*g*, including the use of DMZs, the delegation of security privileges, and the use of Oracle Enterprise Manager 10*g* to manage security.

DMZ Deployment

Oracle Application Server 10*g* enables deployment using a DMZ topology. In the context of computer networking, a DMZ is a server placed between two firewalls and thus separated from the Internet and intranet(s). Its placement means that the server exists in a secure buffer zone.

The word *DMZ* comes from a military term referring to a "demilitarized zone." DMZ was a term used during the Korean War to indicate a no-man's land where troops residing in North Korea and South Korea were not allowed to enter. The DMZ was a zone of security created to prevent attacks or incursions from either side.

In one typical deployment, you might want to use a DMZ to separate an OracleAS Portal repository database from the database containing business data. The DMZ prevents a hacker from gaining access to the OracleAS Portal password in Oracle Application Server and then using the OracleAS Portal's DBA privileges to wreak havoc on corporate data. In another typical deployment, you might use the DMZ topology for intrusion containment.

Figure 4-2 shows a typical DMZ deployment in an Oracle Application Server environment.

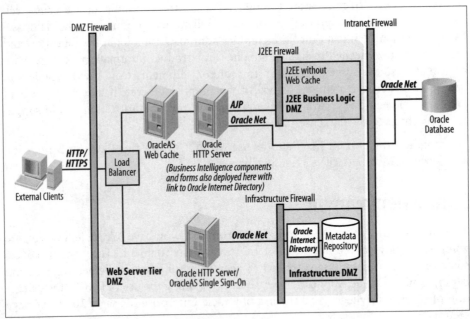

Figure 4-2. Oracle Application Server typical DMZ deployment

For details about DMZ deployment strategies, see the *Oracle Application Server 10g Security Guide,* a part of the standard Oracle Application Server documentation set. (That manual, and many others, are referenced in the Appendix.) In that guide, Oracle provides the following recommendations:

- Make sure that all OracleAS Web Cache, HTTP servers, OracleAS Single Sign-On HTTP servers, HTTP load balancers, and HTTPS-to-HTTP appliances reside in the DMZ.

- If direct Oracle Internet Directory access is needed from the Internet, place the Oracle Internet Directory servers in the DMZ.

- Don't allow J2EE servers to be directly accessible to the intranet. (Instead, place business logic behind a J2EE firewall.)

- Place databases containing metadata and the Oracle Internet Directory database behind a firewall in an infrastructure DMZ.

- Deploy OracleAS Portal on a single HTTP server with OC4J within the web server tier's DMZ; you can also deploy OracleAS Discoverer, OracleAS Reports Services, and OracleAS Forms Services behind an OC4J firewall.

Delegation of Privileges

An Oracle Internet Directory infrastructure may be shared by administrators of applications in different business areas or with different responsibilities. A *delegation model* provided in Oracle Application Server enables the delegation of appropriate levels of privileges within a shared infrastructure.

Delegation is structured as follows:

- The Oracle Internet Directory super user orcladmin creates an identity management realm, identifies the realm administrator, and delegates all privileges to the realm administrator.

- The realm administrator delegates roles for managing Oracle components and grants privileges associated with those roles.

- The context administrators, in turn, delegate Oracle Application Server roles.

- Oracle Application Server user roles include installation administration, application administration, identity management infrastructure administration, and Oracle Application Server application users.

Security Management Through Oracle Enterprise Manager 10*g*

Oracle Enterprise Manager 10*g* provides a single interface for managing multiple Oracle Application Servers through the Application Server Control tool installed for each application server being monitored. We discussed Oracle Enterprise Manager 10*g*, Application Server Control, and other system management tools in more detail in Chapter 3.

You can use Application Server Control for a number of different security management activities. For example, through Application Server Control you can configure application security resources, including JAAS provider services. You can also configure and modify the Oracle Internet Directory and OracleAS Single Sign-On. You can use the Application Server Control Infrastructure page to change infrastructure services if you change the Oracle HTTP Server OracleAS Single Sign-On port number on an identity management installation, the Oracle Internet Directory port number (non-SSL or SSL), the Oracle Internet Directory Mode (dual-mode or SSL), or the host on which Oracle Identity Management or the OracleAS Metadata Repository resides. If you do this, you must perform a variety of manual command-line tasks to prepare the new infrastructure services before using Application Server Control to make the change (those tasks are described in the *Oracle Application Server 10g Administrator's Guide*).

CHAPTER 5

Oracle HTTP Server

The Oracle HTTP Server acts as the web server or listener for Oracle Application Server. Based on the Open Source Apache Web Server (Version 1.3 code base), the Oracle HTTP Server is the heart of Oracle Application Server, directing requests to the appropriate source for the requests. Requests for both static and dynamic content are processed through the Oracle HTTP Server. Static content is served from the local file system, while the Oracle HTTP Server redirects dynamic content requests to the appropriate executable resource.

Oracle isn't the first organization to use Apache as the web server component of their application server. Several others have also used Apache. So why is Apache such an attractive choice for a web server?

- Apache has an extremely flexible architecture; most of its functionality is provided by a set of plugged-in modules, or *mods*. You can add any desired functionality to Apache by creating an appropriate module. Oracle has created several custom mods for Oracle Application Server, as we'll discuss later in this chapter.

- Apache has a very flexible configuration system. Directives specified in a set of text-based configuration files are used to load any desired module and have it process requests using a variety of methods—for example, by location, file type, or other indicators.

- Largely because of its large installed base (more than 64% of all Internet web sites at the time of this writing), Apache has become a very stable and secure web server. Combine this with the ability to leverage a large existing Apache administrator workforce, and it makes sense to use Apache's existing code base as a basis for the Oracle HTTP Server.

This chapter delves into the workings of the Oracle HTTP Server. It starts with an overview of the Apache architecture. Next, it covers the modules Oracle bundles with the Oracle HTTP Server that aren't part of a standard Apache distribution. It touches on how security and management services hook into the Oracle HTTP

Server, and it finishes up with a look at integrating third-party listeners with the Oracle HTTP Server.

Apache Architecture

Before examining how Oracle has extended the Apache server for use in Oracle Application Server, you need to take some time to learn about Apache's basic architecture. The Apache architecture (prefork model) consists of a parent process that starts one or more child processes (Unix) or threads (Windows). The child processes each serve a single request at a time. When a child process finishes serving a request, it once again becomes available to serve another request.

A child process manages a request through its life cycle. The request life cycle can be broken down into phases. Each request is taken through the life cycle phases until the request is completed, or until an error occurs. Figure 5-1 shows the Apache request life cycle. Apache functionality is provided by modules that are plugged into an appropriate phase of the request life cycle.

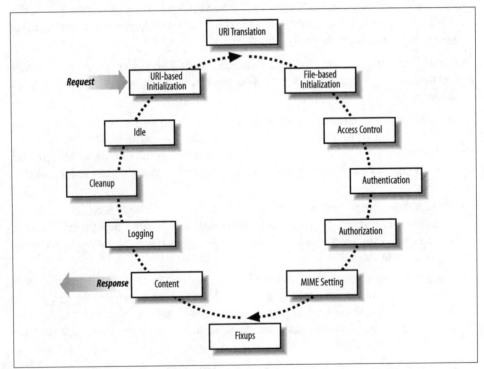

Figure 5-1. The Apache request life cycle

Modules are typically plugged in using an AddHandler or SetHandler directive within a URL mapping directive in the Apache configuration file *httpd.conf*. A module has hooks in the form of callback methods that are implemented for the desired phase of the life cycle. The URL directive activates the handler based on a particular characteristic of a request's URI.

At the end of each request, Apache logs the request URI to an access log file. A different access log can be created for each URL mapping directive you specify in the configuration file. In addition, you can customize the format with directives or replace the logging mechanism altogether with the appropriate directive. If an error occurs, the error is logged to its own error log file.

Tools exist that allow an Apache server administrator to analyze these logs for bad URLs, traffic patterns, and so on. Using these tools, an administrator can eliminate bad links, plan server capacity, or identify malicious activity—to name only a few possibilities.

To learn more about Apache, check out the Apache documentation available online at *http://httpd.apache.org*. You may also want to consult the book *Apache: The Definitive Guide* (O'Reilly)

Oracle-Supplied Modules

Oracle supplies some key, additional modules that turn Apache into the Oracle HTTP Server. Oracle has also made minor improvements to the code base in the area of security and other defect fixes.

The Oracle HTTP Server installs most but not all of the standard Apache modules. Those removed from Apache are either deprecated or have something to do with authentication. OracleAS Single Sign-On has replaced the removed authentication modules' functionality.

What About Apache 2.0?

Those of you who are Apache administrators may be asking why Oracle is using the Apache Version 1.3 code base and not the Apache 2.0 code base. The reason is that at the time Oracle Application Server was first in the works (back in 2001), Apache 2.0 didn't even exist. Oracle decided to use Apache Version 1.3 because, at that time, "it proved highly reliable, secure, and had great performance characteristics."[a] Apache Version 2.0 was released for production in April of 2002. Although it offers improved performance and important new features (e.g., support for IPv6), Oracle has stated that it is still "less reliable and has more security vulnerabilities than Version 1.3." Oracle's current plans are to use Apache 2.0 on Release 10.0.4 of Oracle Application Server, provided that Apache 2.0 is appropriately secure and defect-free at that time.

---

[a] A quote from one of Oracle's Statement of Direction documents for Oracle Application Server.

Third-Party Modules

Oracle includes the following third-party modules that aren't part of the standard Apache distribution:

```
mod_fastcgi
mod_perl
mod_jserv
```

The following sections briefly describe these modules.

mod_fastcgi

mod_fastcgi provides an efficient CGI environment that allows C, C++, or any executable program to run in a performant manner. In a FastCGI environment, each program runs in a cached child process. This improves performance over the CGI environment because it avoids the need to recreate a new process for each request.

Java and Perl programs can be run via CGI, but OC4J (described in Chapter 6) and mod_perl (described in the next section) provide a better-performing environment for these two programming languages.

mod_perl

mod_perl provides an efficient and highly integrated Perl environment. Like FastCGI, mod_perl operates more efficiently by caching Perl processes. Unlike CGI, mod_perl provides complete access to Apache's request life cycle API. This capability allows mod_perl programmers to write both web applications and Apache modules using Perl.

mod_jserv

mod_jserv exists solely for legacy Apache Jserv support. Release 9.0.1 of Oracle Application Server used an Oracle-modified version of Apache Jserv as its servlet container. Jserv has long since been replaced by OC4J; mod_jserv will be discontinued with Release 10.1.2.

Oracle Modules

Oracle also has a set of its own modules that add functionality to the Oracle HTTP Server:

mod_certheaders
> Provides OracleAS Web Cache and load-balancing hardware SSL termination at the Oracle HTTP Server

mod_oc4j *and* mod_plsql
> Provide dynamic content generation

mod_oradav

> Provides Web Distributed Authoring and Versioning (WebDAV) support

mod_ossl *and* mod_osso

> Provide security services

mod_dms, mod_oprocmgr, *and* mod_onsint

> Provide Oracle Application Server management integration

mod_certheaders

mod_certheaders enables OracleAS Web Cache and other load-balancing hardware SSL termination at the Oracle HTTP Server. This allows the Oracle HTTP Server to pass SSL information to the other modules. The information is passed using HTTP headers and is then accessible as CGI environment variables.

mod_oc4j

mod_oc4j routes requests to OC4J using the ajp13 protocol. It allows Oracle Application Server to execute J2EE programs in OC4J in response to a request's URI.

The Oracle HTTP Server uses a separate configuration file for mod_oc4j, appropriately named *mod_oc4j.conf,* that is included into the Oracle HTTP Server's main configuration file *httpd.conf.* URL mapping directives in *mod_oc4j.conf* determine which URI requests are forwarded to OC4J. In addition, mapping of context directories (how the URL is mapped into OC4J) and protocol settings are also entered into *mod_oc4j.conf.* As with all Oracle HTTP Server configuration files, *mod_oc4j.conf* is modified using Oracle Enterprise Manager Application Server Control.

mod_plsql

mod_plsql routes requests to an Oracle database. It executes PL/SQL stored procedures in an Oracle database in response to a request's URI. A stored procedure used in this way is analogous to a CGI program or Java servlet.

mod_plsql has three configuration files:

cache.conf

> Configures mod_plsql's PL/SQL cache

dads.conf

> Contains URL mapping directives with connection information in the form of database access descriptors (DADs) that are automatically used by mod_plsql to log into an Oracle database

plsql.conf

> Contains directives to load mod_plsql and to set its logging location

The *cache.conf* and *dads.conf* files are included in *plsql.conf,* which, in turn, is included in *oracle_apache.conf. oracle_apache.conf* is included in the Oracle HTTP Server's main configuration file *httpd.conf.*

mod_oradav

mod_oradav enables distributed authoring and versioning using the WebDAV proto-col. mod_oradav can read and write files to either the server's local file system or an Oracle database.

mod_oradav has one configuration file, *moddav.conf*. Directives in this file load the module and map a URI to either a local file system directory or an Oracle database.

mod_ossl

mod_ossl provides Oracle SSL support. This module replaces the OpenSSL module mod_ssl. Oracle's implementation of SSL supports SSL Version 3.0, based on Certi-com and RSA technology.

mod_osso

mod_osso enables OracleAS Single Sign-On support. With OracleAS Single Sign-On, a user can use the same authentication credentials to log into all applications sup-ported by the same OracleAS Single Sign-On server.

mod_dms

mod_dms provides a hook into Oracle's Dynamic Monitoring Service. DMS measures runtime performance statistics for the Oracle HTTP Server and OC4J.

mod_oprocmgr

mod_oprocmgr provides legacy support for Oracle-modified Apache Jserv (servlet con-tainer) and provides a hook into DMS. It will be discontinued with release 10.1.2.

mod_onsint

mod_onsint provides a hook into the Oracle Notification Server (ONS), which is a component of the Oracle Process Manager and Notification Server. OPMN starts, stops, and ensures that the Oracle HTTP Server and OC4J are up and running. OPMN provides fault tolerance by restarting an Apache process if it fails.

Third-Party Listener Support

Oracle Application Server can also use two other web servers (listeners) besides Apache:

- Java System Web Server (formerly Sun ONE Web Server)
- Microsoft Internet Information Server (IIS)

Oracle Application Server provides a proxy plug-in that allows you to transparently forward requests from these two servers to the Oracle HTTP Server. In this setup, the

Oracle HTTP Server acts as a reverse HTTP proxy server; it receives and forwards a request to the appropriate content engine, but then points a redirect to the third-party listener. The Oracle HTTP Server as a proxy server mimics the host address and port of these listeners so that the proxy is completely transparent to any applications using the third-party listener.

Oracle Application Server also provides a lightweight single sign-on plug-in for these two servers. The plug-in is a partial implementation of the OracleAS Single Sign-On module. It allows these servers to seamlessly integrate with OracleAS Single Sign-On on the application server.

CHAPTER 6

Oracle Application Server Containers for J2EE

The Oracle Application Server Containers for J2EE product provides the Java environment for the Oracle Application Server. OC4J is a 100% pure Java J2EE Server. As such, it can use—and applications can be developed with—any standard Java Development Kit (JDK). This standardization allows you the option of using the JVM that best leverages your hardware platform. OC4J has J2EE-certified Servlet and EJB containers, and a JSP translator. OC4J provides all the standard J2EE services such as session, transaction, and persistence management.

Table 6-1 lists the various J2EE APIs supported by the OC4J releases at the time of this writing.

Table 6-1. OC4J J2EE API support

	Release			
API	**9.0.1**	**9.0.2**	**9.0.3**	**9.0.4**
Java Development Kit (JDK)	1.1	1.3	1.3	1.4
Enterprise JavaBeans (EJB)	1.1	1.1+	2.0	2.0
J2EE Connector Architecture		1.0	1.0	1.0
Java Authentication and Authorization Service (JAAS)		1.0	1.0	1.0
JavaMail API		1.1.2	1.1.2	1.1.2
Java API for XML Parsing (JAXP)		1.0	1.1	1.1
Java Database Connectivity (JDBC)	1.1	2.0	2.0+	2.0+
Java Message Service (JMS)	1.0.1	1.0.1	1.0.2	1.0.2b
Java Naming and Directory Interface (JNDI)		1.2	1.2	1.2
JavaServer Pages (JSP)	1.0	1.1	1.2	1.2
Java Transaction API (JTA)		1.0.1	1.0.1	1.0.1
Java Servlet	2.0	2.3	2.3	2.3

This information may be out of date by the time you read this, but the list demonstrates Oracle's commitment to support the most current versions of J2EE APIs in a timely manner. If you're interested in knowing what J2EE APIs are currently supported, go to the Oracle Technology Network web site at *http://otn.oracle.com* and look up the information under documentation, application server, *OC4J User's Guide.*

As discussed in Chapter 2, OC4J can be clustered across hosts to provide almost unlimited horizontal scaling to satisfy any level of demand. However, OC4J can also be configured with several instances on a host to ease the management of applications, or to run as a lightweight standalone server for application development purposes.

A great deal of what we describe in this chapter is standard J2EE functionality. Nevertheless, we cover this functionality to ensure that readers of all levels will be able to understand the added value the J2EE portion of Oracle Application Server provides. In addition, this chapter covers Oracle value-added services, touches on server management, discusses how deployment is supported, examines standalone configuration, and finishes up with the impact that clustering the OC4J has on maintaining state in J2EE applications.

OC4J Components

OC4J consists of three components:

- A servlet container
- An EJB container
- A JSP translator

The servlet and EJB containers have access to a standard set of services provided by the J2EE architecture that are managed by the server.

The following sections describe these components and the relationships among them.

Servlet Container

A *servlet* is a server-side Java program that extends the functionality of the application server in which it resides. A *servlet container* is the server-managed environment for executing a Java servlet.

J2EE defines both a generic servlet and an extension called an *HTTP servlet*. An HTTP servlet has all the generic servlet capabilities plus functionality specific to dealing with the HTTP protocol. HTTP servlets are the most common type of servlet used in a servlet container because HTTP is the most common application-level protocol used on the Internet today. When someone requests dynamic content from a Java application server such as OC4J using HTTP, the request is most likely serviced by an HTTP servlet.

A servlet container manages the life cycle of a servlet as follows:

1. It loads any necessary class files from the host file system.

2. After class files have been loaded, it initializes the servlet. At any subsequent time that a request requiring the servlet is received, the already loaded and initialized servlet is executed.

3. When the application server shuts down, the servlet instance is destroyed, and the memory it used is garbage-collected.

A servlet is very performant because the same loaded and initialized servlet, already in memory, is used for each request.

A servlet container also provides a set of standard services to a servlet. A common example is access to data sources, which provide servlets with access to databases. Services are discussed in more depth later in this chapter.

The Hypertext Markup Language (HTML) produced by servlets to provide content for a web browser is sent to the browser by calling an HTTP servlet method that streams output back to the browser. This mechanism implies that a programmer writes Java code to produce web content. Creating web content in this Java-centric fashion may be well suited to programmers, but not web designers. To enable web designers to create dynamic content, an alternate method of designing servlets was created that is HTML-, not Java-centric. This alternative is called JavaServer Pages, described in the next section.

JavaServer Pages Translator

A JavaServer Pages translator parses a JSP file, typically composed of HTML and Java code snippets and/or tags, and creates a corresponding servlet. This servlet is then executed in the servlet container like any other servlet. The difference here is that the source code in a JSP file consists of HTML with embedded Java code instead of Java code with embedded HTML.

JSP also offers a means of using other markup languages such as Wireless Markup Language (WML) for mobile devices or, better yet, XML. If XML is used, an XML technology called the eXtensible Stylesheet Language for Transformations (XSLT) translates the markup into a suitable format for the device on which it's used: HTML for a web browser or WML for a wireless device. See Chapter 10 for a discussion of XML and Chapter 14 for information about OracleAS Wireless.

Enterprise JavaBeans Container

An EJB container is a server-managed environment for executing EJBs. An EJB is a Java program that can be executed as a component in a distributed fashion. A client program, a servlet, or another EJB can remotely execute the methods in an EJB. An EJB can also be executed locally if it exists in the same application server as the calling servlet or EJB. The EJB container provides transaction, security, and persistence management, as well as access to other server services such as Data Sources.

In the J2EE architecture, an EJB can isolate business logic, represent a persistent entity, or process asynchronous information feeds. Appropriately, there are three types of EJBs: session, entity, and message-driven.

Session bean

A session bean, or EJB, is used for business logic. A session bean can be stateful, or stateless. A *stateful EJB* remembers its internal values between invocations, while a *stateless EJB* doesn't. A stateful EJB is typically used to model complex business processes that require several steps to complete, whereas a stateless EJB is used for simple, one-method invocation processes and computations.

Entity bean

An entity bean, or EJB, is used to model a business entity. It typically retrieves its internal values from, and saves its values to, a relational database. Behavior that is intrinsic to the entity is modeled using its own methods. (For some, which methods belong in the entity bean and which belong in a session bean that uses the entity bean can be a source of confusion.) An entity bean can use container- or bean-managed persistence. With *container-managed persistence* (CMP), the EJB container is responsible for creating and executing SQL to retrieve and save values from and to a database. With *bean-managed persistence* (BMP), it's the programmer's responsibility to write the required persistence code using JDBC, Java Data Objects (JDO), or a value-added object-relational mapping tool such as TopLink.

Message-driven bean (MDB)

A message-driven bean, or EJB, processes a stream of asynchronous messages from a queue. The asynchronous nature of messaging systems allows a client to post messages to a queue without waiting for a response. In turn, it allows a message consumer, such as an MDB, to process messages from a queue independent of a conversation with a client program. MDBs process messages delivered via the Java Message Service (JMS) API. JMS provides an implementation-independent API for accessing messaging systems. One of the strengths of MDBs is that they can process messages concurrently, providing a scalable means of handling asynchronous information.

Transactions can be container- or bean-managed:

Container-managed transactions

In such transactions, the EJB container coordinates commits or rollbacks in a distributed fashion.

Bean (or component)-managed transactions

In such transactions, the component is responsible for its own transaction coordination.

In a similar fashion, security and persistence (as mentioned earlier) can be managed by the container or by the component. When the container is responsible for these services, the programmer declaratively specifies the appropriate parameters in a file called a *deployment descriptor*.

Whether exposing its configuration using a deployment descriptor, or being self-managed, an EJB exists as an independent software component that can conceivably be mixed and matched with other components to build an application.

OC4J Component Relationships

Figure 6-1 demonstrates the relationship between these three components and the services to which they have access:

1. A request is sent to the application server's Oracle HTTP Server. The request is identified as a servlet or a JSP by its URI and is appropriately forwarded to OC4J.

2. The servlet, possibly generated by translating a JSP, may access an EJB or other OC4J container services, such as a data source, to produce dynamic content.

3. The servlet, in turn, streams any generated content back through the Oracle HTTP Server to the browser.

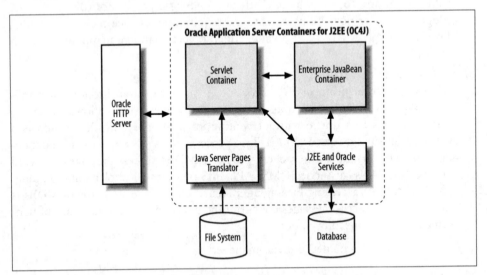

Figure 6-1. OC4J component relationships

OC4J provides access to the J2EE architecture's APIs and to Oracle's own value-added APIs by what it refers to as OC4J Services. These services are described in the next section.

OC4J Services

This section takes a high-level look at each service provided by OC4J to servlets and EJBs. Some of these are standard J2EE services while others are Oracle value-added services. The OC4J services consist of the following:

- Java Naming and Directory Interface (JNDI)
- J2EE Connector Architecture
- Java DataBase Connectivity (JDBC)
- Java Message Service (JMS)
- Remote Method Invocation (RMI)
- Server-side HTTPS
- Java Transaction API (JTA)
- Java Authentication and Authorization Service (JAAS)
- Java Mail
- Java API for XML Parsing (JAXP)
- Java Object Cache

We'll discuss JNDI first because it is often used to access other resources in the list.

Java Naming and Directory Interface

The Java Naming and Directory Interface provides Java programs with standardized access to various naming and directory implementations. Within OC4J, servlets and EJBs can access global resources, such as Data Sources, and environment variables defined in each servlet or EJB deployment descriptor with the default JNDI context. The OC4J's naming mechanism is implemented using an XML file.

If a servlet or EJB requires access to an external directory, such as LDAP implemented by the Oracle Internet Directory, the URI to the external directory can be specified as a parameter in the servlet or EJB's deployment descriptor, looked up via JNDI using the default context, and then used to create a new context that accesses the external directory once again using JNDI.

JNDI can access various naming and directory services using service provider interfaces (SPIs) to abstract the API for the naming or directory service. This capability allows JNDI to use any desired naming or directory service. The service can be enabled by configuring its SPI.

J2EE Connector Architecture

The J2EE Connector Architecture provides a standardized interface for J2EE applications to access existing Enterprise Information Systems (EIS), such as Peoplesoft,

SAP, mainframes, and so on. A Java program can access any EIS for which a J2EE Connector implementation exists. A J2EE Connector is implemented in the form of a driver called a *resource adapter*. A resource adapter is a driver that connects to and communicates with an EIS.

A JDBC driver is an example of a resource adapter that allows a servlet or EJB to connect to a database. However, the JDBC API existed long before the J2EE Connector Architecture, and JDBC drivers are very commonly used, so they have their own configuration facilities.

There are two types of resource adapters:

Standalone resource adapter
This type of resource adapter is globally available—that is, it is available to all applications.

Embedded resource adapter
This type of resource adapter exists within a deployed Enterprise Application aRchive (EAR) file, available to the components within an application, but not to other applications running on the same instance of the OC4J.

Resource adapters must abide by a set of quality of service contracts, which means that they must provide connection pooling, transaction management, and security management as follows:

Connection pooling
Provides a way to efficiently allocate resource adapter instances by caching them in a pool. This ability allows the connections to be checked out of a pool when needed, and then checked back in when they are no longer needed. Connection pooling reduces the instantaneous workload (the number of resources in use at the same time at both ends of a connection) on the OC4J and the host EIS.

Transaction management
Provides a facility whereby the resource adapter implements the Java Transaction API so that an EIS that is being accessed can participate in a global distributed transaction.

Security management
Provides a facility whereby the resource adapter supports authentication, authorization, and secure connections.

In addition, resource adapters must support both component- and container-managed security. Component-managed security is simple enough; all connection information is supplied programmatically. However, with container-managed security, information such as sign-on parameters is specified declaratively in the application's deployment descriptor.

Java DataBase Connectivity

The Java DataBase Connectivity API provides Java programs with standardized access to tabular data sources. Modeled after Microsoft's Open DataBase Connectivity (ODBC) API, JDBC was originally designed to access relational databases. JDBC has evolved, as has ODBC, to handle any tabular data, including comma- and tab-separated values in operating system data files. In addition, with the publication of the new SQL standard, SQL 1999, and Oracle's complete implementation of the new SQL standard, Oracle's JDBC drivers now support even object-relational data.

OC4J supports both Oracle and non-Oracle JDBC drivers. For the Oracle database, the Oracle Thin (type 4) and OCI (type 2) drivers are supported. For non-Oracle databases, Data-Direct (type 4) drivers for IBM DB2 UDB, Microsoft SQL Server, Informix, and Sybase are provided with OC4J. It is entirely possible to use any JDBC driver, because the OC4J is a standard J2EE server implementation.

 Type 2 drivers are part Java and part operating-system executable code. Type 4 drivers are 100% pure Java.

Access to JDBC is configured globally through Application Server Control, which in turn makes an entry in the global *data-sources.xml* file. Configuration can also be made locally in a servlet, EJB, or enterprise application's deployment descriptor. In addition, an application can be packaged with its own *data-sources.xml* file.

A servlet or EJB uses JNDI to look up and retrieve a DataSource at runtime. A DataSource is a JDBC object that represents a logical JDBC connection to a tabular data source. A servlet or EJB manipulates the data in the host database through the methods of objects created by a DataSource.

OC4J has three types of data sources (not to be confused with driver types):

Emulated data sources
> Emulate the XA API without providing a full XA implementation. (The XA API is discussed later in the "Java Transaction API" section.) An emulated data source acts as though it supports JTA, but it doesn't support two-phase commits. This allows the emulated data source to perform better than its nonemulated counterpart, yet still support local transactions.

Nonemulated data sources
> Provide full XA and JTA global transaction support. A nonemulated data source is recommended only for distributed transactions because the additional overhead of full support can unnecessarily impede the performance of transactions when full support isn't needed.

Non-JTA data sources
> Provide no global transaction support.

OC4J supports the caching of data sources to efficiently allocate database resources and to improve application performance. Three caching schemes are available:

Dynamic scheme
> This scheme grows the pool of cached data sources as needed, and later it removes unused data sources when they are no longer used. The minimum pool size can be configured so that data sources are already cached upon startup of the OC4J instance in which they reside.

Fixed wait scheme
> This scheme uses a maximum parameter to limit the number of data sources in a pool. When the limit is reached, and a servlet or EJB requests a connection, it must wait indefinitely until another process returns a data source to the pool.

Fixed return null scheme
> This scheme works in a way that's similar to the fixed wait scheme, but instead of waiting indefinitely, it immediately returns a null data source (effectively no data source) to the servlet or EJB if a data source isn't available in the pool.

Java Transaction API

The Java Transaction API provides a standardized set of interfaces for managing a distributed transaction. Java programs, such as EJBs, are intrinsically distinct components that are assembled into applications at deployment time. You can define transaction scope between various EJBs and their methods in either of two ways:

Bean-managed transactions (BMT)
> Transaction scope is defined programmatically during development in each EJB's deployment descriptor.

Container-managed transactions (CMT)
> Transaction scope is defined declaratively at deployment time in each EJB's deployment descriptor.

OC4J, like any other J2EE-compliant EJB container, supports both bean-managed and container-managed transactions. In addition, the OC4J supports two-phase commits. In the context of OC4J, a *two-phase commit* is a transaction that involves two or more Oracle databases. In other words, when two or more resources involved in a transaction are all Oracle databases, OC4J's two-phase commit process guarantees that all involved databases will commit or roll back a given transaction.

Java Message Service

The Java Message Service provides Java programs with standardized access to enterprise messaging systems. Messaging systems provide a persistent message queue: one or more programs can place messages on a given queue, while one or more programs can retrieve or consume messages from a given queue.

A queue is what gives messaging products the ability to support asynchronous messaging, and asynchronous messaging is, in turn, what makes enterprise messaging systems (EMSs) uniquely useful. An EMS provides guaranteed execution (delivery) of messages, without incurring the waits that an otherwise synchronous procedure call would incur. A servlet or session EJB can act as a JMS client message producer, able to place messages on a queue, or a synchronous message consumer, while a message-driven EJB can act as a JMS client message consumer, retrieving messages from a queue.

JMS provides two messaging models:

Point-to-point model
   One message producer queues messages to one and only one message consumer.

Publish-and-subscribe model
   One message producer queues messages to one or more message consumers.

OC4J provides a Resource Provider interface that allows you to transparently add JMS implementations to the server. JMS resource providers are looked up using JNDI through the local context similar to JDBC resources. Just like JDBC resources, JMS resources can be configured as standalone (available to all applications in an OC4J instance) or embedded (available only to the application in which it is configured).

Oracle JMS (OJMS) is a provider that can be used to access Oracle Advanced Queuing, the Oracle database's enterprise messaging system. Several third-party resource provider interfaces are also supplied that allow access to other systems, including SonicMQ, SwiftMQ, and WebSphereMQ.

As of the OC4J Release 9.0.4, OC4J has its own messaging system, OracleAS JMS, also known as OC4J JMS. OC4J JMS provides an in-memory and/or disk-based persistent JMS implementation in OC4J. With this addition, OC4J has become a complete enterprise messaging system in and of itself.

Remote Method Invocation

Remote Method Invocation is the protocol used by client-side applications, servlets, and EJBs to remotely communicate with EJBs. The remote communication is in the form of remote method execution. While RMI is a standard used by all J2EE-compliant EJB containers, OC4J provides value-added protocol extensions.

As part of the EJB 2.0 specification, EJBs can be configured to use the CORBA RMI/IIOP (RMI over IIOP) protocol to facilitate communication between EJBs deployed on different application servers. Using this form of component-to-component communication allows you to deploy components on any tier, provide dynamic load balancing, and enable horizontal scaling. However, the RMI/IIOP protocol doesn't support all these features when used with OC4J.

The default protocol used by OC4J is RMI/ORMI (RMI over Oracle RMI). Oracle RMI is a proprietary RMI implementation that is highly optimized for use with OC4J. ORMI supports application load balancing and failover between OC4J instances. ORMI also supports RMI tunneling. RMI tunneling enables EJBs to communicate through a firewall using the HTTP protocol, which is passed unscathed through most firewalls.

HTTPS for Client Connections

Oracle HTTPS for Client Connections (Oracle HTTPS) provides an SSL infrastructure inside OC4J to support SSL communication between the Oracle HTTP Server and OC4J, a client-side application program and OC4J, or a servlet residing in OC4J acting as a client program accessing another servlet or web site using SSL. Oracle HTTPS supports the following common cipher suites:

- Key exchanges of 512, 768, or 1024 bits using RSA or Diffie-Hillman
- Null, 40-, or 128-bit encryption using RC4 or DES
- Message authentication using MD5 or SHA1

Oracle HTTP Server SSL certificates are managed with Oracle Wallet Manager (OWM). OWM can generate public/private key pairs and certificate requests. A signed certificate request and the associated trusted certificate are added to OWM's wallet to create a complete wallet. That wallet, in turn, can be exported to use in a Java SSL-based client-side application.

OC4J's SSL certificates are managed using the JDK's keytool. keytool can also generate public/private key pairs and certificate requests. A signed certificate request and the associated trusted certificate are added to OC4J's keystore using keytool. Like OWM, keytool can export a client-side certificate.

Once signed certificates have been created for both the Oracle HTTP Server and OC4J, they can be exchanged to provide SSL communication between the two server components. In addition, configured OC4J can use its SSL configuration to enable SSL communication between a client-side application and OC4J or a servlet inside OC4J and another SSL server.

Java Authentication and Authorization Service

The Java Authentication and Authorization Service is the Java implementation of the standard Pluggable Authentication Module (PAM) framework. JAAS acts as a user-based adjunct to the Java 2 security model. In the Java 2 security model, access control is driven by a set of privileges, called a *policy*, that are granted to a code base. A *code base* is the location from which a Java program is executed.

With JAAS, code-base policies are effectively overridden by policies granted to a particular user logged into an application. As its name suggests, JAAS provides a standardized set of APIs that facilitate user login (authentication) and control over what a user may or may not do while logged in (authorization).

JAAS is a set of abstract classes that are implemented at runtime by a JAAS provider. OC4J supports JAAS with the OC4J JAAS Provider (JAZN).* JAZN supports two provider types:

XML-based provider
> This type of provider stores realm, user, and policy information in an XML file typically named *jazn-data.xml* that is co-located with an OC4J instance.

LDAP-based provider
> This type of provider uses LDAP to access an LDAP directory, such as the Oracle Internet Directory, where it too stores realm, user, and policy information. The LDAP provider type is tightly integrated with OracleAS Single Sign-On, which enables a user to use one user ID and password to log on to all applications.

A *realm* is a high-level identifier that organizes users, roles, and policies. Using an external realm, you can import users from other systems: NT, LDAP, Unix password, DB, and so on.

Using JAAS requires program modifications; it isn't enabled transparently. First, an administrator must configure one or more login modules, and a set of policies for an application. Next, a programmer must make minor code changes so that affected class methods are called with a user's security policy instead of with the code base's policy.

OC4J has its own default login module, RealmLoginModule, but can be configured to use any JAAS-compliant login module. JAZN can be configured programmatically or by using a components deployment descriptor. The JAZN user manager handles authentication and authorization for OC4J. It can be configured through Application Server Control to use JAZN-XML for the XML-based provider or JAZN-LDAP for the LDAP-based provider.

You can configure the XML-based provider's users, roles, and policy using the command line-based JAZN Admin tool. You can configure the LDAP-based provider's users, roles, and policy using the Oracle Internet Directory's Delegated Administrative Service (DAS).

Managing policy assignment by user can become quite cumbersome. To improve manageability, both provider types support role-based access control (RBAC) by allowing you to create a principal (normally a user, but now a role name), add a policy to that principal (a role), and then add other principals (users as members) to that role. Roles can also be added to roles, effectively creating a role hierarchy.

---

* Don't ask how they got JAZN out of OC4J JAAS Provider.

Java Object Cache

Java Object Cache is an Oracle value-added service provided by OC4J that exists to improve the performance of Java-based applications. Java Object Cache caches expensive-to-create or frequently accessed Java objects. Java Object Cache is both a memory- and/or a disk-based cache. It is meant to complement OracleAS Web Cache where applicable.

With Java Object Cache, cached objects can be shared between servlets and EJBs. They can be invalidated—that is, flagged as no longer cached—by the amount of time they have been present in the cache (time-to-live), by the amount of time they have not been accessed (idle), or on demand.

Java Object Cache provides a flexible resource organization structure based on a top-level identifier called a *region*. A region can be subdivided into more regions, appropriately called *subregions*. Each cached object belongs to one and only one region or subregion. Groups can be created that combine regions for mass property manipulation or invalidation of cached objects.

Java Object Cache also provides flexible management either programmatically or through its Java Object Cache properties file. Java Object Cache can be configured as either a local cache or a distributed cache. A local cache is available only to Java programs running in the same OC4J where the cache resides. When the Java Object Cache is configured as a distributed cache, cached objects are available to all OC4J instances that are part of the same cluster.

Web Object Cache is an HTTP-centric object cache implementation that uses the Java Object Cache for its repository. Web Object Cache is used solely with servlets (and JSPs that are actually servlets). It uses information from a servlet's HTTPRequest object to automatically define regions in Java Object Cache.

See Chapter 7 for more information on Java Object Cache and Web Object Cache, as well as a complete description of OracleAS Web Cache.

Other APIs

The previous sections briefly describe all of Oracle's officially designated OC4J services. However, keep in mind that all Java APIs can be used in Oracle Application Server with the appropriate configuration. The servlet API exists as a way to extend Oracle Application Server. Some of the other Oracle components available in Oracle Application Server are themselves J2EE applications. Hence, using J2EE you have basically unlimited capability to create a server-side solution.

Note that we haven't touched on XML or Web Services in this chapter. These two topics are described separately in Chapters 10 and 11, primarily because Oracle Application Server provides more than just Java support for these areas.

Application Deployment

Application deployment is the process of making a J2EE application available to end users on an application server. OC4J can deploy a J2EE application in an EAR file or a WAR (Web Application aRchive) file. When deploying a WAR file, OC4J automatically wraps a WAR file in an EAR file. OC4J provides a mapping mechanism so that differences in deployment environments can be resolved during the deployment process. OC4J also supports application development by accessing servlets and EJBs from an operating system directory without requiring OC4J-specific deployment descriptors. The remainder of this section takes a closer look at how OC4J handles application deployment, starting with standard J2EE deployment.

J2EE Deployment

J2EE applications are typically composed of JSPs, servlets, and EJBs. In a well-written J2EE application, each program unit acts as a separate and distinct component. To facilitate the composition of components into a working application, J2EE components have a descriptor file. A descriptor file exposes any configuration parameters, such as database resources, so that they can be specified declaratively—that is, without changing a line of Java code.

EJBs are placed into a Java ARchive (JAR) file that contains the EJB, with any supporting custom classes, and a deployment descriptor file named *ejb-jar.xml*. There is typically one JAR file for each session or message-driven EJB, whereas a JAR file usually contains multiple entity EJBs because related entity EJBs must be co-located.

All servlets under a particular application context directory in a servlet container use the same deployment descriptor file named *web.xml*; so do any JSP files that reside in the same application context directory because the JSP translator automatically compiles them into servlets. The servlets, JSPs, any supporting custom class libraries, JSP tag libraries, and the *web.xml* file are all placed into a WAR file; such a file facilitates deployment of a web application to another web container.

To create an application that uses both EJBs and servlets, WAR files and any required EJB JAR files are placed into a EAR file, along with an application deployment descriptor file appropriately named *application.xml*.

Applications are usually developed on one server, deployed on a second for quality assurance testing, and then deployed on a third to put them into production. If the environments aren't exactly the same, how do you resolve the differences? It is possible to make the appropriate changes to the individual J2EE descriptor files for the target environment before archiving the files into a WAR or EAR file, but this is at best a deployment nightmare. Another solution is for the host application server to provide a mapping mechanism during deployment. That is how OC4J solves this deployment problem.

OC4J Deployment

In OC4J, each J2EE deployment descriptor has an OC4J-specific counterpart that can map a J2EE deployment resource name to one that is available in the OC4J. Let's look at an example. Suppose that a data source defined on a development server is named DefaultDS and that the appropriate entry in the web application's deployment descriptor file, *web.xml*, references that name, yet on the production server, a dedicated data source named MyAppDS is defined for the web application. You can map the J2EE deployment descriptor reference DefaultDS to the dedicated data source name by specifying the mapping in the appropriate OC4J-specific deployment descriptor file *orion-web.xml*. Table 6-2 shows the relationships between the J2EE and OC4J specific deployment descriptor files.

Table 6-2. Deployment descriptor relationships

Type	J2EE	OC4J
EJB	ejb-jar.xml	orion-ejb-jar.xml
Web (servlet and JSP)	web.xml	orion-web.xml
Application	application.xml	orion-application.xml
Resource adapter	ra.xml[a]	oc4j-ra.xml
		oc4j-connectors.xml

[a] Supplied with the resource adapter

Using this mechanism, OC4J can deploy any J2EE-compliant application without having to modify its deployment descriptors. Deployment mappings are specified during deployment using Application Server Control.

OC4J Development

You can use OC4J as a development environment to compile EJBs, servlets, and so on, in the server directory tree. Doing so requires you to create a standard deployment directory structure and the appropriate J2EE deployment descriptor files, and make a set of manual configuration changes through Application Server Control.

If you create a separate development instance for each development project, you can restart OC4J quickly, without incurring the wrath of developers who may be working on other projects. When using OC4J as a development environment, your application's response times will be slower because nonarchived classes are loaded as-needed, whereas archived classes (that is, classes in JAR files) are cached in memory.

Standalone J2EE Server

While OC4J is normally installed as part of Oracle Application Server, it can also be installed as a standalone J2EE server. This is ideal for creating a lightweight development environment. One member of a development team can install OC4J standalone on his personal computer to produce a fully functional workgroup development environment. Other members of the team can work directly in a development directory, storing and compiling their Java code in place.

When ready, the completed J2EE application can be packaged from the development directory and deployed on a complete Oracle Application Server installation acting as a quality assurance server for testing, then later moved to a production environment. Using OC4J in this fashion gives a development team a great deal of control over their development environment, while not requiring a great deal of expense to duplicate a production J2EE environment.

Oracle provides an OC4J standalone download available on the Oracle Technology Network (OTN) web site for just this purpose. You can download OC4J along with its *OC4J Standalone User's Guide*. As stated earlier, it can be run with any JDK of the appropriate version. This also makes it possible to develop a J2EE application on any platform that supports Java, not just on platforms that support Oracle Application Server.

Clustering

Clustering OC4J instances allows Oracle Application Server to solve both hardware and software reliability and scalability problems. Oracle Application Server can group two or more OC4J instances into a cluster, whether or not they reside on the same host. Clustered OC4J instances appear to the outside world as one application server, providing high reliability and almost unlimited scalability.

Various load-balancing mechanisms are available to direct incoming requests between clustered OC4J instances. If one clustered instance fails, another picks up where it left off, using the appropriate load-balancing mechanism. Clustering OC4J instances across hosts solves both the hardware and software reliability problems. The bulk of what clustering is and how it is employed in Oracle Application Server was covered in Chapter 2, but a few relevant J2EE issues are discussed in this section.

OC4J provides stateful failover for clusters via HTTP session object and EJB state replication. This means that each user's session, and each EJB's state, is replicated between OC4J instances.

The HTTP session objects in a web (servlet) container are selectively replicated across all OC4J instances that are part of the same cluster and processes that are part of the same island. An OC4J island is a way to group one or more OC4J JVM processes. Rather than having to replicate HTTP session objects among all OC4J processes (which can be very resource-intensive), islands allow selective replication. This fine-grained control prevents replication within a cluster from degrading OC4J's performance.

EJB state replication is handled differently. Because of the nature of EJBs—they are all independent components—EJB state is replicated between all OC4J instances in a cluster. There is no fine-grained replication control mechanism.

CHAPTER 7

Caching

For users, performance is the most visible aspect of any IT solution. Developers must make sure that the applications they build provide users with the functionality they need. Unfortunately, if those applications can't achieve adequate performance, the developers' efforts aren't judged as successful. Consequently, the search for ways to improve performance never ends.

Oracle Application Server includes three different types of caches that play a role in improving the overall performance of the product:

OracleAS Web Cache
An in-memory cache for web content of all kinds, including static pages, dynamic pages, and pages assembled from both static and dynamic content.

Java Object Cache
A cache for frequently used or expensive-to-create objects used by a particular Java application.

Web Object Cache
A Java Object Cache implementation used for HTTP-centric Java objects.

All three caches improve performance in the same way—by making commonly used data available more rapidly. This chapter describes the architecture and use of each cache.

OracleAS Web Cache

OracleAS Web Cache is the primary caching mechanism provided with Oracle Application Server. An OracleAS Web Cache instance sits in front of one or more Oracle HTTP Servers, as described in Chapter 2. The responses to all requests directed to the Oracle HTTP Server through OracleAS Web Cache can be cached in OracleAS Web Cache, which means that this cache can handle any web content transmitted with the standard HTTP protocol. Thus, OracleAS Web Cache works with Oracle Application Server as well as with any other HTTP application server.

Web Cache can also act as a load balancer for multiple instances of Oracle Application Server, and it provides some high-availability features as well. By caching selected request responses, OracleAS Web Cache reduces the load on the application server. The load is reduced because cached content no longer needs to be regenerated. CPU cycles and other resources are thus freed, thereby improving performance for those items that can't be cached.

OracleAS Web Cache was designed to work on low-cost machines. Because OracleAS Web Cache works as an in-memory cache, its capabilities are more dependent on addressable, available memory than they are upon CPU speed or number of CPUs. OracleAS Web Cache was designed to use two processors. Oracle's own My Oracle site, for example, uses a pair of two-way Intel machines as its own OracleAS Web Cache cluster.

Basic Principles

OracleAS Web Cache is a server accelerator. OracleAS Web Cache instances act as a front end cache for pages, content fragments, and other objects coming from one or more application servers. OracleAS Web Cache can also be used with third-party web servers, such as BEA's WebLogic or IBM's WebSphere.

In the simplest case, a web server delivers static pages in response to a client request. In this case, the server retrieves a page from disk. For many sources of web content, however, the case isn't nearly so simple. A page may be based on dynamic content, changing either with time or because of the characteristics of the user who has made a request. A page may even be assembled from several sources of content, which can individually be either static or dynamic.

A database uses a memory cache to hold frequently used data, allowing for faster retrieval. OracleAS Web Cache does the same thing with web pages and, more importantly, portions of web pages. This second capability expands the scope of potential performance improvement.

Many web pages are customized: a simple page contains common elements as well as portions specific to the user or the situation. For instance, the home page for an application is largely the same for all users, but may contain special greetings or messages for a particular user. OracleAS Web Cache can assemble the page from different fragments, providing the performance improvement of a memory cache everywhere content is reused.

Several other components of Oracle Application Server may also use OracleAS Web Cache to improve performance:

OracleAS Portal
> OracleAS Portal comes with a set of predefined caching and invalidation rules.

OracleAS Discoverer
> OracleAS Discoverer content can be cached by OracleAS Web Cache.

Oracle AS Wireless

OracleAS Wireless content can also be cached by OracleAS Web Cache. Note, however, that OracleAS Web Cache is used by the OracleAS Wireless server as a repository for content, rather than as a front end, which is the role it plays for normal HTTP requests.

eBusiness Suite

Portions of Oracle's eBusiness Suite are also supported by OracleAS Web Cache.

OracleAS Web Cache also supports a variety of security configurations including HTTPS communications between a browser and itself and between itself and origin servers, as well as redirection for an OracleAS Single Sign-On server. OracleAS Web Cache can also communicate with client programs that use client-side SSL certificates. In this case, OracleAS Web Cache forwards the certificate information in special HTTP request headers, which are then used by the Oracle HTTP Server for authentication.

OracleAS Web Cache can provide scalability and high availability in several different ways.

- OracleAS Web Cache provides rapid response by being able to cache both static and dynamic content, allowing pages to be returned directly from OracleAS Web Cache without having to access the originating application server. This rapid response allows the cache to provide support for more users.

- If a request comes in that can be satisfied directly from OracleAS Web Cache, there is no need to go to the application server for the content. In this scenario, OracleAS Web Cache provides availability even though the application server may be unavailable.

  If OracleAS Web Cache can't contact the required web server (known as the *origin server* in this context), the instance returns a standard apology page. This page can be modified, but it can contain only static HTML. If you want to include other elements, such as an image or a company logo, you can designate another HTTP server to serve up these images and embed the images in your apology page.

- OracleAS Web Cache can load-balance for multiple application servers, increasing the scalability of the overall site.

- OracleAS Web Cache instances can be clustered, with each cache instance providing failover for other cache instances as well as scalability for the entire OracleAS Web Cache.

The following subsections describe how OracleAS Web Cache handles incoming requests and the various topologies that can be used for OracleAS Web Cache and their implications. We also cover the basics of how OracleAS Web Cache moves content out of the cache with invalidation; how OracleAS Web Cache handles static, dynamic, and partial pages; administration of OracleAS Web Cache instances; and other features of the product.

How It Works

OracleAS Web Cache sits in front of a web server, as shown in Figure 7-1. The web server here is referred to as an origin server. The web server could also be a proxy server used to access content outside the firewall.

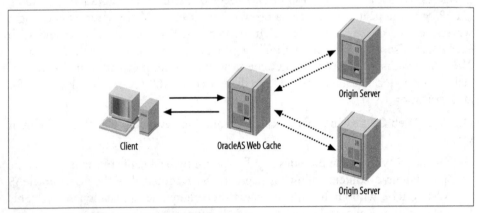

Figure 7-1. OracleAS Web Cache fulfilling user requests

When a request comes into an OracleAS Web Cache instance, it determines whether the request is for a site that uses the instance. That information is provided by the Host request-field header from the request, the host portion of the URL, or the src attribute of the ESI include tag, which is explained later in this chapter.

> ESI stands for *Edge Side Includes*, an open standard specification for defining web-page components for dynamic page assembly. More information on ESI is available at *http://www.esi.org*.

If the request is for a document from a site that uses the instance, OracleAS Web Cache checks to see if the document is in the cache. If OracleAS Web Cache can satisfy the request, it returns the page to the user. If it can't satisfy the request, it requests the object from the application server after appending a Surrogate-Control response-header field to the document. The application server returns the object to OracleAS Web Cache.

If the object is specified as cacheable, by either a caching rule or an attribute in the returned Surrogate-Control response-header, the object is cached for future use. For pages that are constructed of page fragments, using ESI (as described later), OracleAS Web Cache follows the same procedure for each fragment.

Once the document is available, OracleAS Web Cache returns it to the user. If the newly retrieved object is marked as being cacheable, the object is placed in OracleAS Web Cache's cache.

The flow of logic for OracleAS Web Cache requests is shown in Figure 7-2.

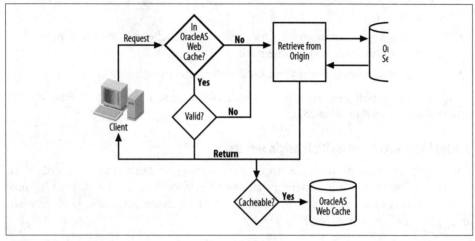

Figure 7-2. Logic flow of requests to OracleAS *Web Cache*

Objects remain in the cache until they are either removed (because of demand for cache resources) or marked invalid, as described later. If the total size used by OracleAS Web Cache exceeds a configurable percentage of the overall memory available for the instance, OracleAS Web Cache will initiate a garbage-collection routine that will select content to be removed. You might want to set the maximum size for any single cached object to avoid using up too much cache memory too quickly.

OracleAS Web Cache lets you set a maximum size for any cached object. Any object that exceeds the specified size isn't cached, regardless of how it is marked or how caching rules apply to it.

Topologies for OracleAS Web Cache

Earlier, Figure 7-1 showed a simple configuration for an OracleAS Web Cache instance, with a single OracleAS Web Cache instance supporting a group of sites. OracleAS Web Cache can be on the same machine with multiple instances of an application server. In this configuration, OracleAS Web Cache uses interprocess communication (IPC) to assign requests to application server instances.

If, instead, OracleAS Web Cache is on a different machine, it uses HTTP to communicate with the origin server. In this configuration, a single OracleAS Web Cache instance can communicate with multiple origin servers. OracleAS Web Cache uses a connection pool for each origin server for faster communication with the server.

OracleAS Web Cache can work in several other topologies to provide additional features and benefits. Although OracleAS Web Cache is primarily used for caching content, you can also use it as a load balancer that supports application server failover. Three common OracleAS Web Cache deployment topologies include:

- Use of OracleAS Web Cache to support load balancing and failover for multiple origin servers
- Use of multiple instances of OracleAS Web Cache for load balancing and failover for OracleAS Web Cache itself
- Use of multiple instances of OracleAS Web Cache in a cluster

Another set of topologies, known as *hierarchies*, is used for specific needs, such as geographic distribution of caching.

OracleAS Web Cache and multiple origin servers

The ability to support multiple application servers is built into OracleAS Web Cache's architecture. This capability allows OracleAS Web Cache to load-balance requests across multiple application servers and to provide automatic failover when an application server instance fails.

Sometimes, a web site is supported by more than one application server. In this situation, a single OracleAS Web Cache instance can manage requests for pages from as many as 100 application servers, and load-balance among them.

OracleAS Web Cache automatically sends requests to the origin server with the most available resources. The quantity of available resources for a particular origin server is determined by the workload and capacity for the server. The workload is based on the number of active connections to the origin server. An OracleAS Web Cache administrator establishes the maximum number of connections for each origin server. The available resources are determined by subtracting the workload from the capacity. If all origin servers have an equal capacity, OracleAS Web Cache uses a Round-Robin method to assign new connections.

If a connection request or a configurable number of read/write requests to an origin server fails, OracleAS Web Cache considers the server unavailable. For an unavailable server, existing requests for documents return errors, but subsequent requests to the server are failed-over to another origin server. The capacity of the failed server is assigned to the failover server. Once the failed server responds to a request to a designated URL on the server, the server is considered available, and capacity for the server is reassigned to it.

The operations we've described so far make sense for stateless requests; one origin server is as good as any other. But what about stateful requests that depend upon earlier interactions with the failed origin server? Stateful transactions require *server affinity* to emulate persistent connections to a server, such as for use with a shopping cart.

You can configure OracleAS Web Cache to perform stateful load balancing using *session binding*. Session binding requires that the origin server use cookies and session IDs to indicate server affinity for a particular request. This is done automatically by Oracle Application Server. Server affinity ensures that a stateful request will consistently return to the server that is maintaining its state.

 If a request requires a connection to a particular origin server, but that server is already handling maximum capacity, the session binding for that request is disabled, and an error message is returned to the user.

Multiple instances of OracleAS Web Cache

Multiple instances of OracleAS Web Cache can be used together, either in a cluster or in a failover configuration. In both configurations, you can use a hardware load balancer in front of OracleAS Web Cache instances, as shown in Figure 7-3. In addition, in both configurations, the load balancer recognizes a single logical OracleAS Web Cache and balances requests across the instances.

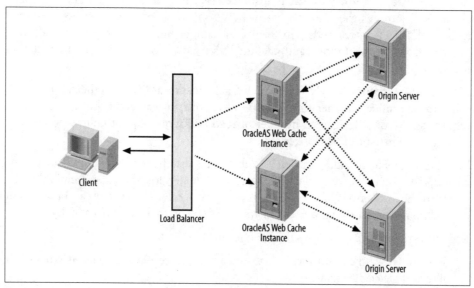

Figure 7-3. Multiple instances of OracleAS Web Cache

OracleAS Web Cache can be configured to automatically restart an instance if a failure has been detected. If you have installed OracleAS Web Cache as part of a complete Oracle Application Server installation, the Oracle Process Manager and Notification Server monitors the health of an OracleAS Web Cache instance and performs the restart when necessary. If you have installed OracleAS Web Cache as a standalone product, a watchdog process restarts the instance. This process can be disabled if desired.

You can configure a hardware load balancer to send only HTTP or HTTPS requests to an instance of OracleAS Web Cache. For example, you might designate an OracleAS Web Cache instance to receive only HTTPS requests if you are going to use some type of SSL accelerator hardware only on that machine.

You can use an L7 switch to route requests to OracleAS Web Cache or an origin server via the Application Layer (Layer 7) of the OSI model. This configuration might make sense if there are certain types of content that you don't want to cache—for example, protected or transactional content—so you would want to completely bypass the OracleAS Web Cache servers.

Clustering

Multiple instances of OracleAS Web Cache can also be combined into a *cache cluster*. A cache cluster uses the same basic hardware configuration used for unclustered, multiple instances of OracleAS Web Cache, but it offers some additional functionality as well.

A cache cluster is a group of cache instances that look like a single cache. A cache cluster still requires the use of a hardware or software load balancer, as described earlier. All the instances in the cluster use the same common configuration information, such as site definitions and caching rules, and receive the same invalidation messages.

In a cluster configuration, OracleAS Web Cache instances can periodically ping each other to determine whether they are still alive, or can wait for either a connection request failure or a designated number of read and write request failures to demonstrate that an instance is no longer alive.

You can dynamically add OracleAS Web Cache instances to an established cache cluster, although you do have to restart the cluster for the new member to be included. Each member of the cluster is assigned a relative capacity, and document ownership is distributed among the instances based on their relative capacity.

Requests are handled as follows for a cache cluster:

- If a request comes into a cache instance for a document it owns, it works just like a single cache instance.
- If a request comes into a cache instance for a document that is owned by another instance, the cache instance passes the request off to the owning instance.
- If a cache instance doesn't respond to a request for a document in a specified length of time, the requesting instance assumes that the other instance has failed. When this occurs, the documents owned by the failed instance are redistributed to the remaining instances according to their designated capacity.

In the last case, the other instances of the OracleAS Web Cache cluster periodically ping a specified URL for the failed server so that they will recognize when the instance rejoins the cluster. When an instance rejoins the cluster, document ownership is again redistributed according to the new relative capacities of the available instances. Keep in mind that while document ownership is redistributed, document content isn't. The new instance will retrieve a document that it now owns once the document is requested.

Although each document is owned by a single cache instance, the content may be needed by other instances. Once the content is requested and returned to another instance, the requesting server caches the content itself, so future requests to that server won't require a redirection. In this way, the same popular content may be contained in multiple cache instances.

The upshot of this design is that the most popular objects in an OracleAS Web Cache cluster are most resilient to the failure of an individual OracleAS Web Cache instance because popular objects typically reside in more than one instance and don't have to be refreshed if one instance fails.

Some operating systems—for example, some flavors of Windows 2000 and Windows 2003—include the ability to load-balance requests across nodes in an operating system-defined cluster. In such a configuration, the operating system also recognizes node failure and uses automatic IP takeover in the event of a failure.

A cache cluster offers a number of benefits not provided by unclustered, multiple instances of OracleAS Web Cache, including:

Increased scalability
> Multiple instances of OracleAS Web Cache can be combined for greater caching capability, but without increasing the number of content requests to the origin server.

Improved maintenance
> Maintenance is easier because all members of a cache cluster share the same configuration, and one member typically receives a single invalidation message. In addition, you can add members to, or remove members from, a cache cluster without having to worry how it will affect management overhead.

Hierarchies

You can use hierarchies of OracleAS Web Cache in two basic configurations:

Remote Cache Deployment
> One configuration of OracleAS Web Cache implements enterprise content delivery networks with Remote Cache Deployment. In this configuration, OracleAS Web Cache can provide better response time by caching frequently used content closer to the eventual user of the data, such as in a remote location or LAN segment, as shown in Figure 7-4.

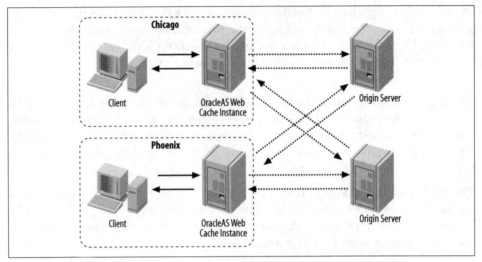

Figure 7-4. Using OracleAS Web Cache as Remote Cache Deployment

Edge Side Includes

A second type of hierarchy uses instances of OracleAS Web Cache on ESI providers (described later) and an instance of OracleAS Web Cache on a subscriber machine, which assembles the ESI fragments into a web page. This type of hierarchy is especially appropriate for an OracleAS Portal deployment, in which complete pages are assembled from different sources. OracleAS Portal is described in detail in Chapter 13.

When you configure a cache hierarchy, the origin servers for the upstream caches, such as the ESI subscriber machine, are the downstream instances of OracleAS Web Cache. If you can't specify a site definition for an ESI provider machine, and there is a firewall between the subscriber instance and the unknown ESI provider, you must configure a proxy server because OracleAS Web Cache uses DNS to locate undefined ESI providers.

Types of Caching

Three different types of information can be cached in OracleAS Web Cache: static HTML pages, dynamic HTML pages, and page fragments.

Static page caching

For static pages, the use of OracleAS Web Cache is straightforward. If a document is cacheable, it is placed in the cache until it becomes invalid, either through receipt of an invalidation message or after a request for the document comes in and the caching rules indicate that it has expired.

Static pages are swapped out of OracleAS Web Cache if the cache becomes full, and the garbage-collection process selects the page as a candidate for removal, as described earlier.

Dynamic page caching

Dynamic pages are pages that can have different content for different situations or different users. These pages can be generated using a variety of scripting and programming languages and modules. Examples include JSPs, Active Server Pages (ASPs), PL/SQL Server Pages (PSPs), Java servlets, and CGI calls.

Sometimes these dynamic pages are completely unique. In these cases, OracleAS Web Cache would have to potentially cache each individual page. Frequently, though, pages are very similar, with only some different areas. In some scenarios, described in the following subsections, OracleAS Web Cache can substitute dynamic values or to recognize when a page can be reused for multiple users.

In other scenarios, developers can combine some static objects with dynamic objects by caching portions of an overall page.

Multiple versions for a single URL. Some web sites create different versions of the same page for different sets of users. These sites either use a cookie with an identifying value or encode the value in the URL.

If a cookie is used, the value for the cookie is passed back from the origin server in the Set-Cookie response header, which is stored with the document. When a subsequent request comes in with a value in the corresponding Cookie request header, OracleAS Web Cache returns the appropriate page. OracleAS Web Cache can also use values in request-header fields to determine which version of a page to return.

If appropriate, you can configure OracleAS Web Cache to ignore embedded URL parameters when determining which page to return. This approach avoids the requirement to cache every version of a web page with distinct URL embedded information, such as a session ID. You can also configure OracleAS Web Cache to ignore POST body parameters, as discussed in the next section.

You can use multiversion caching to support different cached pages for different types or groups of browsers. This technique allows you to build in flexible pages for different browsers while still taking advantage of OracleAS Web Cache.

Personalization in a page. You can specify personalization information in a web page with special OracleAS Web Cache HTML tags. When OracleAS Web Cache receives a request for the page, the specified information is retrieved from a cookie, from a URL embedded parameter, or from POST body parameters.

When you specify the attribute that will be used for personalization, you can also specify whether to return the page for requests that are missing the attribute, or what to use in place of the attribute for pages missing a value.

Session-encoded URLs. Some web pages use session-specific information in internal hyperlinks. You can also configure OracleAS Web Cache to substitute session values in hyperlinks that use session-encoded URLs. As with personalization attributes, you can specify how OracleAS Web Cache should handle a request with missing session information.

Partial page caching

As mentioned earlier, some pages combine static objects, such as a page template and logos, with dynamic objects. These pages use ESI tags to indicate where the dynamic objects are located on the page and where to get their content.

 ESI tags were originally introduced by Oracle and Akamai, and are on the standards track for the World Wide Web Consortium (W3C).

OracleAS Web Cache can work with both include fragments, which are always fetched, and inline fragments, which are identified with a unique name and can be reused by multiple pages without refetching.

OracleAS Web Cache can cache page fragments independently, with each fragment having its own validation rules. This method allows OracleAS Web Cache to cache individual fragments, which can be used in many different pages. Each fragment has its own set of validation rules; these rules can use the same information and logic as a rule for an entire page. This separation means that an individual fragment doesn't have to be re-fetched every time a page requiring the fragment is requested.

For instance, you can have the template and logos for a page cached indefinitely, the news for the day cached for several hours, and stock prices not cached at all. By separating all these fragments into separate ESI fragments, OracleAS Web Cache can intelligently refresh the fragments as appropriate. ESI tags can use XML stylesheets to transform content into HTML.

When you configure the origin servers that OracleAS Web Cache will access, you can specify that the site is an ESI provider only, which prevents browsers from accessing the site directly. You don't have to configure all sites that are ESI providers. However, failing to configure an ESI provider site disables OracleAS Web Cache's capacity heuristics capability, as we discuss in the next section. If there is a firewall between an ESI provider and a OracleAS Web Cache subscriber cache, as described in the earlier "Hierarchies" section, you must configure a proxy server to contact the ESI provider.

For ESI use in JSPs, a set of Java ESI tags, known as *JESI tags*, can implement ESI fragments more productively. JESI tags will automatically create the surrogate control headers that are used by ESI fragments to determine caching characteristics. By using JESI tags with JSPs, you can use JSP expressions for more flexible implementation of caching rules.

Cache Invalidation

Caching is, of course, nothing new in the world of computing. Databases have long used caches to improve performance. In a database cache, the database uses the concept of least-recently-used (LRU) to swap out blocks of data when the cache becomes full.

In Oracle Application Server, OracleAS Web Cache performs the same type of operation when it becomes full, but there are also other options for removing content from an OracleAS Web Cache instance. Some content stored in OracleAS Web Cache changes frequently, while some rarely changes at all. To handle this breadth of "freshness," OracleAS Web Cache lets you specify when content becomes invalid, which marks it as ready to be discarded from the cache.

Validation is the process of verifying whether an object in OracleAS Web Cache is still valid. *Invalidation* is the process used to flag an object as no longer being available. Invalidating an object doesn't necessarily remove it from the cache. Once an object is put into OracleAS Web Cache, it remains valid until it is marked as invalid.

There are basically two types of invalidation:

Predictable
> This type of invalidation can be indicated with an expiration time, either in elapsed time or at a specific time.

Unpredictable
> This type of invalidation occurs in response to some other event. Unpredictable invalidation can be implemented with a message, as described later.

There are two ways to indicate that an object is invalid:

Policies
> These are evaluated each time a request is made for an object.

Messages
> These are sent to OracleAS Web Cache, either manually or programmatically.

If an object in OracleAS Web Cache is marked as invalid, the next request for the object causes OracleAS Web Cache to fetch a fresh version of the object from the origin server.

Just as you assign validation rules to objects and groups of objects, you can mark objects as noncacheable, which means that they are never placed in OracleAS Web Cache.

These techniques are used for the OracleAS Web Cache instance itself to invalidate content. OracleAS Web Cache can use HTTP *validators*, included in the browser request, to ensure that delivery of cached documents is appropriate. OracleAS Web Cache compares the If-Modified-Since value with the value in the Last-Modified response-header field of the cached document, or compares the If-None-Match validator with the ETag response-header field of the cached document.

OracleAS Web Cache has its own set of caching rules (described later), but it can also accept caching directives, either in the Surrogate-Control response-header field in the object returned from the origin server, or in the HTTP Cache-Control header. If there is a rule in more than one of these areas, the Surrogate-Control rule overrides OracleAS Web Cache rules, which override the HTTP Cache-Control header. If a Surrogate-Control response-header rule is used, additional properties in the OracleAS Web Cache rule, such as compression, can be merged with the rule.

If you are using a hierarchy of caches, the top cache instance in the hierarchy receives the invalidation message and then propagates it to the other downstream caches. If you are using cache instances in a cluster, you can choose either to have a cluster member act as an invalidation coordinator (which propagates invalidation messages) or to send invalidation messages to all members of the cluster.

Invalid objects are removed from OracleAS Web Cache by a garbage-collection process. This process runs when the OracleAS Web Cache instance runs out of space. The garbage-collection process uses a heuristic algorithm to determine which objects to remove, which takes into consideration the popularity of an object (how long it has been since the object was requested), whether an object is invalid, and other considerations. An object is marked as invalid, based on rules and messages, but it isn't discarded from the cache until a garbage-collection process is initiated by the load on the OracleAS Web Cache instance.

Cacheability/invalidation rules

You describe the objects that an OracleAS Web Cache instance should cache by specifying caching rules. A caching rule contains four properties:

Selector
> Specifies the pages to which a rule applies. The selector contains a URL expression, which could be based on a URL prefix, a file extension type, or a regular expression (for more extensive logical selection). It can also be based on a URL or POST body parameter, or on a POST body expression.

Caching policy

Indicates whether the selected URL should be cached. You can also indicate whether the URL has an expiration policy or whether it should be compressed. An expiration policy uses a time-based indicator, which can work on the amount of time an object is in the cache, on the amount of time since an object was last requested, or on information in the HTTP Expires or Cache-Control response fields.

Cache key policy

Defines what information OracleAS Web Cache uses to create a unique ID for an object. This ID is used to retrieve the object from the cache for subsequent requests. This information can include the site name, the URL of the object, the POST body expressions, the cookie names and values, and the HTTP request header name and values.

Priority

Defines the order of use of the caching rules. If some objects aren't cacheable, this property specifies their rules first to avoid excess overhead.

OracleAS Web Cache comes with some default caching rules, such as one used with OracleAS Wireless. If you don't specify any caching rules, content isn't cached. Even if content isn't cached, OracleAS Web Cache can still be used as a load balancer to multiple origin servers.

Invalidation messages

To invalidate an object by a message, an OracleAS Web Cache instance must receive an HTTP POST message from one of two accounts—the administrator account or the invalidator account. Both accounts are set up at installation time and can be modified with Web Cache Manager. These messages must be received on the invalidation listening port, which is also configured at runtime.

The message contains information presented in XML that identifies the page to be invalidated. There are two types of XML descriptions:

Basic

Lists the identifying URL

Advanced

Uses pattern and range matching to identify a number of different pages

Invalidation messages can be sent in a variety of ways, including:

- Via Telnet
- From OracleAS Web Cache Manager
- Via application logic
- From database triggers using Oracle's UTL_TCP built-in package
- With scripting languages

OracleAS Web Cache ships with an API for invalidation messages for Java and PL/SQL. An invalidation message sent by OracleAS Web Cache Manager can include a removal time, which must be later than the invalidation time. This time is used for performance assurance heuristics, discussed in the next section.

If you use ESIs, you can invalidate fragments, based on the retrieval of another inline fragment. For instance, if one inline fragment is invalid, you may want to indicate that the other fragments associated with the document are also invalid.

OracleAS Web Cache sends an HTTP response for all invalidation requests. This response contains a status code indicating the outcome of the request. The application that sent the request can use this information in its own logic.

Performance assurance heuristics

Objects in OracleAS Web Cache can be marked as invalid, as explained earlier, but a large number of objects can become invalid at any one time. For example, a bulk application of changes to material used in an online catalog may invalidate all the pages in the catalog. How does OracleAS Web Cache avoid impacting performance when it saturates the origin server with requests for new versions?

The answer is that OracleAS Web Cache uses something called *performance assurance heuristics*. These heuristics are used to create a queue for refresh requests. If the capacity of the origin application server is exceeded, OracleAS Web Cache uses this queue to keep the number of requests to a more reasonable level. Requests are prioritized in the queue based on two factors:

- Levels of invalidation defined for the object
- Popularity of the object

The concept of levels of invalidation is based on the concept of *removal time*. You can specify a removal time for an object, which indicates how long an invalid object can stay in the cache before it is removed. The greater the time since an object has been invalidated, the staler it is. There may be multiple levels of staleness.

For example, a web page may contain the following:

- A logo, which is static
- A news feed, which should be updated on a regular basis
- An account balance, which must always be up to date

If OracleAS Web Cache determines that refresh requests are overwhelming the origin server, it can assemble the page with a stale version of the news feed item, but not the account balance. The only real consequence of this decision for the user is that it provides slightly older news content, while providing better performance for all users.

If objects are equally stale, OracleAS Web Cache uses *popularity ratings* to remove the least-requested object. In this way, OracleAS Web Cache can smooth out the performance it delivers, regardless of the number of objects that are invalid at any one time. In addition, you can use this feature to help address issues associated with surges of traffic. By designating some content as acceptable for stale delivery, you allow OracleAS Web Cache to automatically throttle back its requests as demand grows.

Compression

OracleAS Web Cache uses the standard GZIP compression algorithm to reduce the size of pages returned to the browser (assuming that the requesting browser supports this type of compression). On average, OracleAS Web Cache compression can reduce the size of compressed documents by 75%. A compressed document may contain both cached and noncached elements, or may be a complete page that has not been cached. OracleAS Web Cache itself stores content in a compressed format to save caching space.

If the HTTP header for a request indicates that a browser can expand compressed content, OracleAS Web Cache compresses the content before returning it, reducing bandwidth requirements and potentially improving response time. Most browsers have supported the GZIP algorithm since 1997. However, OracleAS Web Cache caches both compressed and uncompressed version of objects, and returns whichever is appropriate.

You indicate whether you want content to be compressed by supplying the appropriate information in the *cacheability rules* you specify to select the content. Because these rules allow the use of regular expressions for evaluating cacheability, you can use the same flexible expressions to determine whether content is to be compressed. If the origin server has already compressed content, OracleAS Web Cache recognizes this in the response header and does no further compression.

If you are using a hierarchy of caches, you should configure the OracleAS Web Cache closest to the origin server to compress content, and configure the downstream OracleAS Web Cache instances so that they don't compress. This approach delivers the compressed content early on in the flow of the response, and consequently, the transmission benefits over the greatest distance.

Administration

There are three ways to start an OracleAS Web Cache instance:

- Through the command line, using the OPMN Server
- Through OracleAS Web Cache Manager
- Through Application Server Control

Of the three, OracleAS Web Cache Manager (shown in Figure 7-5) is the tool most often used to manage OracleAS Web Cache instances. This tool is the interface to the management process for OracleAS Web Cache, which in turn must be running to use the Manager.

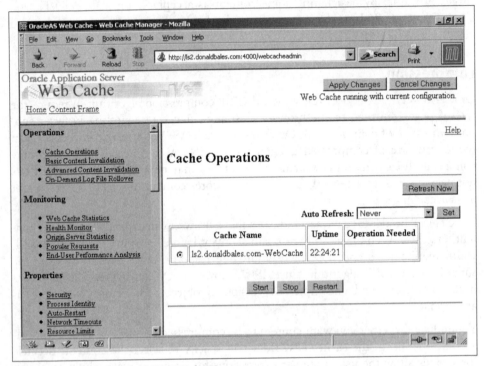

Figure 7-5. Sample OracleAS Web Cache Manager page

You can use OracleAS Web Cache Manager to start and stop OracleAS Web Cache instances, administer invalidation or rollover log files, monitor performance and activity, and configure OracleAS Web Cache instances. You can also use the OracleAS Web Cache Manager to associate specific caching rules with URLs or sets of URLs. In addition, you can create and view caching rules with this tool, as well as edit some of the attributes of the rules, such as expiration policies, compression, and the content of HTTP request headers.

Most changes specified through OracleAS Web Cache Manager aren't applied until an OracleAS Web Cache instance is restarted. However, some of the changes do take effect as soon as the changes are saved. Such changes include setting levels of detail for the event logs, changing the buffering for event logs and access logs, enabling and disabling the inclusion of diagnostic information in the HTML response body, and setting routing to origin servers.

OracleAS Web Cache Manager tracks whether other members of a cache cluster have a different configuration and allows you to bring those members' configuration into conformance. Once you have matched the configurations, you can restart all instances of a cluster with a single button push. You can also choose to stagger the restart of the instance to reduce the impact on operations.

Monitoring OracleAS Web Cache

OracleAS Web Cache Manager can display a list of the most popular documents, based on the number of requests and the most recently received requests. This list can be limited to either cached documents or noncached documents. You can also get a listing of all documents in the cache at the present time, but this list is saved to a file.

To highlight potential performance improvements, OracleAS Web Cache Manager can give you a list of the most popular documents that return cache misses, which provides the information you need to adjust caching rules to reduce the number of misses.

OracleAS Web Cache uses an event log to record events and errors. Events include cache hits, cache misses, and invalidations. Events can be recorded with details of the request that triggered the events, such as the IP address of the browser that made the request and details about the site and URL of the request.

Event log files are periodically rolled over, with the old log file stored. Rollover intervals can be configured to once a week, once a day, hourly, or never. Starting with Oracle Application Server 10g, you can set the level of detail in the OracleAS Web Cache log.

OracleAS Web Cache Manager displays information about the overall health and operations of an OracleAS Web Cache instance. The information includes health and utilization statistics for the instance, error and invalidation statistics, requests for each origin server supported by the instance, and information about fresh and stale documents that have been served from the cache.

For troubleshooting purposes, OracleAS Web Cache includes diagnostic information in the HTTP Server response-header fields by default. If you choose to do so, you can have this information added to the response body.

OracleAS Web Cache and performance monitoring

In addition to the event log mentioned in the previous section, OracleAS Web Cache also keeps an access log, which tracks information about HTTP requests sent to it. OracleAS Web Cache can be configured to use its access log to determine user response times for HTTP requests because the access log includes information about the elapsed time from a request to its response.

The access log can be analyzed through OracleAS Web Cache Manager and can be output into either an HTML file or a comma-separated file for import into a spreadsheet or database. The access log can also be used more fully by Oracle Enterprise Manager 10g's Application Service Level Management feature, which ships with Grid Control, a web-based tool described in Chapter 3. ASLM helps administrators to understand the actual performance their end users are receiving by tracking the time it takes for a response to an end-user request to be returned to the user. The OracleAS Web Cache access logs are used to track time—from the time a request comes into OracleAS Web Cache until the time the response is returned to the user. ASLM can't be used without these access logs, so OracleAS Web Cache contributes substantially to the overall management capabilities of Oracle Enterprise Manager 10g.

Java Object Cache

OracleAS Web Cache improves performance by caching all kinds of content accessed via HTTP. Two other types of caches, Java Object Cache and Web Object Cache (described in the next section), are used specifically to support Java and web objects.

Java Object Cache is a service provided by OC4J. OC4J is the Java servlet, JSP, and EJB environment provided by Oracle Application Server, and was described in Chapter 6. Similar to OracleAS Web Cache, Java Object Cache allows the selective caching of content. However, Java Object Cache caching is performed within OC4J before content is generated by Java code. Java Object Cache also provides disk, pool, and stream-accessed caches in addition to a memory cache.

Figure 7-6 illustrates Java Object Cache's use in OC4J. An HTTP request to a servlet or JSP in the web container, or an RMI request to an EJB in the EJB container, can access a cached object in Java Object Cache. The object in the cache can be loaded by a cache loader class that, in turn, can retrieve virtually any information it needs from any source.

Basic Principles

Java Object Cache exists to cache frequently accessed or expensive objects created by Java code. An expensive object is one that requires a significant amount of CPU resources or a great deal of time to generate. Any Java object type can be stored in Java Object Cache.

A programmatically defined hierarchy of namespaces, called *regions,* organizes Java Object Cache. Typically, a region is created for each application. Then one or more subregions are defined for each part of an application that uses the cache. Regions or subregions can be combined to create a *group*. Groups allow multiple regions to be manipulated at the same time.

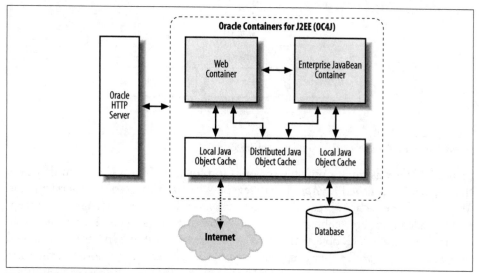

Figure 7-6. Java Object Cache architecture

Java Object Cache can cache objects in four ways:

- You can place objects in memory.
- You can place objects on disk. OracleAS Web Cache, in contrast, stores objects only in memory.
- You can access objects through a pool mechanism.
- You can access objects using streams.

Objects may be placed in the cache automatically by an implementation of the CacheLoader class, or programmatically using the CacheAccess class. The following subsections expand on this very high-level view of Java Object Cache.

How It Works

As mentioned earlier, Java Object Cache is organized by regions, subregions, and groups. Regions define a namespace within the cache. If a region isn't specified, the default region is used.

The first step in using the cache is to define a top-level region, which is typically the name of an application. Once a top-level region has been created, that region can be further subdivided into subregions. A subregion can also be divided into additional subregions, creating a hierarchy of regions, as shown in Figure 7-7.

One or more regions or subregions can be placed into a group. A group definition allows you to apply caching attributes or to invalidate cached objects for the regions in a group. A region (or subregion) can be a member of only one group at a time.

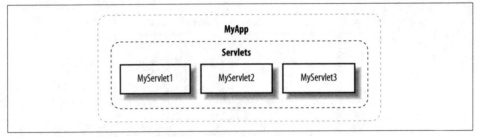

Figure 7-7. Java Object Cache organization example

Figure 7-7 demonstrates a possible organization for Java Object Cache. In this case, the application is called *MyApp*. It has several servlets, *MyServlet1*, *MyServlet2*, and *MyServlet3*. The cache is organized by creating a top-level region *MyApp*. The region is subdivided into three subregions using the names of the servlets. This creates a set of namespaces in which objects that need to be shared between servlets can be stored in region *MyApp*, while objects specific to a particular servlet are stored in the servlets' own region. A *Servlets* group has been created that groups the servlet subregions; this grouping allows all the servlet caches to be invalidated at once.

Types of Caching

Four types of cache mechanisms exist for Java Object Cache: memory, disk, stream access, and pool. You can select the mechanism that best fits your needs and the resource constraints (e.g., available memory and disk space) of your system. Methods exist that allow you to update any cached memory, disk, or stream access object.

Figure 7-8 shows the relationship between the four cache types, described in the following paragraphs.

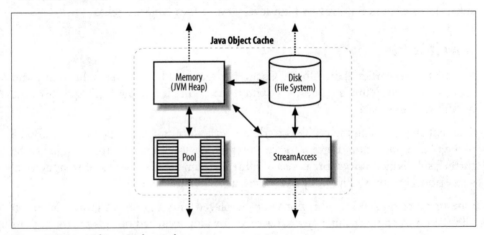

Figure 7-8. Java Object Cache: cache types

Memory cache

Memory cache is stored in the JVM's heap. This is the fastest form of cache, but only if there is enough real memory on the host server so that the operating system isn't required to use its virtual memory mechanism that swaps its real memory to disk. If the cost of creating a memory cached object is significant, you can configure the cache in such a way that it saves the object to disk if it is invalidated, then retrieves it from disk when it is needed. Memory cached objects can be updated by obtaining a private copy of an object, updating it, and then explicitly placing the object back into the cache.

Disk cache

Disk cache is stored in a designated local operating system directory. While not as fast as memory cache, disk cache has some advantages. Any object that requires a significant amount of CPU processing time or that requires a great deal of time to retrieve resources to create, can be cached to disk, eliminating the cost of recreating the object. A LRU algorithm is used, which deletes disk objects when space is needed. Like a memory object, a disk object can be updated by obtaining a private copy, updating it, and then explicitly placing it into the cache.

Stream access and pool are special cache types that use the memory cache, the disk cache, or both:

Stream access cache

Stream access cache solves the problem of dealing with very large objects. This type of cache is accessed using the Java classes OutputStream and InputStream. Class OutputStream places an object into this type of cache, while InputStream accesses an object. Stream access cache objects are automatically loaded into disk cache. How a stream access object is actually stored is transparent to the application using the cache. Java Object Cache determines the best storage method—memory or disk. This determination is based on the size of an object and the available resources in Java Object Cache. Streams can typically access very large objects one small chunk at a time. Such objects would otherwise require a significant amount of memory to materialize all at once.

Pool cache

Pool cache solves the problem of managing a pool of identical resources. Pool cache is accessed through a check-out/check-in system. A pool object contains a collection of like objects. An application-defined factory object creates objects for the collection. The cache provides a minimum and maximum pool size mechanism that allows you to create an initial minimum number of objects in a pool and to set a maximum number of objects allowed in a given pool. A pool cache can also allocate shared resources such as a custom resource adapter.

Cache Initialization

An object can be placed into one of the four cache types automatically using a CacheLoader object or explicitly using the CacheAccess.put( ) method. Because placing objects in the cache is done programmatically, doing so can be coordinated between processes.

When a cache region, subregion, or group is defined, it is given a set of default attributes. These default attributes, in turn, become the defaults for an object placed in the cache at that location. The default attributes can be overridden with object-specific attributes at the time an object is cached. Some attributes must be defined when an object is stored in the cache, while others can be modified after an object is already in the cache.

An object can be loaded automatically by setting its LOADER attribute to an instance of a custom CacheLoader class at the time the object is defined. You create a custom CacheLoader class by extending the CacheLoader class, overriding its load( ) method. Then, whenever the object is accessed, if it doesn't already exist in the cache, Java Object Cache uses the custom CacheLoader to load the desired object into the cache.

An object can be explicitly loaded using the CacheAccess.put( ) method. This requires you to create the object, and then pass it to the cache as a parameter of the put( ) method. There are drawbacks to explicit loading; in particular, you will have to detect and reload the object explicitly if it is invalidated. An event-handling mechanism, the interface CacheEventListener, exists to help with this cache management issue.

After an object is defined by including a LOADER attribute or is placed into a cache explicitly, it can be accessed using the CacheAccess.get( ) method. However, two factors affect its visibility within an application:

- The Java class loader (not the cache loader) used to load the classes placed into the cache
- The value of the DISTRIBUTE attribute

Where a particular class loader exists in the class loader hierarchy determines the visibility of the objects it loads. For an object to be visible in both the web and EJB containers, or even shared between servlets (and JSPs), a system class loader (not a servlet class loader) must load it. This means that any classes used for objects that will be cached in Java Object Cache and shared between servlets, etc., must be placed on a class path that is available to the application server, not just to a web application in a web container.

A cached object's DISTRIBUTE attribute determines whether the object is replicated across clustered instances of OC4J. If OC4J is clustered, and if Java Object Cache is configured as a distributed cache, any object that has the DISTRIBUTE attribute set will be replicated to each instance of OC4J and will therefore be accessible to all.

Cache Invalidation

Invalidation is the process used to flag an object as no longer being available. Invalidating an object doesn't necessarily remove it from the cache. An invalidated object remains in the cache until the resources it has in use are required by Java Object Cache to cache another object. If an object that is currently invalidated is requested, it will be reloaded if its LOADER attribute is set, or it will throw a CacheException error.

Cached objects can be implicitly or explicitly invalidated:

Implicit invalidation
> Implicit invalidation takes place automatically if you have set a time attribute. Two attributes control time invalidation: time-to-live and idle time. You can set the time-to-live or idle time by calling the appropriate method when an object is defined or after it has been placed into the cache. When the time-to-live expires, or when the idle time is reached, the associated object is invalidated.

Explicit invalidation
> An object can be explicitly invalidated by calling the CacheAccess.invalidate() method. An object can be removed from the cache altogether by calling CacheAccess.destroy() instead of invalidate().

You can set invalidation rules for entire regions, subregions, or groups by setting the time-to-live or idle time attributes for the desired organizational unit. You can also explicitly invalidate a region, a subregion, or a group.

Cache Management

Java Object Cache's global configuration is managed manually by setting properties in its configuration file, or programmatically using the Cache class. Unlike OracleAS Web Cache, Java Object Cache isn't managed via Application Server Control or DCM. Either the manual or the programmatic method allows you to specify the cache's memory size, its disk size and location, the cache cleanup interval, and other attributes, as well as to configure the cache as a local or distributed cache.

The contents of a local cache are available only to programs run on the OC4J instance where Java Object Cache resides. When a cache is configured as a distributed cache, its contents are replicated to every other distributed Java Object Cache in the same cluster. Using a distributed cache requires a great deal more resources, so it may make more sense to use a local cache even in a clustered environment.

Web Object Cache

The third type of Oracle Application Server cache, Web Object Cache, is used specifically to support web objects. Web Object Cache is an HTTP-centric Java object caching service for servlets and JSP, provided by the OC4J. We refer to Web Object

Cache as HTTP-centric because it typically uses information from the servlet request object, `HttpServletRequest`, such as the URI, query string, and cookies, to automatically formulate a name to use for storing and retrieving objects in a Java Object Cache.

Web Object Cache caching takes place within the OC4J web container before any content produced from a servlet or JSP is sent. Web Object Cache is best used for expensive-to-create or frequently used Java-generated objects. It isn't a substitute for OracleAS Web Cache, in which rendered content is cached and distributed outside of OC4J. Instead, use OracleAS Web Object Cache only to cache sections of content that need to be merged within an OC4J servlet. Outside OC4J, on the other hand, ESI can be used in OracleAS Web Cache.

A Web Object Cache Java API exists for use in servlets, and a Web Object Cache tag library exists for use in JSPs. A *tag library* is a set of custom tags that effectively extends the tags available when creating a source file such as an HTML file. These tags are preprocessed by a JSP translator, resulting in a servlet that is then compiled and executed.

Java objects are stored in Web Object Cache using block names. Cache policies determine block naming, as well as expiration rules. These policies can be specified declaratively in a policy descriptor file or programmatically using the API or tag library.

To use Web Object Cache effectively, you must split web pages into blocks so that appropriate parts of dynamically generated page content can be cached to improve performance.

Basic Principles

Web Object Cache consists of two components:

Programming interfaces
> These interfaces consist of the Web Object Cache servlet API and the Web Object Cache JSP tag library.

Java object repository
> This repository has two possible implementations: Java Object Cache or File System Cache.

The API and the tag library (which uses the API) can be used to programmatically set block naming and expiration policies. In addition, the API offers a set of general-purpose cache storage and retrieval methods. The tag library further abstracts these into specific tags for storing and retrieving String, XML DOM, and serializable Java object types. The tag library also offers an include mechanism that uses Web Object Cache cached content. Web Object Cache provides a special interface class, `CloneableCacheObj`, which allows the API to completely clone copies of variables to solve the problem of a shared item's being inappropriately modified by multiple users of the item.

The repository used by Web Object Cache can be of any appropriate implementation. As mentioned, two implementations exist:

Java Object Cache
> This cache, described earlier in this chapter, provides both a memory- and a disk-based caching mechanism.

File System Cache
> This cache is strictly a disk-based caching mechanism.

Cache Organization

When items are cached, they are given either an implicit or an explicit block name:

Implicit block name
> Implicit block naming, the default, is controlled by attributes of a `CachePolicy` object. Block naming attributes can be set programmatically using the API or tag library, or declaratively using a policy descriptor file that is deployed with the web application.

Explicit block name
> Explicit naming is performed programmatically using the API or tag library.

You can cache an object with different types of access. The access scope can be session or application:

Session scope
> An object cached with session scope is available only within the current HTTP session.

Application scope
> An object cached with application scope is available to all HTTP sessions in an instance. If Java Object Cache is used as the repository, and it is configured for distributed mode, application scope objects are available to all instances of OC4J that are part of the same cluster.

Caching Policies

The block naming policy is determined in various ways:

- Using the attributes set in a `CachePolicy` object
- Using the API or tag library
- Using a policy descriptor file

Sometimes, the policy is determined using both the API or tag library and the policy descriptor file.

An implicit block naming policy allows you to use any combination of the HTTP request information (URI, query string, and cookies) to formulate an appropriate block name. Even combinations that selectively specify some query string parameters or cookies can be configured. This creates a powerful, adaptable mechanism that automatically determines the block name for a cached object, in effect, relieving the programmer from having to create a custom naming mechanism. If you wish, you can set a block name explicitly.

An important part of a cache policy is the expiration policy. The expiration policy is set using an ExpirationPolicy object, which is an attribute of a cache policy. Like a block naming policy, an expiration policy is set either using the API or tag library or with a policy descriptor file. You can use either of two time-related approaches:

- You can set a time-to-live value. When the time-to-live expires, the cached object is invalidated.

- You can set a fixed day-of-the-month, day-of-the-week, and/or time-of-day. Doing so allows you to invalidate a cached object once a month, once a week, or once a day at a specified time.

Cache Invalidation

Invalidation is the process used to flag an object as no longer being available. Invalidating an object doesn't necessarily remove it from the cache. When an object's expiration policy is met, the object is invalidated. An object can also be invalidated explicitly using the API or tag library. Whether an invalidated object is removed from Web Object Cache depends upon the repository. However, once invalidated (if requested from the cache), an object isn't returned from the cache. Instead, it must be recreated and recached. Fortunately, because of the programming interfaces, this happens transparently.

It is also possible to invalidate several objects at a time. The API and tag library provide methods for identifying and invalidating objects using a partial block name or wildcard specification.

Repository Management

Currently, you can use one of the two repositories that exist for Web Object Cache: Java Object Cache or File System Cache. The desired repository for a web application is specified in a cache repository descriptor file that is deployed with a web application. If Java Object Cache is specified, additional Java Object Cache properties must be set in the OC4J instance's global web application descriptor file and a Java Object Cache properties file whose location is specified in that descriptor. If File System Cache is specified, a location for the disk cache must also be specified in the cache repository descriptor.

Of the two implementations, Java Object Cache is faster because it is both a memory-based and a disk-based cache, and it is more manageable because it allows you to set limits on the resources it uses. Java Object Cache can also be configured to replicate its cached objects across clustered OC4J instances. File System Cache is slower because it is only a disk cache, and it is less manageable because it allows you only to configure where to store serialized Java objects. You have no configurable control over how much disk space it may use. In addition, File System Cache's cached objects are available only to the local instance of OC4J.

CHAPTER 8

Java Development

This chapter explores the myriad possibilities that exist when you use Oracle Application Server as a destination for applications developed using the Java programming language and its application programming interfaces. This richness of possibilities exists for three reasons:

Java programming language capabilities

The object-oriented nature of the Java programming language makes it infinitely extensible. Every class created extends the capabilities of the language. The Java 2 Standard Edition (J2SE) and Java 2 Enterprise Edition APIs are well-engineered classes that extend the language to make it possible to build Java Client and server-side applications primarily through composition. *Composition* is the process of using existing components rather than having to recreate functionality for every program. Typically, only classes that are part of the business problem being addressed need to be created.

OC4J's complete J2EE implementation

The Oracle Application Server Containers for J2EE is a full-featured, highly scalable J2EE environment. Because OC4J provides a complete J2EE implementation, it includes all the classes available in both J2SE and J2EE for creating new applications. Functionality that doesn't exist can be added to OC4J easily because the J2EE environment itself provides a framework to address this requirement.

Oracle Application Server extensions that are accessible via Java APIs

Beyond J2EE, Oracle Application Server provides a set of Java APIs that bring additional functionality to the table. APIs exist to solve business problems using Oracle products such as OracleAS Business Components for Java, OracleAS Messaging, OracleAS Personalization, OracleAS Single Sign-On, and transformation for OracleAS Wireless devices. In addition, Oracle Application Server APIs allow developers to log application activity, report performance statistics, and manage expensive-to-create, long-lived Java objects in a cache.

Combined, these factors make Oracle Application Server, with its certified J2EE environment and Oracle-supplied Java APIs, an ideal platform for building and deploying web-based applications.

This chapter begins by taking a look at the various technologies commonly used in the development of web-based applications. Next, it examines the development tools available that support Oracle Application Server. These tools range from Oracle's own JDeveloper IDE through use of the Sun JDK. The chapter then touches on OracleAS TopLink and BC4J (Oracle's Java data-binding solution) and finishes up with a discussion of Oracle's Java APIs and Tag Libraries.

Developing Web Applications

Trying to understand what technologies should be applied when developing a web-based application is a common dilemma. Should you use HTML, Java, JavaScript, applets, servlets, EJBs, and/or XML? In some organizations there is no dilemma because someone else, someplace else in your organization, has already made the choice for you. If you are given the choice, however, what approach should you use?

Your first step is to understand how Java and related technologies can be used for web-based applications. This section examines the use of Java and related technologies for web-based application development in three layers: the presentation layer, the data and business rules layer, and the control layer, as depicted in Figure 8-1.

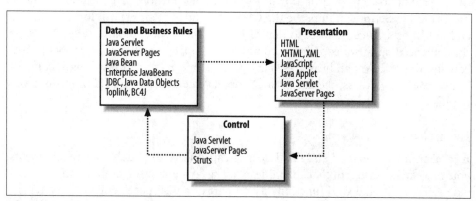

Figure 8-1. Web application architecture

Presentation Layer

The presentation layer represents the interface to the application that will be used by a human being. In a presentation (or view) layer of a web-based application, it isn't uncommon to see a combination of HTML, JavaScript, Java applets, and XML employed to provide a graphical user interface for an end user. The following are some examples:

- HTML can create a data-entry form, a menu, and so on.
- JavaScript can provide client-side (web-browser) based validation and enhanced functionality that is beyond the capabilities of a simple HTML form.
- A Java applet can be used in an HTML form to extend the capabilities of JavaScript or to replace HTML form tags altogether, by providing a rich GUI using Java.

HTML

An HTML form, created using the <form> related tags in HTML, provides a simple user interface. It doesn't allow you to do any fancy client-side validation or dynamic population of drop-down list boxes. It's like using a block-mode terminal from the good old days, where everything in the form must be transmitted to the server to be validated. If a validation error occurs, the server must rerender the entire HTML form and send it back to the end user's browser.

This type of validation can be both time-consuming and resource-intensive. It also creates a poor experience for the user of the application. However, it is extremely lightweight, efficient, portable, and well supported.

JavaScript

By adding JavaScript routines to an HTML page you can perform client-side validation, dynamic loading of drop-down list box values, custom error windows, and so on. Using JavaScript can improve the GUI capabilities of an HTML form so that the end user's experience is closer to that of using a client-server application. Of course, this enhanced end-user experience comes with a price, which is that JavaScript isn't equally supported on all browsers. That, in turn, means that you will have compatibility issues. Regardless, the use of JavaScript as an extension to HTML forms is very popular.

Java applets

If JavaScript can't extend an HTML form's capabilities to match your requirements, you can extend JavaScript's capabilities with a Java applet or use an applet to provide some additional GUI functionality on part of a web page. You can also replace the combination of an HTML form and JavaScript altogether by using a Java applet as a rich-content GUI.

Using a Java applet as a rich-content GUI allows you to provide a client-server application look-and-feel inside a browser. That is how Oracle's Forms applications, for example, are used on the Web, by employing an applet run inside your browser. The one drawback with applets used in this fashion is that they are large, and consequently take longer than HTML pages to download and display in a browser.

JSP and Java servlets

JavaServer Pages are nothing but Java servlets alternatively created by coding HTML with scriptlets and other JSP syntax, instead of by coding Java that outputs HTML, as is done in a servlet. Because JSP is nothing but a servlet, the discussion in this section covers both technologies.

Java servlets can generate the HTML pages that are then presented in an end user's browser. Essentially, you use a servlet to create HTML forms, possibly with embedded JavaScript routines and applet tags, to load an applet. Servlets (or JSPs) allow you to retrieve values from a database, create a form, and send it to the browser. When the user submits the form back to the server, it calls another servlet (or possibly the same one, depending on design) to process the data values and update the database.

You can see from the discussion in the previous sections that HTML, JavaScript, and applets are probably used together, with the HTML generated by a servlet. But what about the data and business rules? How do you retrieve and save an application's data? Where are the business rules kept? That is where JDBC and EJBs are used:

- JDBC allows your program to access a relational database.
- EJBs allow you to create modular, reusable software components that encapsulate business logic and data persistence.

The following sections describe these capabilities.

Data and Business Rules Layer

In the data and business rules layer of a web-based application, it isn't uncommon to see a combination of JDBC, JavaBeans, Java Data Objects (JDO), EJBs, and XML manipulating data and executing business rules. Several approaches can be used to manipulate data used in a web application:

- JDBC used directly in a servlet
- JDBC used in JavaBeans
- OracleAS Toplink, OracleAS Business Components for Java, or another proprietary object-relational mapping tool that implements its solution as JavaBeans or EJBs
- JDO
- EJB

Several of these persistence technologies may also be combined and then used in a servlet. As you go through the options listed here, the complexity, programming required, and infrastructure required all increase.

JDBC used in servlets

You can use JDBC directly in your servlets. JDBC allows you to perform SQL Data Manipulation Language (DML), such as inserts, updates, deletes, and selects, along with stored procedure calls and Data Definition Language (DDL).

If you do use JDBC directly in your servlets, make sure to use prepared statements to prevent SQL injection.

 With *SQL injection*, values entered into fields of your HTML form are actually additional SQL syntax. This maliciously added SQL syntax allows the perpetrator to select all values from a table or damage the validity of data in a table by erroneously inserting, updating, or deleting rows. SQL injection is possible if you use a JDBC Statement which allows you to perform dynamic SQL, but not if you use a PreparedStatement.

JDBC used in JavaBeans

If the size of your application requires multiple servlets to access the same information, you should consider consolidating your JDBC code in a JavaBean that represents a table in the database. Alternatively, use one of the other more complex solutions covered in the following sections.

If you create a JavaBean that represents a table in the database, you can add routines to select, insert, update, and delete entries as well as accessors and mutators. *Accessors* and *mutators* are methods that allow you to get and set column values. This level of abstraction is well suited for JSPs because you can then use JSP bean declarations instead of large embedded scriptlets in your JSPs to retrieve and save data.

Object-relational mapping tools

Object-relational (OR) mapping tools also allow you to use simple JavaBeans for data abstraction. These tools provide a framework that glues JavaBeans to a persistence layer such as a database. Oracle Application Server provides two OR mapping tools: OracleAS TopLink and OracleAS Business Components for Java. Object-relational mapping tools add value because they significantly reduce the amount of time it takes to create code for persisting data in a relational database.

Java Data Objects

Java Data Objects is a more recent public specification and standard for object-relational mapping. It can also be used in the same way as custom JavaBeans. JDO simplifies a lot of the coding required to make your own beans. However, using JDO comes with a price: you have to license a JDO implementation, learn how to use yet another technology, and do some special coding just for JDO.

Enterprise JavaBeans

If your application is one with high transaction volumes or a large user base, or one in which many servlets will need to share the information and business processes, Enterprise Java Beans are your best bet. EJBs provide a business process and data abstraction that treats each EJB as a distributed component that can be called by any program. EJBs provide services that ease management of transactions and deployment of an application.

EJBs allow you to more easily separate data from the business rules that may manipulate the data. This, in turn, leads to a more adaptable and longer-lived application. Once again, this comes at a price. As with JDO, you'll have to learn how to use yet another technology and do some special coding just for EJBs.

Control Layer

The control layer acts as a traffic cop between the presentation layer and the data and business rules layer. One important aspect of a web-based application is how to direct the response of an HTML form to another servlet (or other entity) in the presentation layer. One common approach is to hardcode the URL of the servlet that will process a form in the action attribute of the HTML <form> tag. This approach is referred to as *model 1 programming*. This works just fine, but it makes your application's modules programmatically dependent on each other.

An improvement on this approach is *model 2 programming* with which the same controller servlet is specified in the action attribute of every form. The controller servlet then forwards the HTML form's response on to the desired servlet. The desired servlet's URL is stored in a configuration file, as shown in Figure 8-2.

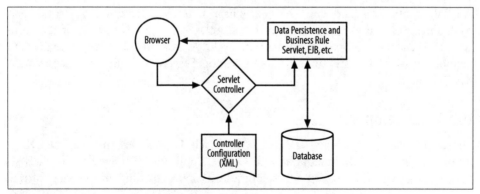

Figure 8-2. A model 2 controller

Struts is a configurable implementation of a model 2, *Model-View-Controller* (MVC) framework. You can find additional information about Struts at *http://jakarta. apache.org/struts/*.

Other Considerations for Web-Based Applications

You might also consider making sure that the output of your servlets is XHTML instead of HTML. XHTML is an XML implementation of HTML, one in which HTML documents are well-formed and valid XML documents. Using XML from the start gives you an advantage if you need to provide a presentation layer of your application to another device, such as a cell phone. In this case, your servlet's output can be forwarded to a filter servlet that transforms HTML (XHTML) to Wireless Markup Language for the handheld device. This process is possible because your HTML is actually XML. Chapter 10 describes XML in more detail.

After reading this overview of Java web-based application development, you may have realized that the most formidable part of web-based application development is the number of technologies you must master to build a user-friendly application. There are many good Java books out there that can help you. O'Reilly, for example, has books on each of these topics. You can find very well-written books on servlets, EJBs, Struts, and JavaScript at *http://www.oreilly.com*. Choosing a development tool that aids you in these technologies can also help tremendously.

Development Tools

Writing programs in Java can be accomplished with something as simple as your favorite text editor and the javac compiler. However, developing business applications with Java (or any other language, for that matter) requires a host of tools and technologies. To simplify management of the tools and technologies required for application development, and at the same time improve the efficiency of the development staff, IDEs were created.

An IDE combines a modeling tool, text editor, compiler, make utility, deployment tool, and so on, into one application that seamlessly integrates the use of each tool with the next during the development life cycle. As you will see shortly, many IDE vendors provide support for Oracle Application Server, typically as a deployment destination.

Oracle JDeveloper

Oracle JDeveloper is Oracle's IDE for Java. Oracle JDeveloper, an excellent IDE in its own right, is tightly integrated with Oracle Application Server. Because it is so tightly integrated, this section will spend a little time providing an overview of this tool.

IDE

Oracle JDeveloper is a J2EE, XML, and PL/SQL development environment that supports the full development life cycle, from modeling a business solution through its deployment. The IDE itself is extensible, so other development tools and technologies can be added to the environment as needed.

Oracle JDeveloper provides tools for source code control, data and object modeling, coding, debugging, profiling, and deployment. The editor does both syntactic and semantic verification of your code as it is entered. It also provides context-sensitive help in the form of access to API documentation. Many complex or mundane programming tasks are simplified with the use of wizards.

Figure 8-3 shows a typical Oracle JDeveloper screen setup. The smaller window sections are called *dockable windows*. You select the dockable windows you desire from the view menu. Displayed in this figure are the Application Navigator, Class Structure, Data Control Panel, Help, Editor, and Error Message windows.

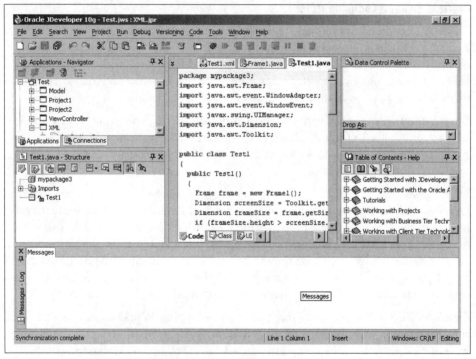

Figure 8-3. An example of the Oracle JDeveloper IDE's GUI

Oracle JDeveloper can build J2EE and/or XML applications or Web Services that can be deployed onto any J2EE server. However, Oracle JDeveloper is also tightly integrated with Oracle Application Server through its Application Development Frameworks that use OracleAS Business Components for Java and OracleAS TopLink.

Application Development Framework

Oracle JDeveloper's Application Development Framework (ADF) allows you to use several combinations of technologies to build web applications. ADF leverages the Open Source, Model 2, MVC implementation, Struts. Using Struts as the controller, ADF employs combinations of other technologies for the model and view, such as:

- EJB as the model and JSP as the view
- OracleAS Business Components for Java (BC4J) as the model and JSP as the view
- OracleAS TopLink as the model and UIX as the view. UIX is a presentation layer developed using XML

OracleAS Business Components for Java

OracleAS Business Components for Java, or ADF Business Components as it is known in Oracle JDeveloper, is an application framework that implements common design patterns. OracleAS Business Components for Java expands on the standard J2EE by providing solutions for data access, network traffic minimization, object-relational mapping, validation, and user-interface data binding.

OracleAS Business Components for Java applications are deployable on any application server. Oracle Enterprise Manager's Application Server Control tool is an example of an application that uses OracleAS Business Components for Java.

TopLink

OracleAS TopLink is an advanced object-relational mapping tool that some may say resides in the same solution space as EJB QL and JDO. However, unlike these technologies, OracleAS TopLink makes mapping relational database architecture to Java's object-oriented architecture easy by providing a superior mapping tool called the Mapping Workbench.* With OracleAS TopLink, it's possible to persist any Java object in any relational database that is also supported by a JDBC 2.0 driver.

OracleAS TopLink's graphical mapping tool, Mapping Workbench, presents relational databases with an object-oriented view. This means that Java programmers with no SQL experience can map Java classes into a relational database structure.

OracleAS TopLink is extremely flexible. It can map JavaBeans as well as EJBs to a relational database. It supports the mapping of both container-managed persistence and bean-managed persistence EJBs. OracleAS TopLink even supports mapping in a Java Client two-tier application.

---

* The OracleAS TopLink mapping editor is fully integrated into Oracle JDeveloper 10g (9.0.5).

Third-Party Support

Many of today's top IDEs provide support for Oracle Application Server. In addition, other products exist that extend the capabilities of Oracle Application Server. The following is a short list of third-party IDEs that support Oracle Application Server deployment:

- Borland's JBuilder
- Computer Associates' COOL:Joe
- Macromedia's Dreamweaver MX and UltraDev
- Rational's Rational Rose
- Sun's Sun ONE Studio
- TogetherSoft's Together ControlCenter

Because a list such as this can change dramatically over time, it's best if you consult it online. You can find an up-to-date list at *http://otn.oracle.com/products/ias/9ias_partners.html*.

As discussed earlier in Chapter 6, you can even code directly in a deployment directory on the server. In this configuration, you can simply use your favorite text editor and the Sun JDK's javac compiler to build your application.

Oracle Application Server APIs and Tag Libraries

In addition to Oracle Application Server's support for J2EE, it also provides access to components of Oracle Application Server and application frameworks via a set of proprietary APIs and JSP tag libraries. The following is a list of these APIs and tag libraries:

- OracleAS Business Components API Reference
- OracleAS Business Components Generic Domains API Reference
- OracleAS Business Components InterMedia Domains API Reference
- OracleAS Business Components Oracle Domains API Reference
- Certificate Authority Java API Reference
- Dynamic Monitoring Service API Reference
- Edge Side Includes for Java (JESI)
- HTTPClient API Reference
- JAAS Provider API Reference
- Support for JavaServer Pages API Reference
- Java Object Cache API Reference

- Oracle JSP Tag Libraries
- Oracle Internet Directory API Reference
- JDBC API Reference
- SQLJ API Reference
- Syndication Services API Reference
- XML API Reference
- OracleAS Personalization API Reference
- OracleAS Single Sign-On API Reference
- OracleAS TopLink API Reference
- UltraSearch API Reference
- Unified Messaging API Reference
- OracleAS Web Cache Invalidation API Reference
- OracleAS Web Clipping API Reference
- Web Services SOAP API Reference
- Web Services Proxy API Reference
- Web Services UDDI Client API Reference
- OracleAS Wireless API Reference
- OracleAS Wireless J2ME SDK API Reference
- OracleAS Workflow API Reference

As you can see from this list, Oracle Application Server exposes all its capabilities to the Java application developer. Oracle Application Server also provides an extensive library of XML and Web Services APIs, which are covered separately in Chapters 10 and 11. In addition to these Java development tools, Oracle Application Server is tightly integrated with the Oracle database, exposing all its capabilities as well. This integration makes the combination of the Oracle database and Oracle Application Server an ideal environment for enterprise application development and deployment.

CHAPTER 9

Oracle Development

Oracle Application Server provides both a development platform and a deployment platform. Many of the components in Oracle Application Server are based on open standards, such as Java and the Apache Web Server, and those are described in earlier chapters of this book.

But Oracle Application Server is an Oracle product, and many users consider acquiring the product because of their past involvement with the Oracle database. Consequently, three areas of Oracle Application Server focus on Oracle-specific technologies:

- PL/SQL, the long-standing language used within the Oracle database
- Deployment services for Oracle Forms applications
- Deployment services for Oracle Reports applications

OracleAS Forms Services and Reports Services come as part of the Enterprise Edition of Oracle Application Server 10*g*. You can install a version of Oracle Application Server specifically to support these services. This installation includes the OracleAS Infrastructure (described in Chapter 2), which is used to implement security services for Oracle Forms and Oracle Reports.

This chapter describes the use of PL/SQL, OracleAS Forms Services, and OracleAS Reports Services in Oracle Application Server.

PL/SQL

The Procedure Language extension to SQL (PL/SQL) is Oracle's proprietary programming language. It is used both server-side and client-side:

On the server side
    PL/SQL is used in the Oracle database to program stored procedures and triggers.

On the client side

PL/SQL is used in Oracle's declarative development tools, Oracle Forms and Oracle Reports, to program behavior.

PL/SQL's strengths lie in its seamless integration with SQL and in its excellent server-side performance. Because Oracle's tools, Oracle Forms and Oracle Reports, also use PL/SQL as their programming language, these tools can leverage both seamless integration with the database and existing PL/SQL database programmer expertise for client-side development.

Using PL/SQL

PL/SQL uses the same datatypes as SQL in the database; hence, no datatype conversions are necessary. PL/SQL effectively adds procedural language constructs, such as IF-THEN-ELSE logic, FOR loops, and so on, to SQL. Because PL/SQL stored procedures are executed in the database, this capability eliminates the data access delays caused by moving data across a network. This makes PL/SQL the superior choice for data-intensive manipulations in the database.

Oracle Application Server provides a way to produce dynamic content via Oracle database stored procedures. The execution of stored procedures for web applications is facilitated through the Oracle HTTP Server module `mod_plsql`; the Oracle HTTP Server was described in detail in Chapter 5.

PL/SQL is a rich and powerful language that we only touch upon in this book. For much more detailed information, see *Oracle PL/SQL Programming* (O'Reilly).

PL/SQL Web Applications

Oracle HTTP Server uses the `mod_plsql` module to route stored procedure requests to an Oracle database. `mod_plsql` provides a CGI environment for stored procedures. A request URI routed to `mod_plsql` from the Oracle HTTP Server is mapped to a corresponding stored procedure in the database as follows:

- The name of the stored procedure—schema, package name, and procedure name (as required to eliminate ambiguity)—is specified in the URI.
- Any HTTP parameter values are mapped to stored procedure parameters with exactly the same names as the HTTP parameters.
- Extra path information, cookies, and CGI environment variables are also made available.

The logic of a stored procedure can use any of this information to formulate a response in the form of text that is then streamed back to the requester through `mod_plsql` to the Oracle HTTP Server, and so on. Two software development kits are available to aid the developer: the PL/SQL Web Toolkit and PL/SQL Server Pages. If you're familiar with Java, note that these can be compared to Java servlets and JSPs, respectively.

PL/SQL Web Toolkit

This toolkit provides a set of Oracle stored procedure packages (e.g., HTP, HTF, OWA_UTIL) that allow a PL/SQL programmer to call procedures or functions to produce HTML output. These packages also provide access to CGI environment variables and cookies. Using the PL/SQL Web Toolkit, a programmer writes a stored procedure that outputs HTML tags and data.

PL/SQL Server Pages

In contrast, PL/SQL Server Pages are HTML files with embedded PL/SQL scriptlets. The *scriptlets* (small pieces of PL/SQL code) may call PL/SQL Web Toolkit procedures and functions. PSPs are compiled into stored procedures when they are loaded into the database using the loadpsp utility.

The difference between using the PL/SQL Web Toolkit and using PL/SQL Server Pages is that PL/SQL Web Toolkit procedures are PL/SQL programs with embedded HTML, while PL/SQL Server Pages are HTML files with embedded PL/SQL. The PL/SQL Web Toolkit is typically a more appropriate choice for programmers, whereas PSPs are a better fit for web designers. Ultimately, every PSP becomes a stored procedure.

OracleAS Forms Services

For many years, OracleAS Forms Services has been one of the most popular 4GL development environments for Oracle database applications. OracleAS Forms Services was designed originally to be closely integrated with the Oracle database. As we mentioned, OracleAS Forms Services uses PL/SQL as the language for its extended logic. The same Oracle sales team that provided the Oracle database was also able to helpfully supply this development tool. But, as the technology environment evolved, OracleAS Forms Services was caught in a bind. Like many client-server tools, OracleAS Forms Services split the runtime functionality of its applications between the client and the server.

The new environment of Internet computing required a slightly different deployment model. To address this new requirement, the OracleAS Forms Services development team created a new deployment model in 1997 with Release 4.1. In this new model, a Java applet talks to a Java servlet on a server. That server, in turn, calls the OracleAS Forms Services runtime. With this new deployment model, OracleAS Forms Services deployment was transformed from a two-tier client-server architecture into a three-tier web-based architecture.

How It Works

The interaction between a web client and an Oracle Forms application through Oracle AS Forms Services is shown in simplified form in Figure 9-1.

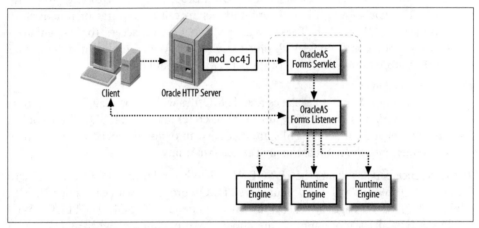

Figure 9-1. Simplified OracleAS Forms Services architecture

Interaction proceeds as follows:

1. The initial contact is between a browser and the Oracle HTTP Server instance, with a URL that indicates an Oracle Forms application. The Oracle HTTP Server instance forwards the URI request through mod_oc4j to the Oracle Forms servlet, which is run in an OC4J instance.

2. The Oracle Forms servlet starts by creating some HTML, based on the application and the browser type. This HTML is passed to the Oracle Forms Listener servlet.

3. The Oracle Forms Listener servlet passes the HTML back to the client. The servlet also creates an Oracle Forms runtime process (written in C) for the application.

4. The HTML passed to the client starts the client-side applet and spawns a client request for a particular form.

5. Once the connection between the Oracle Forms Listener and the client is established, further interaction between the client and the runtime process is done through the Oracle Forms Listener servlet. At this point, the Oracle Forms servlet is no longer needed.

A single Oracle Forms Listener servlet can manage communications between multiple clients and their runtime processes.

Developers can still use the familiar Oracle Forms development environment, but they now deploy Oracle Forms applications as browser-based clients connecting over the Internet or an intranet to a middle tier of Oracle Application Server. This new architecture also brings other features with it, as we explain in subsequent sections.

OracleAS Forms Services applications use a default HTML template to pass environment variables to the browser, but you can also create your own templates by modifying the default template to include either hardcoded values for parameters or dynamic parameters from the Oracle Forms configuration file.

Running Oracle Forms Services Applications

Once you create an application in Oracle Forms Developer, it can be deployed through OracleAS Forms Services. You have to create a configuration for the application either manually or through a portion of the Oracle Enterprise Manager 10g Application Server Control tool (described in Chapter 3). For more information on using Oracle Enterprise Manager to manage OracleAS Forms Services, see the next section, "Managing OracleAS Forms Services."

When a user wants to run an OracleAS Forms Services application, the interaction proceeds as follows, from the user's point of view:

1. The user sends a URL (containing the pathname) to the Oracle Forms servlet. This URL also contains the name of the configuration file or the name of a section of the configuration file.

2. Based on the configuration file, the Oracle Forms servlet returns an HTML page, which is specific for the type of browser being used by the client.

3. The HTML page loads a client-side applet, which runs in a JVM on the client.

The Java client-side applet is used to display OracleAS Forms Services forms and can display multiple forms simultaneously.

The Oracle Forms applet on the client requires a specific version of a JVM to run properly. Because the native JVM on a particular browser may not be appropriate, Oracle supplies a client-side plug-in called Oracle JInitiator. Oracle JInitiator allows the use of an alternative JVM to run the client-side Oracle Forms applet as a plug-in to Netscape Navigator or Microsoft Internet Explorer.

Some parts of a particular form are common across all users accessing that form, such as screen definitions and application logic. Once these parts are loaded for a form, subsequent users of the same form can share these entities in memory, with only their private application data requiring its own dedicated memory.

The architecture for OracleAS Forms Services is different from the standard client-server architecture, and that fact has implications for the performance of applications. In the multitier OracleAS Forms Services environment, the limiting performance factor is frequently the bandwidth from the client to the middle tier. For this reason, OracleAS Forms Services applications optimize the communications between the client and the middle tier. For instance, OracleAS Forms Services applications bundle events together after each navigation event. These event bundles interact between the OracleAS Forms Server and the back-end database without having to communicate with the client applet.

Although each individual user has a OracleAS Forms Services runtime process, you can have multiple instances of OracleAS Forms Services. Because the Oracle Forms servlets are standard OC4J applications, you can use any of the normal load-balancing options for OC4J for these Oracle Forms Listeners.

You can create a pool of runtime engines for a particular application in the configuration file for the application. The runtime engines in this pool service users for the application. You can configure a number of instances to be started when an administrator starts the application from Application Server Control, as we discuss in the following section.

Managing OracleAS Forms Services

The Application Server Control tool lets you set parameters to control the operation of an OracleAS Forms Services application. For example, you can control the look and feel of the client portion of the application or the specific title of a particular HTML page returned to the client. The configuration file can also be used to provide different versions of the same application in different languages.

For most parameters, you can override the value in the configuration file by including the parameter in the URL that calls the OracleAS Forms Services application. You can also specify parameters that can't be overridden for a particular application in this configuration file.

Oracle Enterprise Manager gives you an easy interface for managing the underlying configuration files used by OracleAS Forms Services. You can still manually edit these files, but after making changes, you will have to stop all the DCM processes, as well as Oracle Enterprise Manager, to have the changes recognized by Oracle Enterprise Manager. If you don't do this, any subsequent changes made through Oracle Enterprise Manager will simply overwrite the manually changed configuration files.

You can have multiple configurations in separate sections of the configuration file. You might want to do this if different users have different versions of the OracleAS Forms Services application.

Many different parameters shape the appearance and behavior of your OracleAS Forms Services application. A comprehensive list of these parameters is beyond the scope of this book. Please refer to the OracleAS Forms Services documentation for more information.

The portion of Application Server Control that handles OracleAS Forms Services can be used to limit access to OracleAS Forms Services. You can disallow any new user connections to these services on a particular server, or you can kill specific user sessions.

Configuring Security

OracleAS Forms Services can be configured to use the OracleAS Single Sign-On capability of Oracle Application Server without additional code. In Oracle Application Server, OracleAS Single Sign-On uses the identity management that is based on the Oracle Internet Directory. Although Oracle Forms applications have traditionally used a database username and password for security, the Oracle Forms Listener servlet can take this information and use the Oracle Internet Directory to implement OracleAS Single Sign-On with an OracleAS Forms Services application. Because the handling of OracleAS Single Sign-On is done by the OracleAS Forms servlets, not in the Oracle Forms Runtime Process, existing Oracle Forms applications can take advantage of OracleAS Single Sign-On without any modification. In fact, the form itself is unaware of whether OracleAS Single Sign-On was used, although the form can acquire this information if your logic requires it.

You can create user accounts with connect information in the Oracle Internet Directory, which in turn creates Resource Access Descriptors (RADs) once a user connects to OracleAS Forms Services. As of the Oracle Application Server 10g release, you can configure OracleAS Forms Services to allow all users to create their own RADs on the fly if none exists; previous releases returned an error in such cases. Also new in Oracle Application Server 10g is the fact that updating a password in the database automatically updates the RAD information in the Oracle Internet Directory.

OracleAS Reports Services

Oracle Reports, like Oracle Forms, is a part of the Oracle Developer Suite and has been a part of the Oracle technology stack for many years. We discuss the use of Oracle Reports in the context of business intelligence solutions in Chapter 12, but an in-depth discussion of the use and capabilities of Oracle Reports is beyond the scope of this chapter.

In brief, Oracle Reports enables a developer to combine data from many sources (including an Oracle database, XML data, JDBC data feeds, and even customizable data sources) into a report that can be distributed either on paper or within the web environment. Reports can be generated as HTML, XML, PDF files, RTF format, and many other formats as well.

This section concentrates on Oracle Application Server Reports Services, the component of Oracle Application Server that is responsible for providing a middle tier for deploying Oracle Reports. OracleAS Reports Services is responsible for creating

Oracle Reports engines to generate reports, for distributing reports across multiple servers, and for caching reports for rapid reuse.

How It Works

OracleAS Reports Services can be used either inside or outside a web environment. The architecture of OracleAS Reports Services within a web environment is shown in simplified form in Figure 9-2.

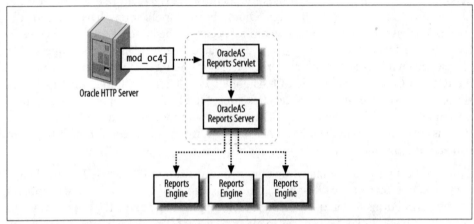

Figure 9-2. Simplified OracleAS Reports Services architecture

Requests come into the Oracle HTTP Server, and are then passed to an OracleAS Reports servlet through the mod_oc4j module. The OracleAS Reports servlet is responsible for coordinating requests with the OracleAS Reports Server. The server handles the processing, scheduling, and distribution of reports. It also maintains the state of all current report requests.

The OracleAS Reports Server is monitored and controlled by the Oracle Process Management and Notification Server (described in Chapter 2), although you can start and stop the OracleAS Reports Server in other ways—for example, with a command-line prompt or from a URL.

The actual creation of reports is handled by Reports engines, which are written in C. There can be many Reports engines for each OracleAS Reports Server. You can configure the maximum, minimum, and initial number of engines for a OracleAS Reports Server, as well as the amount of time a Reports engine can be idle before it is automatically shut down by OPMN.

Several additional components are included in the OracleAS Reports Services architecture but aren't displayed in the simplified version shown in the figure:

OracleAS Reports Cache

Used by the OracleAS Reports Server for caching reports for subsequent use, based on rules established for the report.

Custom Tag Handler

A part of the Reports servlet, used to call Oracle Reports from JSPs with special tags. You can use these tags to gain access to data models developed in reports.

OracleAS Single Sign-On

Because OracleAS Single Sign-On is a part of Oracle Application Server, you can use this security architecture with OracleAS Reports Services. If you choose to use OracleAS Single Sign-On, the Oracle Reports servlet interacts with the OracleAS Single Sign-On service to validate user credentials. If a user doesn't exist in the Oracle Internet Directory, the Oracle Delegated Administration Services, which allow a user to maintain his login credentials, prompts the user for connection information, which is stored in the Oracle Internet Directory. You can also use OracleAS Reports Services with its own security authentication, although OracleAS Reports Services is installed using OracleAS Single Sign-On by default.

 Security can be implemented at three levels in OracleAS Reports Services—on the application that calls a report, on the report and its destination resources, or on the underlying data sources for the report.

Pluggable engines

These are custom engines that can hook into the OracleAS Reports Server to use its capabilities, such as scheduling, distribution, and content. OracleAS Reports Services comes with a URL engine, which lets you distribute content from any publicly available URL using these features of the OracleAS Reports Server.

Reports CGI

Used to call reports dynamically from a browser using CGI, and included for backward compatibility.

You can invoke OracleAS Reports Services from outside a web environment. You can use the command-line argument rwclient to call the OracleAS Reports Server directly. You can also call the OracleAS Reports Server from the SRW built-in PL/SQL package or can expose OracleAS Reports Services as a Web Service.

Handling Requests

A request that comes into an OracleAS Reports Server can include parameters that shape the report. If the request is made from a browser, the parameters can be included in the calling URL, or that URL can use a key to identify a group of parameters. The parameter groups and values are stored by key name in the *cgicmd.dat* file.

When a request comes in to an OracleAS Reports Server, the server first determines if the request can be satisfied either by a currently running job or by a report in the OracleAS Report Cache, described in the next section. If a request can't be satisfied by one of these two methods, the request is placed in one of two queues:

Current job queue
  For immediate requests

Scheduled job queue
  For scheduled requests

OracleAS Reports Services also has two more queues:

Completed jobs queue
  For job history; you can configure a limit to the number of jobs kept in the completed jobs queue

Failed jobs queue
  For failed jobs

OracleAS Reports Server keeps requests that come from a browser in memory. In the event of a server crash, these requests will have to be resubmitted. Requests that are slated for a print queue, a file, or OracleAS Portal will be restarted in the event of an OracleAS Reports Server failure.

You can view the contents of either the current job queue or the scheduled job queue through the Application Server Control tool in Oracle Enterprise Manager. Both of these queues are persistent; if an OracleAS Reports Server crashes, only the currently running jobs are lost.

If a request requires authentication, OracleAS Reports Server calls the mod_osso module before placing the requests in either queue.

You configure the maximum number of Reports engines for an OracleAS Reports Server. If a request is made, and the maximum number of Reports engines aren't currently running, OracleAS Reports Server creates a new engine to run the request at the top of the current job queue. If the maximum number of engines are already running, the top job in the current job queue waits, and the first available engine takes the job.

Internal testing from Oracle has determined that the optimal number of Reports engines is two times the number of CPUs on a server.

With Oracle Application Server 10g, several different Reports engines can exist with different environment conditions, such as the ability to handle reports with different languages. When a report request arrives with a particular configuration, OracleAS Reports Server directs it to an available Reports engine that is appropriate for the request.

Once a Reports engine has completed the creation of the report, the report is placed in the OracleAS Reports Cache, and the OracleAS Reports Server is notified of its availability. The OracleAS Reports Server then distributes the report.

The steps described here are valid for running reports with a paper layout, whether they are standard reports or JSP reports. If you want to display a report with a paper layout in a browser, the report can be sent as an Adobe Acrobat (PDF) file format. If you want to run a report with a web layout, you can save the report definition as a JSP in Oracle Forms Developer and then execute the report like a standard JSP.

OracleAS Reports Cache

A report is a static view of constantly changing data. There may be times when the same report can fulfill more than one request—either by design or by the coincidences of usage patterns. Consequently, OracleAS Reports Services tries to optimize the use of reports and diminish the resource requirements for serving reports to a user community.

As mentioned earlier, the destination for reports created by a Reports engine is the OracleAS Reports Cache. When a report is put into that cache, the report is assigned a cache key. The cache key includes most of the parameters that shape the report, with the exception of destination information, server information, and the TOLERANCE parameter (described later in this section). You can configure an OracleAS Reports Server instance to ignore specified parameters in creating the cache key.

When a request comes in, the OracleAS Reports Server looks in the OracleAS Reports Cache for a report with the same cache key. A report in the cache with an identical cache key can sometimes be reused for another request.

The request itself can include the TOLERANCE parameter. This parameter has a value in minutes, hours, or day, or alternately contains a specific time. If a report has a TOLERANCE parameter, the OracleAS Reports Server searches the completed jobs queue for a report with an identical cache key that isn't older than allowed by the time value specified by the TOLERANCE parameter or earlier than the time specified by that parameter.

The size of the OracleAS Reports Cache is configurable, either by the total size of the cache or by the number of documents the cache is allowed to hold. As the cache is filled, the least-used reports are swapped out of the cache.

Distributing Reports

Once a report is created, it can be distributed to a variety of destinations—for example, to the browser issuing a request, to one or more recipients via email, to a file or a printer, or to OracleAS Portal. You can also create your own custom destinations using the Oracle Application Server Reports Services API. That API supports the distribution of reports to other destinations, such as via FTP or a fax machine.

With Oracle Application Server 10g, the creation of reports is done by the Reports engine, independent of the eventual destination of the report. The OracleAS Reports Server is responsible for distributing the report to its final destinations.

You can create complex types of distributions for reports. Each report has three distinct sections—a header, a trailer, and a body. You can distribute each section separately, and you can also create individual reports based on groups specified in the body of the report. You can send each report or report section to one or more destinations. You can also create destinations based on one or more data values in a variable.

For example, if you have a report on employees by department, you can have a department summary section sent to the appropriate head of the department, as well as individual employee reports, sent to each employee. The department heads and employees can be indicated by data variables within the report. This scenario, sometimes referred to as *bursting* reports, allows a single report pass to generate a wide spectrum of reports.

An XML file is used to describe these complex distributions. You specify the distribution XML file as part of the report request. For more information on these complex distributions, please refer to the Oracle Application Server Reports Services documentation.

XML and Reports Services

The distribution file mentioned in the previous section is an XML file. XML (described in greater detail in Chapter 10), which can also be used as a format for reports or to modify reports with customization files.

Although you can build a report completely from scratch using XML, Oracle recommends following an alternate process whereby you save a report as XML. You can apply one or more XML customization files to the saved report; these files are used to modify characteristics in the report.

For example, you might want to format a particular field using its XML attributes in a customization file. Once you have perfected the XML customization file, you can use it to apply the same formatting to other reports that contain the same field, either by running each report or by applying the modifications as part of a batch process.

Clustering

You can cluster together any number of OracleAS Reports Servers. Each member of the cluster is aware of the other members of the cluster, and all members of the cluster work together to handle incoming requests.

When a request comes in to one OracleAS Reports Server in a cluster, either from a client or off the scheduled job queue, the request will go through the standard set of steps for determining how to handle the request, but will supplement each step with an examination of other members of the cluster. For example, the first step when receiving a request is to see if there is information in the OracleAS Reports Cache to handle the request. With a cluster, this step is followed by a determination of whether there is information in the OracleAS Reports Caches of any other members of the cluster to handle the request. The same process is followed when looking for currently running jobs, for an appropriate Reports engine that is available, and for checking the number of Reports engines running against the maximum number of engines configured for the OracleAS Reports Server.

Each member of a cluster maintains its own local OracleAS Reports Cache, so the failure of any member eliminates the contents of its cache and prevents access by the other members of the cluster to this information. Such failure also prevents access by the OracleAS Reports Server and its engines.

Clusters are formed by appending a cluster name onto the name of the OracleAS Reports Server. You can submit a request to the cluster, rather than to a server in the cluster, by specifying the cluster name as the server.

Calling OracleAS Reports Services

You can access OracleAS Reports Services directly from a browser or from the command line. But you may want to generate or schedule reports based on other interactions and interfaces. OracleAS Reports Services comes with an API that can make a request to the services based on a database event, such as a changed value in the database. Two other interfaces also are frequently used to access reports from OracleAS Reports Services—through OracleAS Portal and as a web service. We describe both of these interfaces in subsequent sections.

Event-based reporting

In general, reports are the way that information in a database is disseminated to groups of users. Oracle Application Server Reports Services brings many helpful capabilities to this task—for example, easily readable presentation, multiple copies, and ease of access. Historically, however, there has been an inevitable problem with reports and the data they represent. A report gives an accurate view of data—at the time the report was generated. This data can change at any point in time after this generation. OracleAS Reports Services has a way to overcome this limitation and make reports more timely.

The OracleAS Reports Services API is a PL/SQL package that can be called from any other PL/SQL procedure. The package lets you submit a request to a OracleAS

Reports Server and pass up to 255 parameter values with the request. Submitting a job returns a job identification, which can check the status of the job or cancel the job.

OracleAS Portal

OracleAS Portal is another component of Oracle Application Server, discussed in detail in Chapter 13. You can call reports from OracleAS Reports Services to be displayed within the OracleAS Portal framework, either within its own portlet or as an item link on another page.

The interaction between OracleAS Portal and OracleAS Reports Services requires a few additional considerations. If you are calling a report from the Portal environment:

- You can limit access to the report through security restrictions on the calling OracleAS Portal page. Because OracleAS Portal uses OracleAS Single Sign-on, a user identity flows to OracleAS Reports Services, which imposes its own set of report and data access security restrictions.
- You must register all OracleAS Reports Servers and reports in your OracleAS Portal environment
- You can use availability calendars in OracleAS Portal to restrict the days and times that reports can be requested from OracleAS Reports Services.

Although you can publish a report to OracleAS Portal, you can't use OracleAS Portal as a destination when you are using an XML distribution file.

Web Services

Web Services are a way to access some kind of functionality or information over the Web, using XML to describe the information requested.

If you want to run OracleAS Reports Services as a Web Service, you run the rwwebservices OC4J servlet. This application provides endpoints for accessing an OracleAS Reports Server as a Web Service. Other applications can use this servlet to get the version of the API used to access the OracleAS Reports Server, get information about the server or any particular job, and submit and kill jobs for the OracleAS Reports Server.

CHAPTER 10

XML Development

EXtensible Markup Language (XML) is a metamarkup language for text documents that allows you to store information in a self-describing format. With XML, you organize information by surrounding it with user-defined, human-readable tags, similar to those used in HTML, but not limited to the tag names used by HTML. Instead, tag names are chosen that best describe the information they organize. XML organizes information hierarchically. In addition, the character set used to encode an XML document is specified within the document. Combined, these features make XML a universal format for information exchange.

This chapter starts with a brief introduction to XML. Next, it introduces the various relevant XML standards that exist and examines the support Oracle Application Server provides for these standards. We cover the support in various programming languages such as C, C++, Java, and PL/SQL. Then we include an overview of the XML tools that Oracle Application Server provides for XML development. The chapter finishes up with a glimpse at how some of the Oracle Application Server components employ the use of XML.

XML, DTDs, and XML Schemas

For an XML document to be used for information exchange, it must be parseable, and to be parseable, it must be *well-formed*. A well-formed document, among other rules, must have an end tag for every start tag, and different start and end tags may not be placed in such a matter as to cross each other's boundaries.

For instance, Example 10-1 is a well-formed XML document that contains information about a person named Jane Doe, born on January 1, 1980.

Example 10-1. An example of a well-formed XML document

```
<?xml version="1.0"?>
<person>
  <name>
```

Example 10-1. An example of a well-formed XML document (continued)

```
    <last_name>Doe</last_name>
    <first_name>Jane</first_name>
  </name>
  <birth_date>1980-01-01</birth_date>
  <gender>Female</gender>
</person>
```

If a document is to be shared with more than one computer program, or shared between organizations, it should also be *valid*. A valid XML document is one that conforms to an agreed-upon format. An XML document is valid if it can be validated against a Document Type Definition (DTD) or an XML Schema.

DTD is the first *schema* standard developed for formally describing an XML document's format. A DTD is narrative document-centric, so while it provides a means to describe a document's structure, it doesn't include the ability to specify datatypes.

To continue with the Jane Doe example, Example 10-2 shows a DTD that can validate the XML document in Example 10-1.

Example 10-2. An example of a Document Type Definition

```
<!ELEMENT person (name, birth_date, gender)>
<!ELEMENT name (last_name, first_name)>
<!ELEMENT last_name (#PCDATA)>
<!ELEMENT first_name (#PCDATA)>
<!ELEMENT birth_date (#PCDATA)>
<!ELEMENT gender (#PCDATA)>
```

XML Schema, a more recent standard, is data document-centric. Not only does it define document structure, it also supports user-defined datatypes and some object-oriented principles, such as inheritance. By validating an XML document against its XML Schema, you can validate its structure as well as the datatypes of its content. This is ideal for computer-to-computer data exchange.

Example 10-3 is an example of a possible XML Schema for the XML document in Example 10-1. If you compare this XML Schema with the DTD in Example 10-2, you'll see the additional specification of the datatypes for each element. Not only do XML Schemas add datatypes, but they also add complex constraints and namespace support, concepts that we will address in the sections that follow.

Example 10-3. An example of an XML Schema

```
<?xml version="1.0"?>
<xsd:schema xmlns:xsd="http://www.w3.org/2001/XMLSchema">
  <xsd:element name="person">
    <xsd:complexType>
      <xsd:sequence>
        <xsd:element name="name">
          <xsd:complexType>
            <xsd:sequence>
```

Example 10-3. An example of an XML Schema (continued)

```
            <xsd:element name="last_name"
              type="xsd:string" minOccurs="1"/>
            <xsd:element name="first_name"
              type="xsd:string" minOccurs="1"/>
          </xsd:sequence>
        </xsd:complexType>
      </xsd:element>
      <xsd:element name="birth_date"
        type="xsd:date"/>
      <xsd:element name="gender"
        type="xsd:string" minOccurs="1"/>
    </xsd:sequence>
  </xsd:complexType>
</xsd:element>
</xsd:schema>
```

A DTD, an XML Schema, or both can be used to define an XML document's vocabulary. This vocabulary, which is a formal specification, is called an *XML application*. This type of application is very different from our normal notion of an application, such as a set of programs coded in a programming language such as Java or PL/SQL. This distinction also brings to light the fact that XML itself isn't a programming language, a protocol, or a database management system.

Because of its capabilities and its promise as a universal data format, XML has suffered more than its fair share of hype. While XML is ideal for storing information in a universal format, making it a perfect choice for information exchange, it makes a poor database. Yes, it can be used as a database to store relatively small amounts of information in an organized manner, but beyond that, information stored as XML is slow to retrieve and/or manipulate when compared to information stored in an object-relational database such as Oracle.

XML Standards

The World Wide Web Consortium, a group of individuals that participate in the establishment of web-related standards, has created many XML-related standards, including XML 1.0, XML's first formal specification, and more recently, XML Schema. Oracle Application Server provides support for these established XML standards both in the database via the mod_plsql module and in the application server for web-based applications written in any of the following:

- C or C++ that runs in mod_fastcgi
- Java that runs in OC4J
- Web Services

XML

XML Version 1.0 is XML's first formal specification (recommendation) from the W3C. It defines the syntax used to create a well-formed XML document. In addition, it defines the structure of a DTD, a schema that, in turn, can validate one of its XML document instances.

Oracle Application Server is XML 1.0-compliant, which means that the server's internal use of XML, along with the tools and APIs it provides, all comply with the XML Version 1.0 recommendation from the W3C.

XML Namespaces

XML Namespaces exist to eliminate potentially ambiguous XML element (tag) names when XML applications are combined to create a new XML application. An XML Namespace associates a URI with a namespace prefix. The prefix is added to an element name in an XML document to maintain the element name's uniqueness within the document. This qualification becomes necessary when element names from two different XML applications used in another XML application use the same element name. Without the prefix, the elements with the same name collide; this creates ambiguity that, in turn, causes confusion about the element's meaning. The associated namespace URI creates a context for an otherwise ambiguous element.

The XML Namespace Version 1.0 recommendation isn't part of the XML 1.0 recommendation. It post-dates XML 1.0 and isn't a dependent specification. XML Namespaces may be used if necessary, but they are by no means required for an XML document to be compliant with the 1.0 recommendation.

Oracle Application Server supports the XML Namespace's 1.0 recommendation from the W3C.

XML Path Language

XML Path Language is a non-XML based language that identifies a particular part, or parts, of an XML document. XPath treats an XML document and its content as a *tree structure*, in much the same way operating systems treat file systems. By doing so, it allows you to write an expression that identifies a specific element, attribute, text, comment, processing instruction, or namespace within an XML document. XPath expressions can also specify Boolean values, numbers, or strings.

Oracle Application Server supports XPath Version 1.0.

Extensible Stylesheet Language Transformations

EXtensible Stylesheet Language for Transformations (XSLT) is an XML application that allows you to specify a set of rules that transform an XML document into another document format. Although typically used for XML-to-XML document transformation, XSLT can be used to create a text document of any kind.

An XSLT stylesheet is an XML document that contains rules for transformation. The rules in an XSL stylesheet use XPath notation to identify the targets of rules. Using an XSL stylesheet, an XSLT processor transforms an input XML document to another format using the rules specified in a stylesheet.

Oracle Application Server supports XSLT Version 1.0.

XML Schemas

An XML Schema is an XML document that describes the composition of a valid XML document in much greater detail than is possible using a DTD. An XML Schema adds the concepts of datatypes (both simple and complex), datatype inheritance, and element and attribute constraints to the structural capabilities of a DTD. However, XML Schemas improve on DTDs at the expense of additional complexity.

Oracle Application Server provides support for parts 0–2 of the W3C's XML Schema recommendation from May 2, 2001.

XML Parsers

XML parsers can read an XML document from an operating system file or stream and present the XML document's information as a tree structure in memory after the entire file is read, or in an event-based fashion as a document is read. Each approach has its strengths and weaknesses:

Tree-structured approach, or document model
> This approach makes it feasible to query any part of an XML document at any time. It also allows you to modify an XML document, but it can require a great deal of memory.

Event-based model
> This approach conserves memory consumption, but it can process a document only as it is read.

Because of the opposing constraints, two types of XML parsers exist: Document Object Model (DOM) parsers and Simple API for XML (SAX) parsers.

Document Object Model

The Document Object Model (DOM) is a specification for reading and modifying (and saving) an XML document as a tree structure. The elements that make up a particular XML document create a hierarchical structure that can be represented as a tree with the first element of an XML document as the root. In many ways, this tree structure, shown in Figure 10-1, is similar to the one presented by most modern operating systems' file systems.

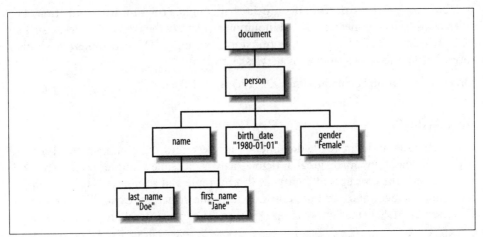

Figure 10-1. A tree of DOM nodes for Example 10-1

At its core, DOM is a set of APIs that represent an XML document as a set of object nodes, as in Figure 10-1. A node type exists for each kind of XML structural and content syntax. DOM's strength is that it allows random access to any part of an XML document.

Oracle Application Server supports DOM Version 2.0. It provides DOM APIs for C, C++, Java, and PL/SQL.

Simple API for XML

The Simple API for XML (SAX) is a specification for reading an XML document that reports each XML artifact—for example, an element or an attribute—as an event as a document is read. The events are reported by calling the callback functions of a programmatically registered document handler. SAX's strength is its low memory consumption.

Example 10-4 lists the callback events generated when parsing the XML document from Example 10-1. The events in this list are named using their corresponding function names in the Java interface org.sax.xml.ContentHandler. Any values passed to the callback functions are shown after the function names.

Example 10-4. A list of SAX events for Example 10-1

```
setDocumentLocator
startDocument
startElement: localName=person, qualifiedName=person
ignorableWhitespace:
startElement: localName=name, qualifiedName=name
ignorableWhitespace:
```

Example 10-4. A list of SAX events for Example 10-1 (continued)

```
startElement: localName=last_name, qualifiedName=last_name
characters: Doe
ignorableWhitespace:
startElement: localName=first_name, qualifiedName=first_name
characters: Jane
ignorableWhitespace:
ignorableWhitespace:
startElement: localName=birth_date, qualifiedName=birth_date
characters: 1980-01-01
ignorableWhitespace:
startElement: localName=gender, qualifiedName=gender
characters: Female
ignorableWhitespace:
endDocument
```

Oracle Application Server supports SAX Version 2.0. It provides SAX APIs for languages that support callback functions: C, C++, and Java.

XML Developer Kits

Oracle provides XML Developer Kits (XDKs) that can develop web applications that leverage XML in four programming languages:

- XDK for Java
- XDK for C
- XDK for C++
- XDK for PL/SQL

These XDKs are used in the Oracle Application Server Containers for J2EE (OC4J) for Java-based web applications, while mod_fastcgi is used for C and C++, and mod_plsql is used for PL/SQL.

Along with the XDK APIs and command-line utilities that execute these APIs, Oracle Application Server provides several XML tools, including:

- XML Class Generator
- XML SQL Utility for performing database queries that produce XML, and also insert XML into an Oracle database
- XSQL Pages that produce web content using XML similar to JSPs

A substantial amount of additional XML functionality is available when you use an Oracle database. However, because that functionality is available only with an Oracle database, it isn't covered here.

Table 10-1 lists the various features supported by the four XDKs. Of the four, the XDK for Java is the most feature-rich.

Table 10-1. XML Developer Kits and features

Feature	Java	C	C++	PL/SQL
XML 1.0	✓	✓	✓	✓
XML Namespaces 1.0	✓	✓	✓	
XML Path Language 1.0	✓	✓	✓	✓
XML Schemas Part 0–2	✓	✓	✓	
XML Parser: DOM 1.0	✓	✓	✓	✓
XML Parser: DOM 2.0 Core	✓	✓	✓	✓
XML Parser: DOM 2.0 Traversal	✓			✓
XML Parser: SAX 1.0	✓	✓	✓	
XML Parser: SAX 2.0	✓	~a	~a	
XML Parser: nonvalidating mode	✓	✓	✓	✓
XML Parser: validation against DTD	✓	✓	✓	✓
XML Parser: validation against Schema	✓	✓	✓	
XSLT 1.0	✓	✓	✓	✓
XML Class Generator	✓		✓	
XML Transviewer Beans	✓			

[a] Partial implementation

XML Parsers

The Oracle XML parsers are composed of two components:

XML Parser
Supports XML 1.0, including XML Namespaces, XPath, XSLT, DOM, and SAX with validation against a DTD

XML Schema Processor
Adds the ability to handle XML Schema documents to the XML Parser; it also enables the parser to validate an XML document against an XML Schema

XML Class Generators

The two available XML class generators, for Java and C++, create source code in the form of class files, from a DTD. The XML class generator for Java can also create class files from an XML Schema. Generated class files can then be used programmatically to construct XML documents in your web applications.

Manually coding a class file (in Java or C++) that represents an XML document can be both tedious and fraught with opportunities for creating errors. Using an XML class file generator removes the burden of coding such classes from a programmer while, at the same time, eliminating possible coding errors.

XML Transviewer Beans

The XML Transviewer Beans are a set of JavaBeans that are part of the XDK for Java. These Beans are components for viewing and transforming XML documents with Java. The XML Transviewer Beans are:

DOMBuilder Bean
> A nonvisual JavaBean wrapped around the XML Parser for Java's DOMParser class that allows you to build one or more DOM trees asynchronously and provides all the functionality of the DOMParser class with a JavaBean interface

XSLTransformer Bean
> A nonvisual JavaBean wrapped around the XML Parser for Java's XSLT engine that allows you to perform one or more XSL transformations asynchronously and provides all the functionality of the XSLT engine with a JavaBean interface

DBAccessBean
> A nonvisual JavaBean that creates CLOB tables in a database and then use retrieves or stores XML documents in one of its CLOB tables

These components may be used server-side in web-based application development.

XML SQL Utility

The XML SQL Utility (XSU), a proprietary Oracle tool that can be used in any application server, allows you to perform a query against a database that is output as well-formed XML. XSU also supports extracting data from any well-formed XML document, then using that data to perform a SQL DML statement such as an INSERT, UPDATE, or DELETE. In addition, using XSU, you can create DTDs from a SQL query and perform XSL transformations.

XSU APIs exist for Java and PL/SQL. A command-line utility, OracleXML, also exists. XSU can be used in any middle-tier web server that supports Java servlets because it is a set of Java classes.

SQL to XML

The XSU can create a well-formed XML document from a SQL SELECT statement. It outputs the XML document as a Java String as a DOM tree in the form of a Java class XMLDocument or as SAX events. When creating an XML document, XSU outputs the columns of a SQL statement as XML elements that use the names or alias names of the columns in the order in which they appear in the SQL statement. Column elements are then enclosed in a <ROW> element, so a <ROW> element exists for each row from a query's result set. All <ROW> elements are, in turn, enclosed by a <ROWSET> element for the SELECT statement. An XML processing instruction is placed at the beginning of the XML document to identify the document as an XML document.

This format of wrapping database result set rows with `<ROW>` and `<ROWSET>` tags is called by Oracle a *canonical* format.

For example, by specifying the query:

```
select last_name, first_name
from   person
order by last_name, first_name;
```

XSU would create a document in canonical format similar to the following:

```
<?xml version='1.0'?>
<ROWSET>
  <ROW num="1">
    <LAST_NAME>Bales</LAST_NAME>
    <FIRST_NAME>Don</FIRST_NAME>
  </ROW>
  <ROW num="2">
    <LAST_NAME>Greenwald</LAST_NAME>
    <FIRST_NAME>Rick</FIRST_NAME>
  </ROW>
  <ROW num="3">
    <LAST_NAME>Stackowiak</LAST_NAME>
    <FIRST_NAME>Bob</FIRST_NAME>
  </ROW>
</ROWSET>
```

If a query is executed against an object table, the result set may consist of a complex datatype structure—a nested table or array. A complex datatype is represented by elements for each column in the user-defined datatype, which are, in turn, enclosed by an element whose name is derived from the name of the user-defined datatype.

A nested table or array is represented by elements for each column in the collection, enclosed by an element whose name is derived by the name of the collection with _ITEM appended to it, with all item elements then enclosed by an element whose name is derived using the name of the collection.

Generated XML can be customized in any of three ways:

- By manipulating the source SQL statement
- By customizing default mappings
- Possibly by postprocessing the created XML document using XSLT

Of the three techniques, the first is the most performant, while the last is the least performant.

Here are some example techniques for manipulating the source SQL statement:

- Using alias names on columns to get the desired element names
- Using the at sign (@) in a column alias to make the column an element attribute instead of an element value

- Using subqueries or the SQL statements CAST/MULTISET to produce nested results
- Using views or object-relational views with user-defined datatypes against relational tables to create new column names, complex datatypes, or embedded collections

XSU mapping customizations allow you to:

- Specify that NULL values should be indicated with a null attribute instead of omitting an element
- Specify the format for dates
- Specify the case used for element names
- Specify that collection elements should contain a cardinality attribute
- Change the name of the ROW element or omit it altogether
- Change the name of the ROW element's attribute num or omit it altogether
- Change the name of the ROWSET element or omit it altogether

You can also register an XSL stylesheet with XSU. The registered stylesheet is then used by XSU to automatically post-transform the XML document generated with the SQL statement.

XML to SQL

The XSU can also be used to apply a SQL INSERT, UPDATE, or DELETE statement against a database based on an XML document in the canonical format defined earlier. If an XML document isn't in the desired or canonical format, any of three techniques can be applied to make it compatible:

- By manipulating the SQL target
- By customizing default mappings
- Possibly by preprocessing the XML document using XSLT

In many ways, these are the inverse of the SQL to XML customizations.

You can manipulate the SQL target by creating a view or object-relational view against a table or set of tables to make the format of the XML input document match the database. You can create INSTEAD-OF triggers to distribute required SQL statements to the appropriate members of a multitable or multiobject view.

In this direction, XSU mapping customizations allow you to:

- Use case-insensitive matching for mapping element names to SQL column names
- Map an alternative element name to the canonical element ROW
- Specify the format for dates

Just as with the SQL-to-XML generation, an XSL stylesheet can be registered with XSU that, in turn, is used by XSU to automatically pretransform the input XML document.

Inserting

To insert data into a database using an XML document, XSU does the following:

1. Retrieves the target table's metadata from the database. XSU uses the metadata to create an appropriate SQL INSERT statement.
2. If an XSL stylesheet is registered, transforms the XML document.
3. Extracts data by matching element names in the possibly transformed XML document to column names in the SQL INSERT statement.
4. Executes the INSERT statement.

By default, XSU tries to map values for all columns in the target SQL object (table, view, object-relational view, etc.). The Java and PL/SQL APIs allow you to specify the column names you want used in the INSERT statement.

Updating

To update a database using an XML document, you must first use the Java or PL/SQL API to set a list of (primary) key columns. Then XSU follows a process that is similar to inserting data, this time creating an appropriate SQL UPDATE statement. The columns to be updated can also be constrained by specifying the desired column names using the API.

Deleting

Deleting from a database using an XML document is similar to updating. Just as with an UPDATE statement, you must first specify the (primary) key column names using the API. XSU then follows the same process it does for inserting and updating.

Committing

XSU normally batches updates. If auto-commit is turned on in the JDBC driver supplying the database connection for XSU, and if the batch execution is successful, a batch is committed. If auto-commit is turned off, you must manually commit, or all SQL statement operations will have to wait to be committed when the JDBC connection is closed.

PL/SQL

The PL/SQL API for XSU is a wrapper around the Java API, so almost all the Java API functionality, as well as how it is employed programmatically, is the same for both APIs. XSU can be accessed in Oracle Application Server programmatically using the Java API in OC4J, using the PL/SQL API used by stored procedures executed through mod_plsql, or using XSQL Pages, described in the next section.

XSQL Pages

XSQL Pages simplify access to the XSU in a web server. XSQL Pages is a framework built on top of XSU that processes XSQL Pages document tags to create dynamic content in the form of XML. The process is similar to the way in which a JSP translator processes JavaServer Pages.

XSQL Pages documents are valid XML documents with a vocabulary that allows you to select, insert, update, and delete against a database using embedded SQL. XSQL tags also provide additional capabilities such as executing stored procedures, including other XML documents, and XSQL Pages.

XSQL Pages documents, by default, end with a .xsql suffix. When these documents are requested from Oracle Application Server, they are automatically processed by the XSQL servlet residing in the OC4J. The XSQL servlet processes the XSQL tags, creating an XML document. If an XSLT processing instruction is found, XSQL uses it to transform the XML document into another format. The resulting XML document is then sent to the requestor. An XSQL Pages file can also be processed using the XSQL Command Line Utility or programmatically using the Java class XSQLRequest.

Configuration

The XSQL Pages configuration is maintained in an XML document named XSQLConfig.xml. XSQLConfig.xml contains information such as database connections, database tuning parameters, stylesheet cache parameters, and so on.

SQL to XML

An XML Pages document can use five action tags to produce an XML document:

`<xsql:query>`
> This tag embeds a SQL SELECT statement. When the SELECT statement is executed, it produces canonical XML content that incorporates the rows and columns of the SELECT statement.

`<xsql:dml>`
> This tag executes any other kind of SQL statement: DML or DDL.

`<xsql:ref-cursor-function>`
> This tag allows you to use a PL/SQL reference cursor returned from a stored procedure to produce XML just as with the use of a SELECT statement described earlier.

`<xsql:include-owa>`

This tag allows you to call a stored procedure that, in turn, uses the Oracle PL/SQL Web Toolkit functions in packages `HTF` and `HTP` to produce XML.

`<xsql:include-xsql>`

This tag allows you to include another XSQL Pages document in your current XSQL Page.

The first four action tags require a connection to a database. A database connection for these tags is specified with an attribute called `connection`. The value of the `connection` attribute corresponds to an alias for a database connection configured in XML document `XSQLConfig.xml`, as described earlier.

Parameters can be bound to embedded SQL statements or stored procedures with a `bind-params` attribute. Lexical substitution parameters can also be employed. These start with an at sign (@).

Parameter values can come from any of the following:

- An explicit XSQL Pages `<xsql:include-param>` declaration
- An HTTP cookie
- An HTTP session object
- An HTTP request object
- A default value attribute

If no parameter value is found, a NULL value is used for a bind variable, while an empty string is used for lexical substitution parameters.

Default values can be specified for bind variables and lexical substitution parameters. A default value is specified including an attribute with the same name as the bind variable or lexical substitution parameter in question. This seemingly duplicate attribute's value specifies the desired default value. The database `connection`, `bind-params`, and default value attributes can be placed within the tag that requires them, or within one of its enclosing parents' tags.

XML to SQL

XSQL Pages can take a valid XML document in the canonical format or any valid XML document, such as XHTML, and transform it into the canonical format from an HTTP POST and use it to perform a SQL INSERT, UPDATE, or DELETE statement against a database. The XSQL servlet can also transform HTTP POST parameters into a valid XML document, transform the document into the canonical format using XSLT, and then use the canonically transformed XML document to perform these SQL operations.

The SQL INSERT, UPDATE, and DELETE statements are accomplished using the `<xsql:insert-request>`, `<xsql:update-request>`, and `<xsql:delete-request>` tags, respectively. In addition, a valid XML document sent as a request parameter in an HTTP GET request can insert data into a database using the `<xsql:insert-param>` tag.

Custom XSQL action handlers

You can create a custom action handler for XSQL pages by creating a Java class file that implements the `oracle.xml.xsql.XSQLActionHandler` interface. You then access the custom handler with the `<xsql:action>` tag, specifying the fully qualified name of your `XSQLActionHandler` class in the attribute `handler`.

Integrating XSQL Pages with JSP

A JSP calls on the services of XSQL Pages using a `<jsp:include>` or `<jsp:forward>` tag. In these tags, a programmer calls upon the XSQL Pages' XSQL servlet. In turn, the XSQL servlet either retrieves the requested data or applies the requested DML statement against the database.

Oracle Application Server Components and XML

Several of the Oracle Application Server components use XML in various ways. Their use of XML ranges from simply using XML documents (to save configuration data) to creating XML documents as output. The most notable use of XML by Oracle Application Server components is found in OracleAS Portal and OracleAS Report Services. These two Oracle Application Server components can use XML as a data source, and produce XML documents for output. This capability makes it possible to use the XML SQL Utility or XSQL Pages to produce input for OracleAS Portal and OracleAS Reports Services or use output from OracleAS Portal and OracleAS Reports Services to update a database with XML SQL Utility or XSQL Pages, or both.

The OracleAS Wireless component, covered separately in Chapter 14, uses XSLT transformation bidirectionally to enable alternative presentation layers for web-based applications to wireless devices such as handheld computers and cell phones. Web Services, the topic of Chapter 11, employ XML to provide a computer-centric, rather than human-centric, view of the Web. Web Services enable heterogeneous computer systems to exchange data over an intranet or the Internet.

OracleAS Portal's Portal Developer Kit Integration Services (PDKIS) allows you to extract data from an external source identified by a URL. If the URL points to a well-formed HTML document, the HTML document can be parsed and used for content in a portlet. PDKIS can also transform an HTML document into an XHTML document. (As mentioned earlier, XHTML is an XML version of HTML.) The XHTML document can then be further transformed using an XSL stylesheet to create content for a portlet.

OracleAS Reports Services can use an XML document as a data source for a report. It can also output reports as XML documents and perform XSL transformations on report output.

CHAPTER 11

Web Services

Web Services are functions or procedures that are accessible to other computer programs over a network, using a standard transport protocol and encoding. Typically, the transport protocol used is HTTP, the encoding is XML-RPC or SOAP, and the messages communicated between programs are exchanged as XML documents.

Web Services are all about interoperability. By encapsulating programming language-specific function or procedure call syntax into a standardized XML document syntax, Web Services allow any program deployed on any operating system to utilize a candidate function or procedure exposed as a Web Service.

Exposing program functions or procedures to be called remotely isn't a new idea. Database stored procedures and EJBs are two longstanding examples of remote procedure calls. What's new with Web Services is the level of interoperability built into them.

To call a database stored procedure, you must use a proprietary or standardized API such as JDBC. However, such APIs allow your program to call only functions or procedures that exist in a target database. These APIs also require a proprietary network protocol. Corporate firewalls typically don't allow proprietary protocols to pass through them, so their use can limit the level of interoperability.

To call an EJB, you can either use the EJB API or CORBA, but this solution allows only an Enterprise Java program, or a program written with a programming language that uses a CORBA API, to use the target EJB. Once again, a network protocol, RMI, is used that may not be supported by a corporate firewall.

In contrast, Web Services allow any programming language on any operating system in which a Web Services client implementation exists to call a target Web Service. In addition, the use of HTTP as a transport protocol, which is generally supported by all firewalls, allows easy access to Web Services.

Of course, this highly interoperable, lowest-common-denominator approach comes with a price: slower performance. Web Services as remote procedure calls are significantly slower than database stored procedures or EJBs. This is understandable because extra steps are involved:

- Encoding a remote procedure call into the XML document on the client-side
- Parsing the XML document to call the desired function on the server-side
- Encoding the result into an XML document on the server-side
- Parsing the XML document to retrieve the desired result on the client-side

Regardless, Web Services are an ideal solution when it comes to integrating heterogeneous computer applications.

This chapter begins by taking a brief look at the architecture used by Web Services. Next, it covers the commonly used protocols and standards used for Web Services, highlighting Oracle Application Server's support for each. It finishes up by examining Oracle Application Server's implementation of Web Services, including programming and management tools.

Web Services Architecture

A well-documented architecture is central to interoperability. From a simplistic viewpoint, the Web Services architecture consists of a client that sends a request in the form of an XML document—a message—over a network to a server that hosts a Web Service. The hosted Web Service processes the request and returns the result as an XML document to the client, as shown in Figure 11-1.

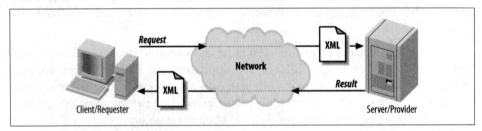

Figure 11-1. A Web Service client and service interaction

In many ways, especially when HTTP is used as the transport, this process is similar to a person using a web browser to look at a dynamically generated HTML page, except that it is a computer requesting the result, not a human being. A Web Service client can be a database stored procedure, a servlet or EJB in an application server, a Java client application, or another Web Service, to name just a few possibilities.

From this simplistic explanation you may have noted that a Web Service requires:

- A method call in the form of a function or procedure to act as the service
- A standardized encoding to ensure that both the client and the service understand the format of the data
- A standardized protocol for transporting the serialized data

But how do you know that a particular Web Service even exists? And if you do know that it exists, what are its specifications? These requirements are addressed using a layered architecture, as shown in Figure 11-2 and described in the sections that follow.

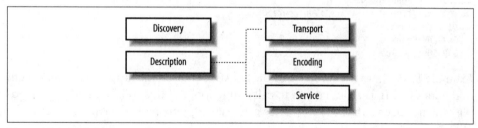

Figure 11-2. Web Services architecture stack

Service

For Web Services, the actual service provided can be written in any programming language that has a Web Services implementation, or that can create valid XML documents and stream them to and from a network. Nowadays, that's just about every commonly used programming language. For example, you can use a simple Java class with a function, as in Example 11-1.

Example 11-1. A sample service method written in Java

```
public class Stateless {
        public Stateless() {}
        public String sayHello(String param) {
                return "Hello " + param + "!";
        }
}
```

The method sayHello( ) returns a String in which the passed parameter is prefixed with the word *Hello*, and then returned.

Encoding

For both the Web Service requester and provider to understand a conversation, they need to use an agreed-upon vocabulary and syntax. This is where the XML becomes useful. Two popular encoding standards exist: XML-RPC and SOAP. Example 11-2 shows a SOAP-encoded request to execute the sayHello( ) service method from Example 11-1.

Example 11-2. A sample sayHello() SOAP request

```
<?xml version='1.0' encoding='UTF-8'?>
<SOAP-ENV:Envelope xmlns:SOAP-ENV="http://schemas.xmlsoap.org/soap/envelope/" xmlns:
xsi="http://www.w3.org/2001/XMLSchema-instance" xmlns:xsd="http://www.w3.org/2001/
XMLSchema">
```

Example 11-2. A sample sayHello() SOAP request (continued)

```
<SOAP-ENV:Body>
<ns1:sayHello xmlns:ns1="urn:test-Stateless" SOAP-ENV:encodingStyle="http://schemas.
xmlsoap.org/soap/encoding/">
<param0 xsi:type="xsd:string">Don</param0>
</ns1:sayHello>
</SOAP-ENV:Body>
</SOAP-ENV:Envelope>
```

Example 11-3 shows the response to the SOAP request in Example 11-2. It may seem that a lot of XML is required just to call a function, but this well-thought-out encoding scheme ensures that a Web Service can exchange any type of data.

Example 11-3. A sample sayHello() SOAP response

```
<?xml version='1.0' encoding='UTF-8'?>
<SOAP-ENV:Envelope xmlns:SOAP-ENV="http://schemas.xmlsoap.org/soap/envelope/" xmlns:
xsi="http://www.w3.org/2001/XMLSchema-instance" xmlns:xsd="http://www.w3.org/2001/
XMLSchema">
<SOAP-ENV:Body>
<ns1:sayHelloResponse xmlns:ns1="urn:test-Stateless" SOAP-ENV:encodingStyle="http://
schemas.xmlsoap.org/soap/encoding/">
<return xsi:type="xsd:string">Hello Don!</return>
</ns1:sayHelloResponse>
</SOAP-ENV:Body>
</SOAP-ENV:Envelope>
```

Transport

A transport protocol is used to send a request across a network to the server and back again to the client program. HyperText Transport Protocol is commonly used as the transport protocol for Web Services. However, it isn't a requirement. Simple Mail Transfer Protocol (SMTP), File Transfer Protocol (FTP), and, more recently, Blocks Extensible Exchange Protocol (BEEP) may also be used. Which protocol is used is simply a matter of the Web Service implementation's capabilities.

Service Description

A *service description* is a document on how to access a Web Service. With XML-RPC, this usually consists of a well-written specification in the form of a word processing document. For SOAP, the Web Services Description Language (WSDL), an XML application (vocabulary) can describe SOAP-encoded Web Services in a standardized computer-readable way. Both document types are typically available on the same server as the hosted Web Service. They identify the names of the available services, the encoding used, the transport protocol, and the location of the service. Example 11-4 is a WSDL document for the service in Example 11-1.

Example 11-4. A sample WSDL document

```xml
<?xml version="1.0" encoding="UTF-8" ?>
<definitions name="Stateless" targetNamespace="http://test/Stateless.wsdl" xmlns="http://
schemas.xmlsoap.org/wsdl/" xmlns:tns="http://test/Stateless.wsdl" xmlns:xsd="http://www.
w3.org/2001/XMLSchema" xmlns:soap="http://schemas.xmlsoap.org/wsdl/soap/">
<documentation>WSDL for Service: Stateless, generated by Oracle WSDL toolkit (version: 1.
1)</documentation>
<types>
<schema targetNamespace="http://test/Stateless.xsd" xmlns:tns="http://test/Stateless.xsd"
xmlns="http://www.w3.org/2001/XMLSchema" xmlns:xsd="http://www.w3.org/2001/XMLSchema" />
</types>
<message name="sayHelloInput">
<part name="param0" type="xsd:string" />
</message>
<message name="sayHelloOutput">
<part name="output" type="xsd:string" />
</message>
<portType name="StatelessPortType">
<operation name="sayHello">
<input message="tns:sayHelloInput" />
<output message="tns:sayHelloOutput" />
</operation>
</portType>
<binding name="StatelessBinding" type="tns:StatelessPortType">
<soap:binding transport="http://schemas.xmlsoap.org/soap/http" style="rpc" />
<operation name="sayHello">
<soap:operation soapAction="urn:test-Stateless/sayHello" />
<input>
<soap:body use="encoded" encodingStyle="http://schemas.xmlsoap.org/soap/encoding/"
namespace="urn:test-Stateless" />
</input>
<output>
<soap:body use="encoded" encodingStyle="http://schemas.xmlsoap.org/soap/encoding/"
namespace="urn:test-Stateless" />
</output>
</operation>
</binding>
<service name="Stateless">
<port name="StatelessPort" binding="tns:StatelessBinding">
<soap:address location="http://www.myserver.com:7779/test/Stateless" />
</port>
</service>
</definitions>
```

Service Discovery

The top layer of the Web Services architecture is about discovering what Web Services are available. This functionality is currently accomplished with Universal Description, Discovery, and Integration (UDDI). UDDI is a specification for a network directory of available Web Services.

Web Services Standards

The work of establishing basic standards for Web Services isn't complete. Specifications exist for discovery, description, transport, and encoding. Some of these specifications have been submitted to the W3C to become standards (recommendations).

Extensible Markup Language

Both encoding schemes, XML-RPC and SOAP, are XML 1.0 applications. XML-RPC is a fairly simple XML application, so it uses only basic XML syntax. SOAP is a more complex application that makes extensive use of namespaces and XML Schemas.

XML-RPC

XML-RPC is a Web Service specification that uses a small XML vocabulary to encode its request and result messages and HTTP as the transport protocol. XML-RPC is a lightweight Web Service implementation that has limited datatype support. Regardless, it is effective and has implementations for most programming languages and operating systems.

Oracle Application Server doesn't provide direct support for XML-RPC; however, that doesn't mean you can't use it with Oracle Application Server. Because XML-RPC has implementations in C, C++, Perl, and Java, you can deploy any of these implementations on Oracle Application Server.

You can find the specifications and a list of implementations for XML-RPC at *http://www.xmlrpc.com*.

SOAP

SOAP 1.1, originally called Simple Object Access Protocol when IBM and Microsoft, among others, submitted it to the W3C in April of 2000, is now an acronym without a name. SOAP 1.2 was released as an official recommendation in June of 2003. The working group decided that the name did not correctly describe the standard, so they dropped the name but kept the acronym.

Oracle Application Server currently supports SOAP 1.1 with two implementations:

OracleAS SOAP
> An enhanced version of the Apache organization's SOAP

OC4J Web Services
> Oracle's own highly performant implementation, which supports JavaBeans, EJBs, database stored procedures, and the JMS.

Of course, as with XML-RPC, you can also deploy on Oracle Application Server any third-party SOAP implementation, or *agent* as the W3C calls it, that is written in C, C++, Perl, or Java.

You can find specifications for SOAP at *http://www.w3.org/2002/ws/*.

Web Services Description Language

Web Services Description Language, an XML application, describes a Web Service specification in a computer-readable format. A WSDL document describes:

- The service methods available
- The datatypes used for requests and results for each service method
- The transport protocol to be used
- The location of a Web Service

The WSDL 1.1 specification submitted by IBM, Microsoft, and Oracle, among many others, to the W3C in March 2001, has been in working draft status for a Version 2.0 since November 2003.

At the time this book is being written, Oracle Application Server tools currently support WSDL 1.1. Oracle Application Server Web Services deployments expose a service's WSDL document at the service's endpoint.

You can find the specification for WSDL at *http://www.w3.org/2002/ws/*.

Universal Description, Discovery, and Integration

Universal Description, Discovery, and Integration is a specification for a network-accessible directory of available Web Services. UDDI contains information about several entities in its XML Schema:

businessEntity
    Contains information about organizations

businessService
    Contains information about the Web Services these organizations provide

bindingTemplate
    Contains information about the location of a Web Service

tModel
    Contains information about where to find the Web Service's technical specifications

This information is usually found in the form of a WSDL document. The additional entity, publisherAssertion, defines relations between two business entities. The relationship between these entities is outlined in Figure 11-3. As of this writing, the UDDI specification has not been submitted to the W3C.

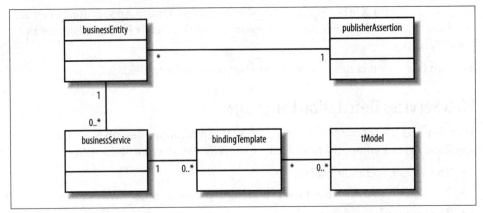

Figure 11-3. A UDDI data model

Oracle Application Server tools support UDDI 2.0. In addition, Oracle Application Server provides a UDDI directory that can be used to publish Web Services on your corporate intranet or be synchronized with UDDI directories on the Internet. The Oracle Application Server UDDI agent is managed through Application Server Control.

You can find the specification for UDDI at *http://www.uddi.org/specification.html*.

Service Provider

As mentioned earlier, Oracle provides two implementations for Web Services on Oracle Application Server: OracleAS SOAP and OC4J Web Services. Oracle's official stand on OracleAS SOAP, an enhanced version of the Apache organization's Java-based SOAP implementation, is that it is in maintenance mode. In other words, Oracle will continue to maintain OracleAS SOAP for the time being, but you are strongly encouraged to use OC4J Web Services instead. For that reason, we cover only OC4J Web Services and its tools in the remainder of this chapter.

OC4J Web Services Agents

Web Services are implemented in OC4J by seven servlets for the following seven types of service objects:

A stateless Java class
    Using an RPC-style XML message

A stateless Java class
    Using a document-style XML message

A stateful Java class
    Using an RPC-style XML message

A stateful Java class
Using a document-style XML message

A stateless session EJB
Using an RPC-style XML message

A stateless PL/SQL stored procedure
Using an RPC-style message

Java Message Service (JMS)
Using a document-style XML message

As demonstrated in Figure 11-4, an OC4J Web Services servlet is responsible for parsing an incoming request in the form of an XML message, calling the appropriate service, encoding the result into an XML document, and then sending the XML document back to the requester through the Oracle HTTP Server.

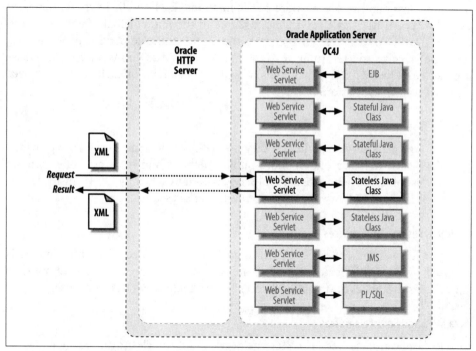

Figure 11-4. OC4J Web Service architecture

By creating seven different servlets for these seven different service types, Oracle has simplified the process of creating a Web Service so that it consists only of programming the service method, configuring the service via an XML file, and then generating a deployment Enterprise Application Archive file. The resultant EAR file is then deployed on Oracle Application Server using Application Server Control. In addition, a different servlet for each service type makes the servlet's code base smaller and more efficient, which leads to better performance.

RPC-style versus document-style

Two styles of Web Services calls are supported:

Remote procedure calls
> As mentioned earlier, an RPC is a parameterized encoding in which the parameters for a service are encoded with elements in the XML message sent to and received from the service.

Document (literal)
> The document or literal style doesn't encode parameters. Instead, it sends an entire encapsulated XML document as the message payload.

Stateless Java class services

Stateless Java class services, whether they are RPC- or document-style, are provided by a Java class that has one or more public methods. Each public method is exposed as a service. An RPC-style service can use one of the many default datatypes specified in the SOAP schema. In contrast, the document-style service must receive, return, or receive and return an XML document passed as an instance of Java class `org.w3c.dom.Element`. OC4J maintains a cache of instances of each stateless service for reuse to increase performance.

Stateful Java class services

Stateful Java class services, whether they are RPC- or document-style, are provided by a Java class that has one or more public methods and maintains one or more instance variables. Instances of stateful services aren't cached by OC4J. Instead, they are stored in the HTTP session object for each user's session.

Stateless session EJB services

Any stateless session EJB can be used as an RPC-style service. The public methods exposed by the EJB's remote interface are accessible as services. As with stateless Java classes, instances of stateless session EJBs are cached by OC4J for reuse.

Java Message Service services

Oracle Application Server Java Message Service and Oracle Advanced Queuing, as well as any desired third-party messaging systems, are supported by OC4J Web Services. JMS Web Services expose JMS sends and receives as services, for both queues and topics. A JMS Web Services client can act as producer or consumer.

Stateless PL/SQL services

Any Oracle PL/SQL stored procedure that is part of a PL/SQL package can be used as an RPC-style service. Both PL/SQL procedures and functions declared in a package's specification are exposed as services. These services are executed through a dedicated servlet that uses a JDBC data source to access the host database.

Web Services Assembler

Oracle Application Server provides a command-line tool written in Java called WebServicesAssembler.jar that packages services into a Web Services EAR file for deployment on Oracle Application Server. Using the Web Services Assembler, Web Service development becomes a matter of doing the following:

- Creating a JavaBean, EJB, or stored procedure to provide service methods
- Editing the Web Services Assembler configuration file, adding directives required for the type and style of service
- Executing the Web Services Assembler to create a deployment EAR file
- Deploying the EAR file using Application Server Control

Service Description

In addition to configuring your Web Service, you can also edit the Web Services Assembler configuration file to specify whether a WSDL file is automatically generated as part of the packing process or if the Web Services Assembler is to include a WDSL file you already created during the creation of the EAR file. You can also direct it to create Web Service proxy JAR files.

A *Web Service proxy* is a class generated by the Web Services Assembler that is a complete client-side SOAP implementation for the specified Web Service. With the proxy, you can create a working client by simply instantiating a copy of the proxy and then calling a proxy method with the same name and the same parameters as the target service.

Both the generated WSDL and the proxy JAR files are available at a Web Service's endpoint. Figure 11-5 is an example of a Web Service's endpoint for the service method in Example 11-1. The WSDL file is available at the Service Description link. You can test an RPC-style Web Service by following its service method link. In this case, the link is *sayHello*. In addition, two proxy JAR files are made available, one containing the Java source for the proxy and the second containing the compiled class files.

Service Discovery

Oracle Application Server provides a UDDI directory you can use to publish your Web Services on your corporate intranet. Appropriately, the UDDI directory is maintained using its own set of Web Services. Additions, updates, deletions, and queries all take place using SOAP over HTTP.

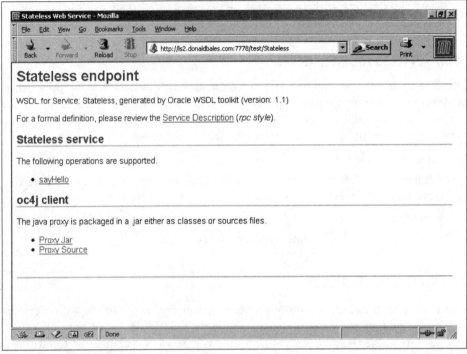

Figure 11-5. OC4J Web Service endpoint

Oracle provides a Java API for the UDDI SOAP-based Web Services as a convenience for Java programmers. However, any programming language that can access a Web Service using SOAP can interact with the directory.

Publishing a Web Service

Web Services can be published to the UDDI directory with a user-written program that uses the Java API and the UDDI publish web service, or during the last step of the EAR file deployment in Application Server Control. If an EAR file contains references to one of the Web Services servlets, Application Server Control displays an additional set of screens where you can publish Web Services during the deployment of an EAR file.

Looking Up a Web Service

Consumers can look up available Web Services using a user-written program that uses the Java API and the UDDI inquiry Web Service. The inquiry Web Service allows you to programmatically perform a query against the UDDI directory as one of the following:

A *White Pages search*
  Using an organization's name, contact's name, address, etc.

A *Yellow Pages search*
  Using standardized classifications such as NAICS, ISO-3166, and UNSPSC

A *Green Pages search*
  Using technical information about a service

Oracle Application Server also provides a Java Client library that allows you to easily build your own directory search engine.

Updating a Web Service

A published Web Services entry in the UDDI directory can be updated with a user-written program that uses the Java API or with the UDDI Registry in Application Server Control. Using the UDDI Registry, you search for an existing service in the directory by one of the categorization taxonomies deployed with the registry. Once you find an entry, you can update any of its fields. You can also add a service to additional organizational categories.

Figure 11-6 is an example of the UDDI Registry update screen available through Application Server Control. This figure shows the update screen for a published service from Example 11-1.

Directory Management

The UDDI Registry itself is managed with the `uddiadmin.jar` Java command-line tool; it allows you to manage properties for the directory. Here are some examples:

- Add and delete directory users
- Specify quotas
- Modify properties about the registry's own directory entry
- Import entities
- Configure and enable replication

In addition, the UDDI Registry supports deployment on Microsoft SQL Server, IBM DB2, and noninfrastructure-related Oracle databases.

Service Requester

Oracle Application Server makes creating a Web Services requester, or client program, extremely easy. As mentioned earlier, OC4J Web Services provide a Web Services home page for each deployed Web Service as shown in Figure 11-5. On this home page are links to a WSDL file, and Web Services proxy files generated by the Web Services Assembler program. The Web Services Assembler tool can even

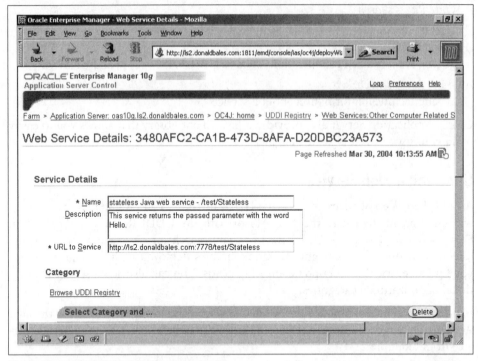

Figure 11-6. Oracle UDDI Registry page

generate a Web Service proxy for Web Services not published on Oracle Application Server. In addition to supporting service calls, a proxy generated by the Web Services Assembler also supports SOAP headers.

Oracle Application Server defines two types of clients that can execute a Web Service: a static client and a dynamic client. These clients are described in the next sections.

Static Client

A *static client*, in Oracle's terminology, is one that is created with all the information necessary to execute a Web Service. To access an OC4J Web Service as a static client, all you need is to create a Java program that makes a copy of the proxy object for the service and then use the proxy to call a method by the same name and with the same parameters as the service.

Dynamic Client

A *dynamic client* is one that looks up an available Web Service and executes it at runtime. In this case, the client doesn't know the location of the Web Service or may not even know the name of the Web Service until the time that it looks up available Web Services in a UDDI directory. Once it locates a service (either because it's the first service found or because it uses some other type of determination to choose one of multiple services), the dynamic client looks up its specification via a link to a WSDL file and then uses the specifications in the WSDL file to invoke the desired Web Service.

Oracle Application Server provides two Java packages, `oracle.j2ee.ws.client` and `oracle.j2ee.ws.client.wsdl`, that work in concert to dynamically invoke a Web Service given the location of a WSDL file. If you combine these with the use of the UDDI API, you can indeed dynamically identify and execute a Web Service at runtime.

Web Services Security

Oracle Application Server supports authentication and authorization for Web Services using the same mechanisms as for other Oracle Application Server applications. Authentication is enabled using JAAS as implemented in OC4J. Web Services can ensure data privacy and integrity by using SSL.

Chapter 4 describes overall Oracle Application Server security.

CHAPTER 12
Business Intelligence Components

The use of business intelligence systems has been steadily gaining in popularity as companies use increasingly larger amounts of data to make strategic and tactical decisions. Business intelligence systems allow business analysts to answer fundamental business questions, such as:

- How many of a company's products have been sold in specific geographic areas over particular periods of time?
- Who are the company's most reliable suppliers?
- Have particular product campaigns been successful?
- Who are the company's most valuable customers?

Analysts work with both prebuilt reports of real-time and near-real-time transaction data (in online transaction processing systems and operational data stores) and historical data (often accessed from data warehouses and data marts). They may also wish to pose their own questions through ad hoc query tools, perform more sophisticated trend analysis and forecasting through online analytical processing (OLAP) tools, and possibly build and leverage custom mathematical models to predict outcomes in which a very large number of variables are present through data mining. All this information can then be pulled together for viewing in a single desktop via a dashboard or a portal.

Oracle Application Server enables the deployment of business intelligence tools used by business analysts, as well as the business analysis applications created by software developers. Because the Oracle database is the typical target database for such analyses, more analysis capabilities have, over time, moved from Oracle's tools into the database itself. Today, the Oracle database includes a variety of advanced query optimization capabilities, including:

- Parallel bitmap star join support
- Understanding of summary-level tables in facts and dimensions called *materialized views*

- Advanced analytics and statistics enabled through SQL
- Embedded OLAP and data mining capabilities

You can take advantage of these advanced capabilities with the business intelligence components available in Oracle Application Server.

Business intelligence components in Oracle Application Server include:

OracleAS Portal

OracleAS Portal provides an integration point for custom-built business intelligence applications using OracleAS Reports Services, OracleAS Discoverer, and other tools. It also provides access to a number of other applications and web sites through its interface and is evolving into a workplace manager that is highly customizable by users. Chapter 13 contains a full discussion of this product.

Reporting tools

Reports are typically created in IT organizations using Oracle Reports Developer and are then deployed for general business usage with OracleAS Reports Services. The OracleAS Reports Services are a part of Oracle Application Server and is described in greater detail in Chapter 9. Oracle Reports Developer is included in the Oracle Development Suite.

Query and analysis tools

More savvy business analysts may choose to submit their own ad hoc queries and to generate reports via OracleAS Discoverer using data residing in the database. Some query and analysis tools available from Oracle partners can also be deployed using Oracle Application Server.

Oracle Application Server can also serve as a deployment platform for custom-built OLAP and data mining applications. Advanced application developers can also use Oracle JDeveloper (part of the Oracle Developer Suite) with OracleAS Business Intelligence JavaBeans (BI Beans) to develop applications that leverage the OLAP Option. In addition, they can develop data mining applications using JDeveloper with Data Mining for Java (DM4J).

The Oracle Warehouse Builder (OWB) is an important tool you can use to build and maintain the business intelligence infrastructure. Bundled with the Oracle Developer Suite or the database, this tool can be used to design target operational data stores, data warehouses, and data marts, and build extraction, transformation, and loading (ETL) scripts. Oracle Warehouse Builder allows you to exchange data stored in its Metadata Repository with OracleAS Discoverer and other tools. The product includes detailed metadata reporting capabilities.

This chapter describes the various business intelligence components available in Oracle Application Server as well as the use of Oracle's data mining and data warehouse tools. It closes by looking briefly at the management of the business intelligence infrastructure.

Reporting

Of the tools that business analysts and executives need, reports are the least glamorous but the most often accessed. Analysts sometimes prefer to avoid reporting software if that software requires help from the IT staff, especially if the process of creating and deploying the reports is more time-consuming and less flexible than manipulating the data directly would be. On the other hand, prebuilt reports often appeal to executives because they require no special IT skills or knowledge to view them. As web-based report generation has become commonplace, the distribution of such reports within an organization has been greatly improved. Users now need be familiar with only a browser.

The OracleAS Reports Services components in Oracle Application Server include the following:

Oracle AS Reports Servlet running in OC4J
> The OracleAS Reports Servlet acts as the intermediary between the Oracle HTTP Server and the OracleAS Reports Server.

OracleAS Reports Server
> The OracleAS Reports Server processes client requests and forwards them to a Reports Engine.

Reports Engine
> The Reports Engine actually fetches requested data from data sources, formats the reports, and notifies the OracleAS Reports Server when jobs are complete.

Multiple Reports Engines can be associated with a Reports Server instance, and you can have more than one server if you need them for load balancing and availability.

Reports can leverage multiple data sources; these include the Oracle database via SQL or PL/SQL, the Oracle Database OLAP Option, Oracle Express, XML, JDBC, and text sources. For example, a report might be generated using SQL queries that leverage analytics in the Oracle database (inverse percentile, hypothetical ranking, etc.). You can also leverage data sources not supported out-of-the-box by programming to a Java API called the Pluggable Data Source (PDS) API.

Report Generation and Deployment

Oracle Reports has a wizard-based frontend called Oracle Reports Developer that can build reports. Oracle Reports Developer is part of the Oracle Developer Suite. The reports created with Oracle Reports Developer can be deployed to the Web using OracleAS Reports Services support in Oracle Application Server.

Developers can use the Oracle Reports wizards to step through the process of defining Reports structures, sources of data, break groups, and summaries. A page frame model enables a variety of formats. A *Live Previewer* displays report layout and a page of data after the initial format selection. The product provides re-entrant wizards to allow further modifications. Available formats include tables, matrixes, grouped reports, graphs, and combinations.

You can add graphs to reports through a graphing wizard that features more than 50 different graph types. The graphs in Oracle's tools are built as "Presentation" Java Beans that enables common graph types among each Oracle business intelligence tool. The major supported graph categories include the following:

Bar
Horizontal bar
Pie
Line
Area
Combination
Scatter/bubble
Stock
Circular
Pareto
Three-dimensional

Figure 12-1 shows a typical report generated by Oracle Reports with an associated graph.

Reports deployed for web use can be specified at runtime to be output in a variety of formats, such as PDF, plain text, HTML, HTML extension, or Cascading Style Sheets (HTMLCSS). By default, PDF output from Oracle Reports is compressed.

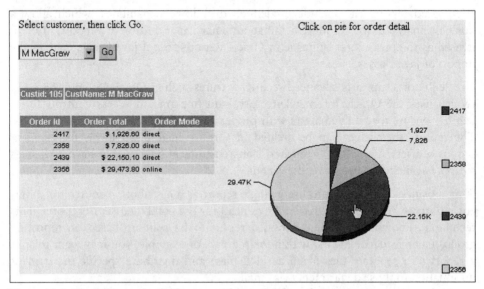

Figure 12-1. Oracle Reports' typical report with associated graph

You can also produce reports in formats more commonly used for printing, such as RTF or PostScript, or in data-oriented formats such as XML or delimited text. Multi-byte character support exists for HTML, PostScript, and PDF.

You can use JSP-based Web Source Reports to create highly customizable and flexible tagged output formats such as HTML and XML. Using JSPs offers a number of advantages, including:

- Separation of static and dynamic content
- Support for scripting and tags
- Reuse of components and tags
- Compilation for permanent execution enabling excellent performance

JSP-based web reports can be created from within Oracle JDeveloper. Version control during the development of reports and impact analysis is provided via the Software Configuration Manager in the Oracle Developer Suite.

You can direct a report to a number of different destinations—for example, to files, WebDAV URLs, printers, email destinations, and FTP destinations. You can use an XML distribution file to name the report destinations. Other report destinations can be created using the Pluggable Destination Java API for Report Engines.

You can also deploy reports of any format to OracleAS Portal. The JSP capabilities in Oracle Reports enable deployment as HTML if you decide to use them as portlets. This capability allows you to publish web-based reports with dynamic access to data as it is changed in the database.

Web-based reports can include predefined drill-down capabilities, which allow a business analyst to ask for more detail about a particular portion of a report. PL/SQL is used as the procedural language in Oracle Reports, but a Java bridge enables the import of Java classes.

Oracle Reports supports advanced security features such as OracleAS Single Sign-On (which uses the Oracle Internet Directory) and fine-grained access control. These features ensure that only analysts with proper access rights can see specific reports. The reports themselves can be created in various customized forms for users or groups of users. These can be created using customization files that have XML tags to apply against the specific report version.

Some businesses may want to use a single report as a distribution source for different reports, which can lower overall overhead for the combined set of reports. This technique, known as *bursting*, allows a report to be split up based on reporting groups (such as departments) within the report. For example, you may want to split a report into separate files (such as PDF files) and distribute specific department information to those departments via email.

In some cases, you may want to generate reports in reaction to specific business events. Oracle Reports provides an Event-Driven Publishing API that's available as a

PL/SQL package. Report "jobs" are submitted via HTTP. Reports in these jobs are then published when triggered by specific database events or by Oracle's AQ query mechanism. The Web Services interface to the OracleAS Reports Server in Oracle Application Server 10g also enables integration into Java applications.

Query and Analysis

Business analysts often want to pose their own "what-if" questions, such as:

- What sales volume occurred in the Midwest subregions in 2004?
- How did sales compare to 2003?

To answer such questions, analysts need ad hoc query tools that can slice and dice the data, pivot the data, and drill down to the detailed level. Initially developed as client-server tools, tools of this kind are now mostly browser-based (though they provide similar functionality to the earlier versions). Because ease of use is very important to most business analysts, these tools are designed in such a way that queries are typically posed by selecting from lists of available data (tables and contents) and analysis selections or icons. Users need to know where their data is stored and what it represents. SQL is generated behind the scenes.

OracleAS Discoverer

Oracle's tool for query and analysis is OracleAS Discoverer, which supports several different client interfaces for different architectures:

Discoverer Desktop
> This interface is the oldest of the three. It is a client-server version and isn't part of Oracle Application Server.

Discover Plus
> This interface is browser-based and is part of Oracle Application Server. It is deployed via a Java applet.

Discoverer Viewer
> This more limited interface is an HTML browser client that is also part of Oracle Application Server.

Discoverer Plus and Discoverer Viewer are much more popular than Discoverer Desktop and are the focus of this chapter.

Each Discoverer interface leverages a common End User Layer. The EUL is a metadata layer that provides business definitions, hiding underlying technical descriptions while providing a map to those specific database fields. Although OracleAS Discoverer is most often used to query an Oracle relational database, it can also leverage Heterogeneous Services support in the Oracle database and use ODBC to connect to non-Oracle databases. Note, however, that some capabilities tied to the Oracle database—in particular, the management of summary tables and query prediction (described later in this section)—aren't available when OracleAS Discoverer is implemented via ODBC.

OracleAS Discoverer access to data is controlled through security that is regulated at both the application level and the database level through defined roles. OracleAS Discoverer can leverage the OracleAS Single Sign-On, and can detect and change expired database passwords.

Information concerning connections to the database is stored in the Oracle Application Server Metadata Repository, which is a part of the OracleAS Infrastructure introduced in Chapter 2. This information includes the database name, database username and password, Oracle Applications responsibility (included only when used with Oracle's ERP Applications), language, and metadata information. Connections can be private and available to specific users, or can be public and available to all OracleAS Discoverer users. Users can create their own private connections.

As such tools gain importance in making day-to-day decisions, you may want to consider highly available deployment. If you are deploying OracleAS Discoverer to Oracle Application Server in a highly available manner, make sure to do the following:

- Configure the Oracle Process Manager and Notification Server to monitor and restart OracleAS Discoverer processes on each middle-tier node. OPMN is described in Chapter 2.
- Use the OracleAS Web Cache for load-balancing OracleAS Discoverer requests. OracleAS Web Cache and the other Oracle Application Server caches are described in Chapter 7.

Manipulating and displaying data

Discoverer Plus is a browser-based ad hoc query tool that is deployed via a Java applet. This tool provides an easy-to-use interface for picking and choosing data items (exposed via the EUL) around which to build queries. These queries can be stored as "workbooks" for reuse as the underlying data changes. Business analysts can manipulate these workbooks or simply view the contents, depending on their access rights. Workbooks can be scheduled for execution at specific times using OracleAS Discoverer's Scheduling Manager.

Discoverer Plus's wizards can create more than 50 different graph types for viewing the data in a graphical form (the same graph types described earlier in the "Report Generation and Deployment" section). Figure 12-2 shows a typical OracleAS Discoverer view of data and an associated graph.

You can generate OracleAS Discoverer's reports with Discoverer Plus and deploy them to the Web as HTML files. You can also export them from Discoverer Plus as Excel files, PDF files, or XML for use with Oracle Reports' distribution capabilities. Information passed via XML includes layout, formatting, exceptions, and parameters.

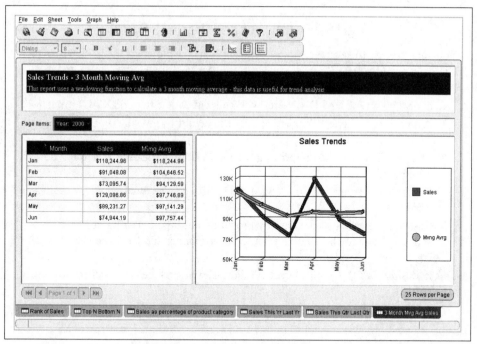

Figure 12-2. OracleAS Discoverer showing data and associated graph

Discoverer Viewer is an HTML-based browser client that is used mainly to view workbooks and worksheets, although some additional capabilities (e.g., sorting) are provided. The Viewer can also export data to formats such as XML and Excel. Discoverer Viewer can be customized to meet corporate standards using a CSS file to define fonts, colors, and graphics. XML is used to represent application state; the XSL is used for formatting the user interface.

A Discoverer Portlet Provider included with Oracle Application Server allows you to publish workbooks to OracleAS Portal. Two types of portlets are provided:

Worksheet
    This portlet can contain tabular or cross-tabular data, graphs, or both.

List of workbooks
    This portlet contains the names of available workbooks.

Using analytics and OLAP

As business analysts become more sophisticated, the questions they ask may evolve from "what happened" to "what trends are present and what might happen in the future." OLAP tools provide the ability to handle time-series and mathematical

OracleAS Discoverer and OracleAS Portal

You might want to leverage Oracle Reports when deploying OracleAS Discoverer results to the OracleAS Portal framework in order to display data in a more visually pleasing way. You can do this as follows:

1. Export your OracleAS Discoverer worksheet in Oracle Reports XML format.
2. Within Oracle Report Builder, modify the layout to give the worksheet a more "published" look.
3. After you have finished improving the look of the worksheet, save the report in JSP format.
4. Register the report in OracleAS Portal through the Builder and Administer interfaces.
5. Customize the link to the data by providing automatic passing of identification and password to the database source in a manner hidden from the OracleAS Portal user.
6. If desired, add prebuilt OracleAS Portal styles to be consistent with other portlets.
7. Add the report definition file to the OracleAS Portal framework.

analysis for understanding past trends and forecasting the future. OLAP tools use two types of data:

ROLAP
   Relational online analytical processing. These tools use data stored in relational databases in a star schema.

MOLAP
   Multidimensional online analytical processing. These tools use predefined multi-dimensional cubes.

Popular MOLAP engines include Oracle's Express Server, Hyperion's Essbase, and Microsoft's Analytic Services. These MOLAP engines handle queries extremely quickly, and they traditionally work best when the data isn't updated frequently (because the cube-generation process takes time). Since Oracle9i, Oracle has supported MOLAP cubes stored *within* the relational database via the OLAP Option; use of this option provides better scalability and more timely access to this type of data.

When building a relational query in OracleAS Discoverer, business analysts can select analytic functions provided in the Oracle database, use predefined functions provided by the administrator, or create their own calculations. Prebuilt templates are provided for the commonly used analytic calculations provided by the Oracle database. These calculations include:

Rank
Percent rank
Difference
Percent difference
Preceding value
Following value
Running total
Percent running contribution
Percent contribution
Moving total
Group total
Band by value
Band by rank

The Oracle database's OLAP Option object contains predefined facts, dimensions, and cube structures stored in an *analytic workspace*. These features greatly speed pivoting and provide other multidimensional functions. OracleAS Discoverer support for access to the analytic workspace is a new capability added in 2004.

Managing and improving query performance

OracleAS Discoverer uses a *cubic cache* to maintain query performance in a way that is transparent to both business analysts and administrators. In a typical three-tier web deployment, the cubic cache is in the middle tier. Because it is tied to the analyst's session, the cube allows subsequent analysis against the same data without requiring repeated queries.

OracleAS Discoverer also provides additional facilities that can be used to improve performance. For example, query performance can be greatly improved when the query is redirected to data that is preaggregated in the database at a summary level. OracleAS Discoverer can automatically redirect queries to these summary tables. You can use a wizard in OracleAS Discoverer to simplify creation by defining a summary policy. After setting aside a portion of the database for summaries (20 MB is typical), OracleAS Discoverer can then analyze available space and recommend, create, and maintain the summary tables.

A business analyst might want to figure out how long a query will take before actually running it. OracleAS Discoverer's *query governor* can predict the amount of time a query will take based on comparisons to previous query times of similar queries. This data is kept in the Oracle database server and is updated so that the predictions become more accurate over time. The administrator has the option of placing limits on the time allowed for queries to complete. This provides a safeguard because an analyst could (either intentionally or accidentally) request incredibly complex and lengthy queries for a particular report. Long-running queries can negatively impact overall database performance for other business analysts.

Using Administrator Edition

Administrators of OracleAS Discoverer can use the Oracle Discoverer Administrator Edition, a part of the Oracle Developer Suite. Oracle Discoverer Administrator lets administrators perform such functions as formatting business areas, creating or editing business areas, creating summaries, setting privileges, and managing scheduled workbooks. Administrators can also set end-user privileges—for example, the ability to use OracleAS Discoverer clients, create or edit queries, collect query statistics, perform item drills, grant workbooks, schedule workbooks, save workbooks to the database, and change passwords.

The Oracle Discoverer Administrator Edition also provides the ability to set up and maintain the End User Layer. Wizards guide the administrator through the process of building the EUL. The EUL can be populated from an Oracle data dictionary, via a gateway to another source or via the Oracle Warehouse Builder Common Warehouse Metamodel (CWM) bridge. As an alternative, the EUL can also be created and managed using Oracle Application Server 10*g*'s EUL command line for Java.

Administrators also control access to workbooks and worksheets through the Discoverer Administrator Edition. As mentioned earlier, they can put limits on resources available to analysts monitored by the OracleAS Discoverer query governor.

 If there is no client activity for a period of time, an administrator may want to have an OracleAS Discoverer "time out" because an OracleAS Discoverer session is a live connection into your corporate data source. For Discoverer Plus, a timeout value can be set in seconds (Timeout=*X*) in the *pref.txt* file. The minimum allowed is 180 seconds. For Discoverer Viewer, the *Web.xml* file contains a session-timeout tag that is set in minutes.

Oracle Application Server Business Intelligence Partners

The continued popularity of the Oracle database for business intelligence and data warehousing is driving a growing number of partnerships among tools vendors. Such partnerships sometimes extend to support of Oracle Application Server.

Business Objects (*www.businessobjects.com*) provides an ad hoc query and OLAP capability that can be deployed in Oracle Application Server in various ways. For example:

- The Business Objects' Enterprise analysis tool can be used to generate queries against Oracle relational and OLAP Option data through SQL.

- The Business Objects "Universe," or metadata layer, can be created to enable transparent drill-through from OLAP data to detailed data stored in relational tables.

- An OracleAS Portal toolkit is also available for the viewing of Business Objects-generated reports.

Custom OLAP Applications

Instead of using standard tools to access OLAP, some organizations choose to deploy applications-oriented solutions. Often, these custom-built solutions are designed to make operations as easy as possible for less-skilled users—although often at the cost of providing less flexibility.

Back when Oracle's Express Server was popular, custom OLAP applications were built via Oracle's Express Objects. For today's Oracle database OLAP Option, such applications are now built using Oracle JDeveloper and Business Intelligence beans. These JavaBeans provide prebuilt components for manipulating tables, crosstabs, and graphs, and for building queries and calculations similar to the functionality previously found in Oracle Express. Oracle JDeveloper generates Java code using these building blocks that maps to the Java OLAP API provided by Oracle's OLAP Option. The J2EE-compliant applications that are produced can be deployed to Oracle Application Server.

Data Warehouses and Oracle Warehouse Builder

The database schema used for business intelligence may be one of several types:

Third normal form (3NF)
In such a model, data is stored once and appears much the same as in online transaction processing. Third normal form is typically used for operational reporting.

Star schema
In such a model, a large transaction fact table is surrounded by multiple lookup or "dimension" tables. This model is common in data warehousing. The star schema is especially popular when used with ad hoc query and analysis tools that explore historical data because the model typically matches the kinds of questions that business analysts want to ask (see Figure 12-3 for a typical example). This model often includes hierarchies with summary levels. These models are extremely useful when the business analyst wants to determine, for example, the number of sales (in a fact table) made by a sales channel (dimension) over a certain period of time (dimension).

OLAP schema
The analytic workspace in the Oracle OLAP Option takes the star schema model one step further by enabling the storage of multidimensional cubes (MOLAP) as objects within the same relational database. This approach further speeds query performance.

If you want to perform business analysis on your data, you typically have to create a data warehouse with a star schema model. Oracle Warehouse Builder, included with the Oracle Developer Suite or the Oracle database, is Oracle's tool for designing these schema, importing the metadata describing data sources, and designing

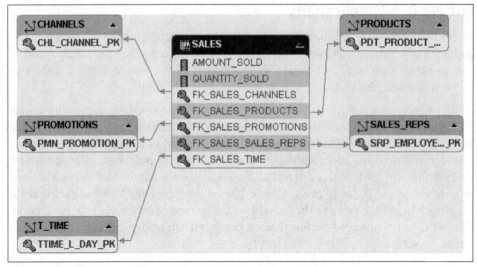

Figure 12-3. Star schema viewed through Oracle Warehouse Builder

extraction, transformation, and loading source-to-target maps. Oracle Warehouse Builder can then automatically generate PL/SQL scripts for ETL from relational sources, and SQL*Loader files for loading from flat files. SQL*Loader's *direct path load* capability can provide rapid parallel loading and bypass the buffer cache and rollback mechanism by writing directly to the datafile.

Data models and mappings are stored in OWB's Metadata Repository, which is based on a version of the Common Warehouse Metamodel standard. OWB provides metadata reports, impact analysis, and data lineage diagrams through a web browser. Metadata interchange to a variety of repositories is available via third-party integration tools. Metadata of designs may be directly imported from tools such as Oracle Designer, CA's ERwin, and Sybase's PowerDesigner.

If you create an OLAP Option analytic workspace schema, you will typically use OWB and an Analytic Workspace Manager. Using OWB, you start by first creating a relational dimensional model, then running an OLAP bridge to create an OLAP catalog and populate the analytic workspace.

In any typical ETL building process, you do the following:

1. Import metadata that describes source tables, including Oracle (via database links) and other relational databases (through ODBC or gateways), flat files, or application-specific tables (such as those in SAP).

2. Design target tables.

3. Map source metadata to target metadata, including mapping functions. The set of mapping functions in OWB includes a joiner, filter, aggregator, reduplicator, sorter, splitter, sequencer, inline expressions, transformations, and name and

address cleansing operator. Figure 12-4 provides an example of how a typical mapping looks.

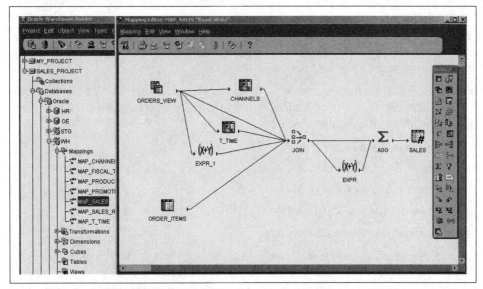

Figure 12-4. Typical Oracle Warehouse Builder source table-to-target table mapping

4. OWB then validates the source-to-target mappings.

5. Once the validation has been performed, generate any of the following:

- DDL if target tables are to be created
- SQL*Loader control files for the loading of flat files
- PL/SQL scripts for ETL from relational sources

OWB can leverage ETL functionality in the Oracle database, such as support for external tables, table functions, merges (inserts or updates, depending on whether a data item exists), and multitable inserts.

Scripts are deployed to, and run at, the target data warehouse, typically scheduled using the Oracle Enterprise Manager job scheduler. Although batch jobs are more common, OWB can also create trickle feeds (data is fed nearly continuously and in near-real time) through the use of advanced queues. For more complex scheduling of ETL jobs where certain prerequisites must be met, OWB includes an interface to Oracle Workflow. (See the discussion of Oracle Workflow in Chapter 15)

Data Mining

Data mining, as we define it in this chapter, is the use of mathematical algorithms to model relationships in the data that solve difficult problems involving large numbers of variables with unknown relationships. You might need such techniques if you are trying to solve such business problems as fraud detection, customer churn analysis, and marketing contact response prediction. The algorithms used to solve such problems include clustering techniques that show how business outcomes can fall within certain groups (such as for market basket analysis) and logic models (if A occurs, then B or C are possible outcomes), validated against small sample sets and then applied to larger data sets for prediction.

Since the Oracle9i database release, Oracle has provided a set of data mining algorithms in the database's Data Mining Option for solving such problems. Algorithms now embedded in the database include:

- Naïve Bayes Associations
- Adaptive Bayes Networks
- Clustering, Support Vector Machines (SVM)
- Nonnegative Matrix Factorization (NMF)

These algorithms are accessible via a Java API.

Data mining applications can be custom-built using Oracle's JDeveloper in combination with the Data Mining for Java interface. DM4J is used to develop, test, and score the models. It provides the ability to define metadata, tune the generated Java code, view generated XML files, and test application components. The J2EE-generated applications can be deployed within the database, to Oracle Application Server, or to other J2EE platforms.

OracleAS Personalization is one application of data mining that is bundled with Oracle Application Server. It provides the tools necessary to instrument a web site, gather data on how a web-site visitor traverses the site, and then use the data gathered to provide a "personalized" web experience by presenting specific pages that are determined to be of likely interest to the visitor.

This solution is implemented in three tiers, as shown in Figure 12-5. The Recommendation Engine API (REAPI) is a set of Java classes that are integrated into the web application on the web site, enabling the gathering of needed data and specific actions based on recommendations from the middle tier. The data that is gathered as a web-site visitor traverses the site is captured and sent to an Oracle database installed with the data mining algorithms. There, scoring takes place to create a sorted, ordered list that is then applied to the middle-tier Recommendation Engine. That engine services the web site in real time, providing recommendations based on similar, previously analyzed trends.

An OracleAS Personalization Administration User Interface (OPUI) accesses the Mining Object Repository (MOR) in the backend. The MOR schema contains business model information and is used for configuration and report administration. A

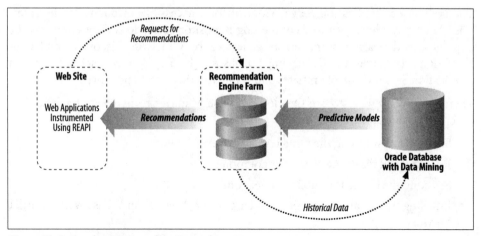

Figure 12-5. OracleAS Personalization architecture

Mining Table Repository (MTR) contains the basic schema needed to create the model of the business, also referred to as a *taxonomy*.

Managing Business Intelligence Components

The latest release of Oracle Application Server, Oracle Application Server 10*g*, was designed to ease the overall management burden by automating many management tasks for large-scale grid computing deployment. These include:

- Software provisioning, including installation, configuration, cloning, patching, and upgrades
- User provisioning, including security and identity management
- Application management and monitoring
- Workload management, including dynamic resource allocation and failover notification
- Systems management and monitoring

Oracle provides Oracle Enterprise Manager, a management tool and framework, as part of every application server and Oracle database. Management capabilities in Oracle Enterprise Manager include not only generic monitoring of Oracle Application Server (e.g., CPU and memory usage), but also extended support of specific BI components deployed as part of Oracle Application Server. For example, configuration of OracleAS Discoverer and OracleAS Reports Services is performed via Oracle Enterprise Manager. OracleAS Reports Services performance can also be monitored, and job queues can be viewed and managed through Oracle Enterprise Manager.

The web-based Application Server Control tool, accessible through Oracle Enterprise Manager, allows you to view the Log Repository error logs. These logs can be populated with warnings and errors generated by OracleAS Discoverer and OracleAS Reports Server for debugging purposes. The Log Loader, started through Application Server Control, initiates and populates this Log Repository.

There are myriad ways to use Oracle Enterprise Manager to manage OracleAS Discoverer; here are some examples:

- Starting and stopping the OracleAS Discoverer Service
- Enabling and disabling client-tier components
- Selecting the locale for public connections
- Enabling or disabling graphs in Discoverer Viewer and Discoverer Portlet Provider
- Managing connections for Discoverer Plus and Discoverer Viewer
- Specifying the number of stylesheets to pool for Discoverer Viewer and Discoverer Portlet Provider
- Specifying a delay value for the query progress page in Discoverer Viewer
- Specifying the communications protocol for the middle tier for Discoverer Plus
- Specifying the maximum number of Discoverer Portlet Provider sessions to pool
- Starting and stopping Discoverer Servlets
- Searching for and analyzing the log files

See Chapter 3 for more information about Oracle Enterprise Manager.

CHAPTER 13

Oracle Application Server Portal

Oracle Application Server Portal is one of the more visible components of the Oracle Application Server product. Because OracleAS Portal includes a wizard-driven development environment, it is an easy part of Oracle Application Server for people to begin using quickly. Certain parts of OracleAS Portal can even be used by end users, and this component is also easy for the Oracle sales team to demonstrate. Because OracleAS Portal provides a complete visual environment for accessing all kinds of information, end users can quickly see how the addition of OracleAS Portal can change their computing environment.

If you are unfamiliar with OracleAS Portal, you are likely to pose two immediate questions: what is OracleAS Portal and, more basically, what is a portal?

Let's answer the second question first. A *portal* is a way to centralize access to a variety of information sources, from a collection of web pages to user interfaces with applications. In this sense, a portal is a type of desktop, but with an important difference. You can think of a portal as a server-resident desktop. Portals are hosted on servers, so they are under the direct control of the IT organization. This architecture makes them easier to manage and control. Of course, the more flexible a portal is, the more likely that end users will be satisfied with its appearance and functionality.

OracleAS Portal is the end result of an evolutionary process across revisions and years:

- The first version of OracleAS Portal was created by an internal consulting group at Oracle. The purpose of this version was to provide an easy way to create HTML-based applications to access and interact with data in an Oracle database. This version was not a public product.

- The second version of OracleAS Portal, known as WebDB, was publicly released in 1999. WebDB had more complete application-building capabilities, but also had the beginnings of a system to organize and classify data.

- The current version of OracleAS Portal appeared with the third release of the product. At this point, the organizational powers of OracleAS Portal had matured, and the idea of portals in general was emerging in the marketplace. This version has been advanced in the Oracle Application Server 10g release.

OracleAS Portal is a way to present information from a number of sources in one or more HTML-based pages. The place to start understanding this product is by examining the structure of a page, which we'll do in the next section. In subsequent sections we'll describe more details of portals, portlets, and the deployment of OracleAS Portal, including security issues.

An OracleAS Portal Page

OracleAS Portal presents information by the page. A *page* in OracleAS Portal has the same scope as a standard HTML page—a page is what a browser holds at any one time.

In OracleAS Portal, though, pages can be assembled from many different sources. Most importantly, a page is a part of a structural hierarchy, as shown in Figure 13-1.

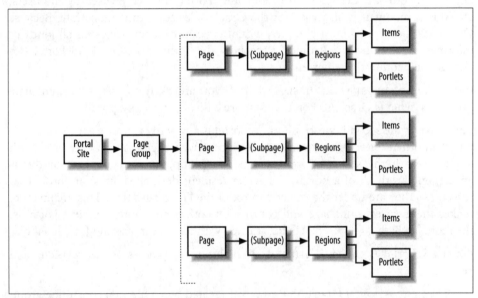

Figure 13-1. OracleAS Portal hierarchy

The top level in the hierarchy is known as an OracleAS Portal *site*; it indicates a single installation of OracleAS Portal, referenced by a specific URL prefix.

The next level in the hierarchy is a page group. A *page group* contains a group of related pages, as well as any supporting objects required for the page group, such as styles or page templates, which are described in subsequent sections. The *root page* of a page group is typically the home page for that group. You normally organize your OracleAS Portal sites so that a user can remain within one page group.

Each page group contains pages, and each page can contain subpages. A subpage can be reached from its parent page. Whenever you copy a page with subpages, you have the option of also copying all subpages associated with the page. Whenever you delete a page group or page with subpages, you also delete its subordinate pages.

A page, or a portlet within a page (we'll describe portlets later in this chapter), can have parameters assigned to it, and the value of a parameter can be included in the calling URL for the page. This capability allows you to link to a subpage or portlet while maintaining some state information. For instance, a click on an item may act as a link to another page with more detail about the item. The parent page can pass the item identifier to the child page through a parameter.

Clicking a button is an example of a particular OracleAS Portal *event*. You can write code to execute in response to an event. Event code can be implemented in JSP code, to execute in response to user actions on the client.

Page Layout and Regions

Each OracleAS Portal page can contain one or more regions, as shown in Figure 13-2.

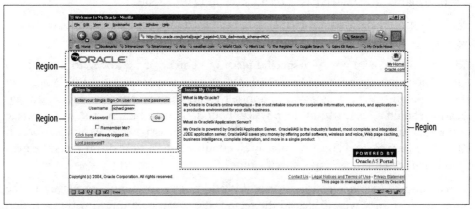

Figure 13-2. An OracleAS Portal page, with regions highlighted

The *regions* in a page provide the basic layout for the page. You can specify where a region goes on a page, in relation to other regions, and what percent of the width or height of a page a region occupies. A region can automatically have a banner, as can a grouping of items within a region.

A region contains one of two types of objects—either one or more portlets or one or more items (we'll describe both of these later in this chapter). A region can contain tabs, each of which brings up its own set of portlets or items. You can also have a region automatically mark a new piece of content with an icon for a specified time after the content is initially added to the region.

There are two other specific types of regions:

Subpage region
> This type of region automatically contains links to all the subpages for the owning page and nothing else. A subpage region can contain one or two levels of subpage links.

Tab region
> This type of region can't contain anything other than objects but can be configured to include rollover objects for information about the tab.

A page can't contain another complete page, so if you want a page to appear within a region on another page, you have to publish the subordinate page as a portlet, and then add that portlet to the region.

Items

An *item* can do any of the following:

- Contain content, such as text or an image
- Be a URI that points to another piece of information
- Be dynamically created based on a piece of PL/SQL code

You can also create a region that uses a search to automatically add items to the region.

An item can either point to a specific piece of content or be a way to navigate to another location, within the OracleAS Portal framework or outside of it. When you create an item that navigates you to another location, you can specify whether that location should appear within the physical boundaries of a region or in its own page or browser instance. When you create an item, you can assign it an expiration, which allows the item to be displayed for only a certain length of time or prevents the item from being seen on the site at a specific time.

Items within a region are either sorted by title or size, or simply displayed in the order in which they were added to the region. Items can be grouped within a region by author, date, category (which is described later in this chapter), or item type, as well as not grouped at all.

An item region, by default, automatically displays each item in the page on its own row. You can specify that a region has more than one column, which causes the items in the region to be evenly distributed across the columns. You can also assign both the number of columns and the number of rows. Doing so limits the display to the number of items that can be shown in the specified columns and rows.

For convenience, OracleAS Portal enables you to load a group of items at one time by uploading a ZIP file containing the group. Once the file is loaded, you unzip the items, which maintain the same directory structure they had in the ZIP file.

Page Appearance

As mentioned at the start of this chapter, OracleAS Portal presents a common interface to many different sources of data. If you had to create each individual page independently, it would be difficult to establish a standard look and feel to your OracleAS Portal site. OracleAS Portal has several features that give a standard look and feel to all the pages within a site: page templates, styles, navigation pages, shared objects, and translations.

Page templates

A *page template* assigns a standard arrangement of regions within a page. If a page is based on a page template, the template must contain all the regions that will be in the page. A developer or user, with the proper privileges, has the option to not display all the regions in a page template, but he can't add additional regions to a page based on a template.

If you make changes to a template, the changes ripple down to all the pages based on that template. You can remove the association between a page and a template, which stops the propagation of template changes to the page.

Many templates assign specific regions within a page to provide navigation within a page group or site. For instance, there may be a region at the top of the page that provides access to the home page for the page group, or to a login and logout page, as well as a region to the left of the page that provides navigation to different parts of the page group.

For convenience, OracleAS Portal allows you to create a page template from an existing page. A page template created in this manner doesn't include everything in the page but does represent the basic layout of regions in the page.

Styles

Styles define overall look-and-feel attributes for a page or region. A style defines the colors and fonts used within the page or region and can be applied to a single page, to a page group associated with a page template, or to a region within a page.

There are style properties for items, tabs, and portlets, as well as properties that apply to all of these groups. When a style is changed, the changes ripple down throughout the items, tabs, and portlets within the area controlled by the style.

When you create or modify a page, you can assign a style to the page or have the page take on the default style of the user accessing the page. A page template can require a particular style and not allow any changes in it. If a page isn't based on one of these restrictive templates, a user can select his own page style from a list of candidate styles. A user can select a default page style to be used when she views a particular page group or an individual page.

If you don't assign a specific style to a page, the page style uses a default style, either for the page group or, if there is no default style for the page group, the style defined as the default global style.

Navigation pages

Frequently, a page group will have a set of *navigation pages* that are used throughout the group. You can implement this functionality by creating a page with the navigation links. These navigation pages also can contain other prebuilt items, such as a login link; a search box; or an object map, which lists all the page groups and pages in the site.

Shared objects

Shared objects can be used in many pages and page templates. Typically, shared objects implement uniform look and feel (as with color and font definitions or images) or functionality (as with JavaScript form- and field-level validations).

Translations

OracleAS Portal can display in different languages, as well as allow users to enter information in different languages. You enable this capability by creating *translations* for a page group. Once a translation is created for a page group, a user can choose a language at sign-in, or by selecting a language with the built-in Set Language portlet. Once a user has selected a particular language, subsequent contributions of content are kept as part of the specific translation for the language he has selected.

The translation capability in OracleAS Portal requires manual translation and applies only to text defined for a portal page, such as category or perspective names or item display names.

Page Groups

A *page group* is basically a collection of pages, along with objects that support those pages. A page group is analogous to a root folder in a file system. Page groups represent the highest level in the hierarchy of OracleAS Portal organization, as shown earlier in Figure 13-1. Each page group contains a root page, which is the top page in the page hierarchy. A single OracleAS Portal site can have many different root pages.

The key to creating page groups is identifying business units that each should represent. For example, some companies create separate page groups for each region they serve. Others create page groups for each intranet their portal supports. Through the use of security, page groups can be hidden from one another. Each page group has its own security model, which can add administrative overhead to support more page groups.

You can share objects between page groups by either creating them in or promoting them to the Shared Objects page group. Objects (including page templates, styles, and navigation pages) within this group can be shared with other page groups to provide a wider scope of reuse and standardization across an entire site.

Types and Attributes

When you create either a page or an item, you must create the object based on a predefined *object type*. An object type does several things:

- Helps you to classify the information based on its characteristics
- Allows you to add information, or metadata, about a particular type of object
- Enforces some basic requirements on the type

For instance, if you define a page as a URL page type, you must have a URL indicating where the content for the page is coming from.

OracleAS Portal comes with a set of standard types, which are associated with pages, items, and regions. You can also create your own customized types. These customized types can inherit the attributes of an existing page or item type. You can also include different types of procedures to a page or item type, which automatically adds the procedure to any page or item of that type.

The page type indicates the source of the information, such as a standard page type for items or portlets, a URL page type for displaying the contents of other pages on the Web, or a PL/SQL page for displaying the results of a PL/SQL procedure. The item type performs a similar function for items, specifying whether the item is text, a file, an image, a link, or one of several other item types.

The type of a page or item specifies some of the attributes associated with the object. An *attribute* is essentially metadata about the particular object, such as the name of the object and the author of the object. As with types, OracleAS Portal comes with a standard set of attributes, and you can also add your own attributes.

There are two classifications of attributes:

Content attributes
> These attributes are stored pieces of information about an object. They are associated with page types and item types.

Display attributes
> These attributes can be displayed to an end user and are associated with regions. Administrators can specify which display attributes are actually available for a particular region.

Portlets

We introduced the concept of a portlet in the previous section. Basically, a *portlet* is a reusable program that delivers information. This information can come from a variety of sources. A portlet works with and leverages the services provided by the OracleAS Portal runtime to integrate its information into the overall OracleAS Portal environment. The portlet is one of the key enablers for OracleAS Portal's display of information.

A portlet displays information that is collected from a source, known as a *portlet provider*. The portlet provider collects the information and then passes it to the portlet, which displays the information. This architecture, and the two types of portlet providers, are shown in Figure 13-3.

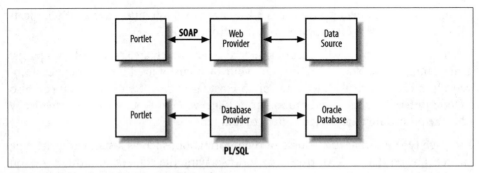

Figure 13-3. Portlet architecture and provider types

A portlet provider can provide information to many different portlets. Portlet providers can be organized into Provider Groups, which combine related providers. A Database Provider, described later, can be shared between multiple instances of OracleAS Portal.

Each portlet is registered in the Portlet Repository, which is a part of the overall OracleAS Infrastructure. When you build a page, you can select any of the portlets in the repository for inclusion in a region.

An individual instance of a portlet can be shared across multiple pages in a page group. By sharing a portlet, you both ensure a consistent view of the information the portlet is providing and reduce the resources required to retrieve the information and create the portlet for the end user.

Providers

Portal providers act as the link between a content source and an OracleAS Portal page via portlets. OracleAS Portal includes many portal providers and can create additional providers to run within the OracleAS Portal environment or to register external providers. There are two basic types of providers, Web Providers and Database Providers, described in the following sections.

Web Providers

A Web Provider collects information from someplace on the Web and delivers information to its portlets using SOAP over HTTP. Because it uses the common protocol of SOAP, a Web Provider can be written in virtually any language. A Web Provider runs in its own environment, while a Database Provider, written in PL/SQL, runs in the Oracle database that holds the Portal Repository.

The OracleAS Portal Development Kit (PDK), described later in this chapter, comes with a Java framework that makes it easier to create Web Providers in Java. This framework includes interfaces to use such Oracle Application Server features as OracleAS Single Sign-On.

Database Providers

Database Providers, as their name implies, retrieve information from an Oracle database and are written in PL/SQL. These Database Providers supply information for portlets based on PL/SQL or JSPs.

Database Providers run in the Oracle database that is also used for the OracleAS Portal Repository. You can access Database Providers running on other OracleAS Portal instances through a feature called the Federated Portal Adapter.

Using Prebuilt Portlets

Although the overall thrust of OracleAS Portal is now to provide a consolidated interface to many sources of information, earlier versions of OracleAS Portal put a lot of effort into making it easy to create your own portlets using a set of *portlet wizards*.

These wizards prompt you for information and then create PL/SQL packages to implement the portlet. The wizards are entirely HTML-based, so you can build portlets from any browser.

You can build a number of different types of portlets with OracleAS Portal wizards:

Form portlets
> These portlets include simple forms, master detail sets of forms, and forms based on PL/SQL procedures.

Report portlets
> These portlets can be built using the Query Wizard, which doesn't require knowledge of SQL or can be based on an SQL query. You can also create a Query-By-Example report, which provides a form interface for users to implement their own selection criteria. An item in a report can be used as a link to another portlet page with detailed information about the item.

Chart portlets
These portlets can include links from chart values to more detailed information.

Hierarchy portlets
These portlets display multiple levels of related information.

Frame driver portlets
These portlets create a page with two frames, with the content of one frame driving the display of information in the other frame.

URL page portlets
These portlets display the content of a URL.

Data component portlets
These portlets display data in a spreadsheet format.

Calendar portlets
These portlets include links to underlying information based on date.

Dynamic page portlets
These portlets display dynamically created HTML pages.

XML page portlets
These portlets are based on XML.

The most recent version of OracleAS Portal includes two new prebuilt portlets that give a broader range of functionality:

OmniPortlet
This portlet can access data from a variety of sources, including a database, an XML file, a comma-separated variable file, web pages, or Web Services. The OmniPortlet can display the information in a variety of ways. OmniPortlet provides some of the same functionality as some of the prebuilt portlets mentioned previously, such as reports, charts, and forms.

Web Clipping portlet
This portlet makes it easy for a developer to select a web page and have some or all of its content displayed in a portlet. With the Web Clipping portlet, any web page can be a data source.

These two new portlets are also Web Provider portlets, which means they can exist outside the Oracle database.

OracleAS Portal also includes wizards that help you build portlets that are meant to be part of a page, such as menus, links, and list-of-values portlets.

Once you have created a portlet, you can use the OracleAS Portal environment to edit the portlet and make changes to its look, feel, or functionality. For Database Provider portlets, Portal automatically stores each version of a portlet, and you can recall earlier versions if necessary.

The end result of building a prebuilt portlet with one of the development wizards is a PL/SQL package that is stored in the OracleAS Portal Repository and run when the portlet is called. The OracleAS Portal development environment includes an option to compile the PL/SQL package to ensure that any code you may have added to the package compiles without errors.

In addition to the prebuilt portlets that come with OracleAS Portal, you can download third-party portlets from the Portal Studio site; it's described in a later subsection.

The development wizards make building portlets fairly easy, and you can include a lot of functionality in these declaratively created portlets. You can even go so far as to include PL/SQL routines to run at various times during the processing of a page.

 You can access any of the data values on a page, or session values for the page, in PL/SQL code.

Although you probably shouldn't think about creating mission-critical OLTP applications with portlets, the ease of creation makes them a viable option for helping users to interact with information in the database through a browser interface. Also, the Database Provider portlets require that the data they are accessing exist within the Portal Repository Database, which is frequently not the case. You can use OmniPortlet to access data outside the Portal Repository Database, because OmniPortlet is a Web Provider.

OracleAS Portal Development Kit

The wizard-driven interface that comes with OracleAS Portal is powerful and productive, but there may be times when you want to implement some type of functionality that is beyond the scope of these built-in wizards. For these occasions, the OracleAS Portal team has created the OracleAS Portal Development Kit.

The PDK contains all the information and APIs you need to create your own customized portlets, in either PL/SQL or Java. Using the PDK is significantly more complex than the simple creation of portlets with the built-in wizards, but it offers almost unlimited flexibility.

Java Portlets

Two new Java standards, Web Services for Remote Portlets (WSRP) and Java Specification Request 168 (JSR 168), provide the Java world with specifications for portlets to run in different portal environments.

OracleAS Portal comes with an Oracle JDeveloper Portlet Wizard, which helps you create a portlet out of Java code in Oracle JDeveloper. This wizard is an add-on for Oracle JDeveloper that allows you to create Java portlet code. This code can be run against any JSR 168-compliant portal, which includes OracleAS Portal. Portal Studio, described in the next section, has a section that lets you test a Java portlet to make sure it can properly interoperate with a JSR 168-compliant portal.

The Oracle JDeveloper Portlet Wizard can also create portlets that use the Oracle PDK, rather than JSR 168, as the basic API for the portlet. Regardless of which type of Java portlet you create, the portlet is run in the Java Portlet Container servlet.

Portal Studio

To encourage the creation and sharing of portlets and providers, Oracle Corporation provides the Portal Studio site (*http://portalstudio.oracle.com*). Portal Studio is intended to be a full-service support site, containing the latest versions of the PDK, a discussion area for developers, integration tools for other applications, and even a way to register and test your own portlets. Portal Studio includes third-party portlets and providers in its Portal Catalog. The OracleAS Portal development team and product managers are continually updating this site with new explanations, tutorials, and sample code.

Classification of Data

OracleAS Portal provides access to information. The more information that is available, the greater the potential aggregate value of the information. However, large amounts of information can also be hard to organize and understand. To help make data more accessible, OracleAS Portal comes with two default ways to classify data—categories and perspectives:

Categories
> Each item in an OracleAS Portal site must belong to one, and only one, *category*. In this way, categories provide a taxonomy for content in OracleAS Portal. OracleAS Portal comes with its own set of built-in categories, and you can add your own categories. You can create a hierarchy of categories to further organize your content. Categories can be made available to specific page groups, or to all page groups.

Perspectives
> Perspectives provide a way to organize content based on an idea of who might be interested in the content. For instance, you might have one perspective for managers, another for developers, and another for sales within your company. By selecting a particular perspective, a user can quickly focus on the content that is most pertinent to him.
>
> An item can be assigned to more than one perspective. As with categories, you can create a hierarchy of perspectives.

Whenever you create either a category or a perspective, a page is created for the item. This page lists the content for that category or perspective.

In addition to categories and perspectives, you can add specific search terms, which may be used to find data, or you can use the functionality of Oracle Text to provide further search capabilities. Searching is described in the next section in the context of end-user interaction.

End-User Interaction

OracleAS Portal is designed to present information to end users. Although an administrator controls the basic creation and deployment of an OracleAS Portal site, end users can also take advantage of OracleAS Portal to customize their user experience, to search for information, or even to add content to an existing site.

Customization

End users have a habit of wanting things shown to them in a particular manner, and not all users in a community agree on what this exact manner should be. OracleAS Portal can help solve this problem by enabling end users to customize many aspects of their OracleAS Portal interaction.

You can grant the user the ability to customize the appearance of any of his pages. Customization can cover a wide range of possibilities, from setting the home page to changing the style of a page or page group, to actually moving, adding, or deleting portlets from a region. You can limit the degree of customization that any particular user has, as well as lock down any region in a page to prevent user customization of the content of the region.

Working with Content

OracleAS Portal was designed to be user friendly, from the way it displays information to the way it implements wizard-driven interfaces for developing some types of portlets. Individual end users can also work within the framework of an OracleAS Portal site to directly interact with content items.

With proper permissions, an end user can manipulate the items in a region. A user can add items to a page. An item can be text, a link to a file, or a link to another source of information on the Web. An administrator can specify a limit to the total amount of space allotted to store items for a particular page group.

Of course, not all users should be allowed to add items, willy-nilly, to managed OracleAS Portal sites. To ensure that added content is appropriate and relevant, a user can be given the privilege of adding content only with approval. Content approval can be specified for an individual page or for an entire page group.

The approval can be a simple sign-off from another user or an entire approval process involving many different users. When a user creates a content item, she is automatically informed of the progress of the item through the approval process, as well as whether the item has been approved or rejected at each step.

End users can also move items from one page or region to another or rearrange the order of items within a region. Users can also delete items with proper permissions. For existing items, a user can change the item's category, add or delete an item from a perspective, or add or delete search keywords for the item.

OracleAS Portal also enables users to "check out" a piece of content. If checkin/ checkout is enabled for an item, this ability can be downloaded by only one user at any given time. OracleAS Portal can implement version control on items, in which older versions of edited items can be saved and retrieved.

There may be times when a user will want to know if a particular page gets new content items. You can set up a page so that a user with the proper privileges can subscribe to the page and be automatically notified when the contents of the page change. The notifications come to the user via a built-in notification portlet.

OracleAS Portal supports the use of Web-Distributed Authoring and Versioning (WebDAV) clients to edit content accessed through OracleAS Portal. WebDAV allows users to view OracleAS Portal as a web folder within Windows Explorer. This displays OracleAS Portal and portal pages in the same manner as desktop file explorers. Pages are rendered as folders and items as files. Via this interface, users can seamlessly interact between OracleAS Portal and their file system by dragging and dropping content, files, and folders.

OracleAS Portal essentially supports WebDAV in parallel with its built-in features for content manipulation, and there are some restrictions on the types of pages and content that can be used.

Searching

The overall purpose of any OracleAS Portal site is to centralize the display of information. As we suggested earlier, all this aggregation of content can lead to information overload, as a result of the sheer volume of information. OracleAS Portal includes the classification schemes mentioned earlier, but also has a built-in search capability to help users find the information they need quickly.

An OracleAS Portal user can search through an OracleAS Portal site to find specific content. A search can look through items, pages, categories, and perspectives for a specific word or words.

 You can add keywords to a particular item to help a user find the item. A user search can include keywords.

The user can limit the search results to specific page groups, categories, perspectives, or item types, among other selection criteria. This basic search capability can be accessed through a built-in Search portlet or through a built-in Search box object built into a page. You can perform more complex searches with the built-in Advanced Search portlet. You can also limit the results the Advanced Search portlet can return for users.

A user can save a search, which allows her to repeat it without having to reenter all the search criteria. A built-in portlet provides access to saved searches.

Oracle Text

You can enable Oracle Text for an OracleAS Portal site, and doing enables you to offer significantly more sophisticated searches. With the added capabilities of Oracle Text, a search can automatically look for related words or use functionality such as the nearness of words to each other, or the sound of the words (known as *soundex*).

Oracle UltraSearch

Oracle Application Server also comes with a component called UltraSearch, an extensible search engine that uses a crawler to index documents. The documents are indexed from within their own repositories. The crawled information can build indexes that stay within an Oracle database.

Deployment Architecture

As the discussions in previous sections have illustrated, OracleAS Portal lets you combine information from different sources into a single, server-based interface. But how, exactly, does OracleAS Portal assemble these pages at runtime? The workflow is shown in Figure 13-4 and is described in the following sections.

Creating Portal Pages at Runtime

When a browser sends a request for a page to OracleAS Portal, the request is routed to the Parallel Page Engine (PPE), a Java servlet. The PPE is responsible for implementing and overseeing the creation of a single page from the different sources of information shown on the page.

The first step in the process is for the PPE to get the metadata for the page. The *metadata* describes the overall layout of the page and the portlets used within the page. The PPE builds a structure to hold the page and its information, as described by the metadata.

Once the metadata is retrieved from the OracleAS Portal Repository, the PPE sends a request to the provider for each portlet. When the provider has returned the requested portlet, the PPE adds it to the structure it has created for the page. Once the entire page has been assembled, the PPE returns the page to the requester.

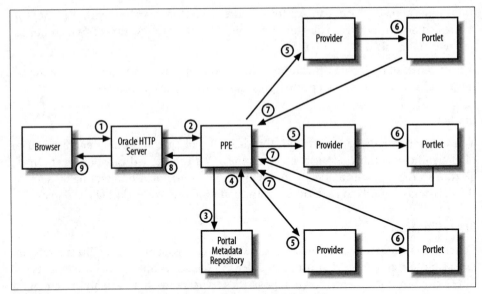

Figure 13-4. Requesting and receiving a page from OracleAS Portal

As you can see from this description, the PPE is central to the overall runtime operation of an OracleAS Portal site. To ensure adequate performance, you can have more than one PPE for an OracleAS Portal site. Each PPE has a default number of fetchers, which request data from providers. You can increase this number if the performance of your OracleAS Portal site seems to be suffering from a lack of fetchers.

Caching

The earlier description shows that creating a page involves a number of different resources. There may be pages or portlets in an OracleAS Portal site that contain the same content for all users. You can reduce the overhead of creating these pages by caching the pages at a system level.

You can specify the following types of caching for a page or portlet:

Cache page definition at the system level
> This approach caches the page metadata once for all users. You can also set an expiration time for this type of caching.

Cache page definition only
> This approach caches the metadata that build the page for each individual user.

Cache page definition and content for a specified length of time
> This approach is helpful for pages that are somewhat dynamic, such as pages listing current news items.

This caching is implemented through the file system on the Oracle Application Server server that is running OracleAS Portal, and is separate from the caching performed by OracleAS Web Cache (described in Chapter 7). Like other pages, portal pages can be cached in OracleAS Web Cache as long as they are defined there as being cacheable. You can set a PPE parameter to prevent OracleAS Web Cache from caching OracleAS Portal pages if desired.

OracleAS Portal Security

OracleAS Portal allows you to assign security to items and pages based on user identity. When a user enters an OracleAS Portal site, he typically logs in, although a site can also accept anonymous users. OracleAS Portal security uses the OracleAS Single Sign-On and Oracle Internet Directory facilities built into Oracle Application Server and described in Chapter 4.

OracleAS Portal supports security for both individual users and groups of users. You can define groups of users through the OracleAS Portal administration interface.

For each user or group, you assign one of several security levels, including:

- The ability to completely manage the page, which allows a user to perform any action on the page
- The ability to manage content on the page, with or without an approval process
- The ability to customize portlets on the page
- The ability to customize styles applied to the page
- The ability to view only the page

Each item can have security restrictions attached to it if you have enabled item security for its page. You can have every item on a page or tab inherit the security restriction of the page or tab. Alternatively, you can allow the person contributing the item to assign a specific security level to it. As with styles, you can assign access privileges in a page template and force those security privileges to be assigned to all pages that use the template.

Portlets also have access rights. By default, a portlet inherits its security settings from its provider, but you can assign specific rights to any individual portlet.

CHAPTER 14

Oracle Application Server Wireless

As Oracle Application Server has evolved, new components have extended the standard capabilities of an application server to handle new areas of technology. One area of explosive technology growth today is the deployment of wireless-enabled applications. This growth has been aided by an increase in the sophistication of wireless devices, including cell phones and Internet-attachable PDA devices, and the growing availability of public wireless connection sites. Usage of such applications and infrastructure is now becoming commonplace. Oracle Application Server Wireless provides a platform that enables the deployment of mobile applications.

Of course, the value of OracleAS Wireless applications is that information can be made available to, and can be updated by, remote users. Advanced OracleAS Wireless features can enable targeted data delivery based on device location. For example, you may want to provide a guide of local movies available in a particular area based on the current physical location of a person's cell phone.

The OracleAS Wireless features in Oracle Application Server enable the deployment of a variety of mobile applications, including:

- Browser-based applications
- Voice applications
- Applications written using Java 2 Micro Edition (J2ME)
- Two-way messaging applications using asynchronous services (ASK), alerts, and notifications

Mobile applications can function entirely disconnected, occasionally connected, or fully connected, depending on the application.

OracleAS Wireless provides components in three areas:

Foundation services
> These services are required in the development and deployment of wireless applications. Foundation services include location-based services, alerts, content

syndication, provisioning, personalization, synchronization, analytics (providing mobile usage reports), and commerce utilities.

Development tools and sample wireless applications
Applications are built using a variety of supported languages and the OracleAS Wireless Development Kit (WDK).

Support of multiple protocols
These protocols enable access to wireless applications from a variety of devices. For example, OracleAS Wireless provides the underlying infrastructure for mobile deployment of Oracle's Collaboration Suite and E-Business Suite applications.

Deployed applications are accessed using a variety of delivery methods via the Multi-Channel Server (see Figure 14-1), which is described in detail in the "Wireless Deployment" section later in this chapter.

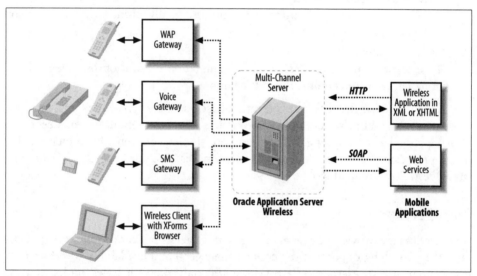

Figure 14-1. OracleAS Wireless Multi-Channel Server deployment

This chapter describes the OracleAS Wireless Foundation Services and the OracleAS Wireless application development tools, deployment process, and administration tools.

OracleAS Wireless Foundation Services

The Foundation Services in OracleAS Wireless provide a library of key functions and capabilities needed in the development and deployment of mobile applications. Services are accessed through APIs provided with the services. The Foundation Services fall into a number of categories: location-based, alert, content syndication, provisioning, personalization, synchronization, analytic, and commerce. The following subsections briefly describe each service.

Location-Based Services

Location-based services allow mobile applications to be location-aware. For example, you might want to build an application that notifies you when a parcel delivery is within a mile of its destination. Here are the services that can build such an application:

Location framework
These services consist of a set of Java APIs, JSP Tag libraries, and Web Services interfaces for geocoding, reverse geocoding, mobile positioning mapping, routing, and business directory services.

Static and dynamic location detection
These services enable the input of location manually, from an application, or from a positioning system such as a GPS.

Privacy management
These services enable or disable the determination of location by others, either permanently or for certain defined time frames

Functionality in OracleAS Wireless location-based services typically is implemented through an external provider. OracleAS Wireless includes prebuilt drivers needed to leverage providers of mapping, routing, and positioning solutions. Examples of solutions providers for such location-based services include InfoUSA, MapInfo, MapQuest, Ericsson, and Nokia.

Alert Services

Alert services are provided by an alert engine in Oracle Application Server that facilitates the publishing of content (by content managers) and availability to subscribers (the content users). Alerts can be triggered at certain times or based on location or threshold values. For example, an application can be built to send an alert to your cell phone when an employee submits an unusually large expense report while you are on vacation.

Content Syndication Services

Content syndication services allow content to be repurposed or reused. You can specify content sources using a wizard provided in OracleAS Wireless Foundation Services to specify a content provider. Two types of content services are provided by OracleAS Wireless:

Transcoding services
These services allow applications developed in WML or cHTML to be dynamically reformatted for use with phones, PDAs, or voice.

Web clipping services

These services enable you to clip and scrape standard web content using a browser interface and then reuse this content for display to mobile devices.

Provisioning Services

Provisioning services support configuring the Wireless Application Protocol (WAP) settings on certain phones (e.g., Ericsson or Nokia) to enable access to email and text-based web pages. OracleAS Wireless includes APIs to extend this support to other devices. Provisioning services also enable integration over-the-air (OTA) that is useful in tasks such as updating Spatial Information Management (SIM) cards in your device. Provisioning is supported for J2ME-developed applications or native applications such as icons, MIDI applications, and ring tones.

Personalization Services

Personalization services enable *quicklinks* that provide shortcuts to applications are commonly used by users. Using these services, you can enable profiles or portal views, and alert notification for services subscribed to by specific users. Personalization services also support managing user devices, user application defaults (such as home location), and user location marks.

Synchronization Services

OracleAS Wireless synchronization services allow you to synchronize J2ME applications and Oracle Lite (Oracle's mobile database). You can use these services to ensure that devices have up-to-date data and that backend data is made consistent with locally updated data.

Analytic Services

Analytic services enable the reporting of system usage, response time, user behavior per channel, and user profile/application matching. Data gathered using these services enables system administrators and planners to determine the level of service and the popularity of applications.

Commerce Services

OracleAS Wireless commerce services allow Mobile Wallets to be stored in a triple-DES encrypted format in an Oracle database for added security. You can retrieve such a wallet after providing a PIN. Commerce services also support the automatic population of forms using wallet data and integration to other systems such as billing systems.

OracleAS Wireless Development

OracleAS Wireless applications can be developed in a completely custom fashion or you can leverage prebuilt applications that are provided with OracleAS Wireless. Markup languages supported for mobile applications include the following:

- XHTML Mobile Profile
- XHTML with XForms
- XML

The OracleAS Wireless engine provides translation to the appropriate device markup language.

 XForms, as defined by the W3C, enables the creation of rich, device-independent forms interfaces through data and processing logic that is separate from presentation logic. Auxiliary scripting isn't needed with XForms, which is an improvement over previous HTML forms creation methods.

When developing an OracleAS Wireless application, you typically follow these general steps:

1. Define business and technical requirements.
2. Design the mobile application needed to fulfill the requirements.
3. Identify prebuilt business logic for reuse, as appropriate, along with needed Web Services.
4. Decide if the application will be accessed via small-screen browsers, messaging devices such as Short Message Service (SMS), or a mixture.
5. Build the mobile application using the Oracle JDeveloper Wireless Extension and device simulators.
6. Test the mobile application using the Mobile My Studio.
7. Deploy the mobile application into production for use on real devices.

OracleAS Wireless Development Tools

The primary tools available for OracleAS Wireless development are Oracle JDeveloper, the Wireless Development Kit, and My Studio.

Oracle JDeveloper

Oracle JDeveloper (packaged in the Oracle Developer Suite) is the primary tool used to build OracleAS Wireless applications. The GUI-based JDeveloper Wireless Extension (JWE) enables you to create mobile applications through wizards and templates. You can use this tool to edit applications. Its device simulators also allow you to test applications and advanced systems and to view log files used in the debugging process. You can deploy applications from the JWE user interface.

OracleAS Wireless Development Kit

The Wireless Development Kit can be used with Oracle JDeveloper, as well as with other development environments and device simulators. You can obtain the WDK at the Oracle Technology Network Wireless web site at *http://otn.oracle.com/tech/ wireless/index.html*.

The WDK includes the following:

- XHTML and J2ME samples
- Device detection
- Error logging
- Location services
- A wireless client
- Java messaging APIs
- Web Services

Web Services components include a J2ME SDK and a J2ME Web Services Proxy Server.

A small-footprint version of OracleAS Wireless Multi-Channel Server is provided in the WDK and enables the testing of wireless applications without requiring deployment of the full Oracle Application Server. The Multi-Channel Server is described in the later "Wireless Deployment" section. The industrial-solution version of the WDK enables developers to build applications using XForms embedded within XHTML documents and then test them in a Telnet emulator.

Figure 14-2 shows the home page for the Mobile area of the OTN, a free service for developers. The figure shows some of the mobile resources available through OTN.

My Studio

After you have created your application, you deploy it to a web server for voice or browser access, or for messaging. Applications can be deployed anywhere they are accessible from the Internet. The next step is to test your application.

Oracle provides an online testing facility, the Oracle Mobile My Studio. You can obtain My Studio from *http://studio.oraclemobile.com*.

This web site provides test facilities for voice, mobile browser, and two-way SMS. Real-time logs are generated as you test the applications that you view when debugging your application.

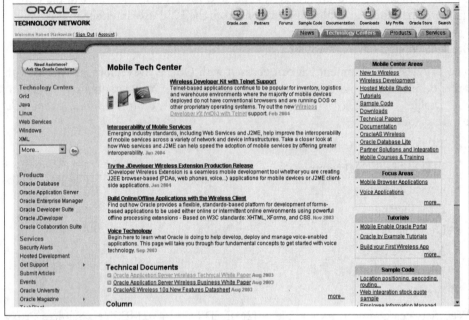

Figure 14-2. Oracle Technology Network Mobile web site

When you come to the My Studio web site for the first time, you need to register on the Welcome page. Once you are a registered user, you can log in. You will then see tabs for Applications, Samples, and Webservices (see Figure 14-3). Exploring the My Studio tabs leads you to the following:

Applications
> Provides a list of existing configured applications that you can view and test. Alternatively, you can configure new applications for voice and browser access (by providing the name and URL) or SMS and email (by providing the short name and HTTP parameters your application expects).

Samples
> Provides sample application code you can view and test.

Webservices
> Enables the registration of new J2ME Web Services and the downloading of registered hubs. Also provides a link to download the J2ME SDK.

My Studio includes online directions for how to test applications. Other online documentation provides help getting started, developing applications, and advanced topics related to voice, messaging, and J2ME Web Services. A link to the Mobile Studio Forum allows you to communicate with other OracleAS Wireless developers.

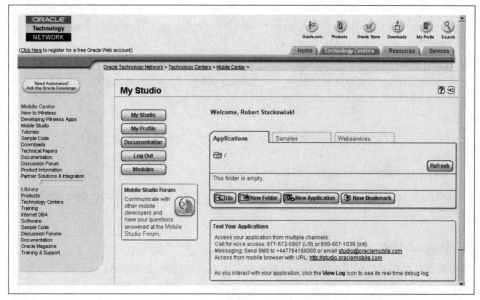

Figure 14-3. Home page for My Studio online testing of OracleAS Wireless applications

Prebuilt Wireless Applications

OracleAS Wireless provides a set of prebuilt applications that can be deployed on their own or that can serve as a starting point for building other applications. These applications are:

- Mobile Office
- Mobile Messaging
- Mobile Location

These applications are described in the following sections.

OracleAS Wireless also provides the underlying infrastructure for mobile and voice access to Oracle's Collaboration Suite and E-Business Suite.

Mobile Office

Mobile Office provides wireless, voice, and messaging applications used to access common office productivity systems. Supported systems and interfaces include:

Email
Through support of email servers supporting SMTP, POP3, or IMAP4, such as Oracle Collaboration Suite, Microsoft Exchange, and Lotus Domino

Calendar
Through support of Oracle Collaboration Suite, Oracle Calendar 5.2, and Microsoft Exchange 5.5 and 2000

Directory

Through access to a Corporate Directory deployed using the Oracle Internet Directory or any LDAP directory

Address Book

Through support of Oracle Collaboration Suite, Oracle Calendar 5.2, Microsoft 5.5 and 2000, and Lotus Domino Release 5 and 6

Tasks

Through support of Microsoft 5.5 and 2000 and Lotus Release 5 and 6

Files

Through support of WebDAV and Oracle Files

Published interfaces are available to extend the use of these applications to nonsupported systems.

Mobile Messaging

Mobile Messaging applications provide message exchange via email, SMS, MMS, voice, or fax. You can choose target destinations from address books or directory entries, or you can specify your own. Alerts and notifications can include email alerts, calendar appointment reminders and new appointments, and custom alerts using the Alert Service.

Mobile Location

Mobile Location applications are location-aware and can be deployed via wireless, voice, or messaging interfaces. These applications can provide driving directions, find nearby businesses (along with directions to those businesses), and show locations on maps.

OracleAS Wireless Deployment

OracleAS Wireless applications can be deployed for many different types of access, including wireless Internet browser, two-way ASK messaging, voice, J2ME devices, and delivery of alerts and notifications. Because of this flexibility, it is desirable to have a single application delivery via multiple channels. The Multi-Channel Server is designed specifically to meet this need.

The Multi-Channel Server delivers device-independent content based on the device's capabilities and ensures compatibility with new and emerging devices. In effect, the Multi-Channel Server provides a common interface that eliminates the need for device-specific applications. It enables the adaptation of text, images, ring tones, voice grammars, and audio/video streams for each device type. For example, if an application generates GIF images, and the device supports only Wireless BitMap (WBMP) format, the adaptation engine adapts the image to WBMP before it is sent to the device. The Multi-Channel Server also supports standard markup languages and provides the XForms engine. Devices are detected as they make requests. The Multi-Channel Server supports URL caching and can be deployed within existing portals.

Browser-based applications are developed using the OracleAS Wireless XML or XHTML languages. Data is accessed using these applications in a synchronous fashion via wireless Internet-connected devices. The typical communication protocols used for deployment include CDMA and 1xRTT; GSM with GPRS and UMTS; CDPD; Mobitex; and 802.11 a, b, and g.

Applications that access data using ASK message protocols via the Multi-Channel Server can operate in disconnected mode. Messaging devices used for an ASK application might include two-way pagers, email clients, instant messaging clients, and mobile phones with SMS. Once the Multi-Channel Server receives an incoming message, it parses the message and sends requests to applications via HTTP. OracleAS Wireless then transforms the content of the response (initially defined by XHTML tags) and matches it to message services available on the mobile device.

Voice applications respond to requests made via speech or a phone's keypad. Once a request is recognized at a voice gateway, the request is sent via HTTP to the Multi-Channel Server. From there, it is relayed to the appropriate application. When the application responds, OracleAS Wireless receives it in XML and transforms it to a user device markup language (commonly VoiceXML).

Rather than deploying to proprietary device interfaces, some developers prefer to use J2ME as the runtime environment. OracleAS Wireless makes this possible by extending Web Services to J2ME devices through a Proxy Server in the J2ME Development Kit.

Three OracleAS Wireless components are used to deliver alerts and notifications:

Data Feeder
    Retrieves alert content from a database, file, URL, or other source

Alert Engine
    Manages alert subscriptions and triggers

Multi-Channel Server
    Formats messages and delivers alerts to specified devices over appropriate channels

Security safeguards are crucial to successful mobile application deployment. In securing your applications, you must ensure the three fundamental goals of security: privacy, data integrity, and authentication:

Privacy
    You can ensure the privacy of your mobile applications by implementing appropriate encryption and decryption of data.

Data integrity
> You can ensure data integrity using various forms of digital security.

Authentication
> You can ensure authentication using digital certificates.

OracleAS Wireless Administration

You can manage OracleAS Wireless using a variety of administrative tools that are available to developers and administrators:

Service Manager
> Provides a visual interface for creating and managing OracleAS Wireless users, user groups, adapters, transformers, and services including applications, notifications, and data feeders.

System Manager
> Allows system administrators to perform configuration management and performance monitoring of the Multi-Channel Server, Asynchronous Listener (a preprocessor of asynchronous requests inside the OracleAS Wireless runtime server process), Location-based Service Provider (providing the actual computation for location services), and standalone OracleAS Wireless processes. These processes include the Notification Engine, the Messaging Server (dispatching application invocation requests and responses), and the Location Event Server (generating events based on location). The System Manager is accessible via the Application Server Control tool and through Oracle Enterprise Manager. See Chapter 3 for a discussion of these management tools.

Content Manager
> Enables the creation of application categories, access points, and bookmarks.

Foundation Manager
> Used by "Foundation" developers to create, modify, and delete devices, transformers, regions, digital rights policies, and API scan policies.

User Manager
> Used to edit user profiles, reset PINs and passwords, manage user access and user devices, and view user application links.

Wireless Customization Portal
> Allows users to register with OracleAS Wireless to personalize their own applications and manage their personal profiles. Users can create their own accounts and manage their devices, locations, and contact rules.

CHAPTER 15

Integration Components

Within your organization, you may have a mixture of business applications based on various technologies deployed in different areas of the business. You may also need to share data and business processes with other organizations and partners. To allow you to successfully manage the entire business, such disparate systems must be able to access and share business processes, data, and services. An integration strategy is key to making effective use of these resources.

Oracle Application Server integration components provide the framework needed to bring together such resources in a variety of ways:

- Enterprise Application Integration (EAI) is enabled through collaborative interaction between applications.

- Business-to-business (B2B) collaboration is enabled by an exchange of documents among "trading partners," two parties that take part in a business transaction. Oracle sometimes refers to this scenario as *OracleAS PartnerConnect*.

- Web Services integration enables business processes to incorporate Web Services present in local networks or externally over the Internet.

This Oracle Application Server integration framework allows you to establish a common view of data and business processes by providing these capabilities.

Two specific integration platforms are provided in Oracle Application Server 10*g*:

Oracle Application Server InterConnect
> OracleAS InterConnect, available since the Oracle9*i*AS application server, provides high-speed message exchange (e.g., exchange of hundreds of messages per second) via brokers that are available for a variety of applications, queuing mechanisms, and data movement protocols.

Oracle Application Server ProcessConnect
> An addition to Oracle Application Server 10*g*, OracleAS ProcessConnect enables business process integration and automation through the use of J2EE Connector Architecture-based adapters.

OracleAS InterConnect is most commonly used for database-to-database (data) integration or application-to-application integration (EAI). It can synchronize data through transformations involving multiple trading partners.

OracleAS ProcessConnect provides a single middleware software solution targeted for business process integration within an enterprise or with trading partners. This platform can enable Business Activity Monitoring (BAM) through the retrieval of such runtime data as the number and status of activities and the current state of an integration object. Business Process Optimization (BPO) reports can also be produced, indicating business process efficiency (e.g., fulfillment completion time).

> BAM is the aggregation and correlation of data from many sources to produce key performance indicators (KPIs). The KPIs can provide business advisories or to trigger specific business processes designed to improve business results when predefined threshold values are reached. This automatic triggering of business processes is called Business Process Optimization.

An alternative to using OracleAS ProcessConnect for defining and deploying business processes and events is to use a combination of OracleAS InterConnect with Oracle Workflow. The InterConnect iStudio tool provides a single interface to build such processes. An Oracle Workflow for Java (OW4J) engine, introduced with Oracle Application Server 10g, complements the PL/SQL-based Oracle Workflow engine previously available with the Oracle database. OW4J enables Oracle Workflow deployment to the middle tier. It also supports the execution of methods in Java classes, EJBs, and Web Services.

This chapter describes the various integration facilities available with Oracle Application Server: OracleAS ProcessConnect, OracleAS InterConnect, iStudio, and Oracle Workflow for Java. It also outlines some sample deployment sequences for business process integration.

Oracle Application Server InterConnect

You can use OracleAS InterConnect to integrate applications from Oracle, other software providers, or custom-built applications using message-oriented middleware. OracleAS InterConnect enables integration through modeling rather than relying on extensive programming techniques. Integration logic is separate from the integration platform. OracleAS InterConnect components include a hub, adapters, and a Development Kit. Figure 15-1 shows a typical deployment configuration.

The OracleAS InterConnect design and modeling tool, called iStudio, features easy-to-use wizards. Intended for use by business analysts, iStudio largely eliminates the need to write code when creating business rules and transformation integration logic. Users of iStudio can define and map data to be exchanged between applications, and can configure and deploy the integration. Objects can be locked within the tool, thus

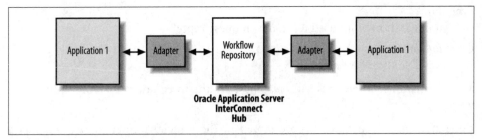

Figure 15-1. Typical OracleAS InterConnect deployment

enabling multiple users to model and design simultaneously. OracleAS InterConnect supports metadata versioning so that multiple versions of the same object can coexist or be active at the same time. If business process collaboration is desired, Oracle Workflow can define the business processes. The *i*Studio tool is then used to associate semantic maps with these business processes.

Components connected with OracleAS InterConnect and created in *i*Studio are called *application views*. Application views include interest in specific messages, internal datatype identification, and information on how a message should be mapped to or from an internal datatype. A *common view* is a hub view in which each spoke is an application view participating in the integration. Figure 15-2 shows the hub-and-spoke nature of OracleAS InterConnect deployment between the common view and application views.

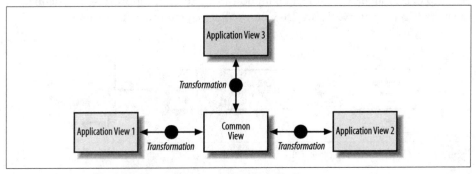

Figure 15-2. Typical OracleAS InterConnect hub and spoke

Common views can contain the following components:

Business objects
> A collection of logically related integration points—logical occurrences that trigger communications between applications

Event
> An integration point used to model "publish and subscribe"

Procedure
> An integration point used to model "request/reply"

Common datatype
> Data definition for reuse

Transformations, sometimes call *mappings*, are the integration points to application views.

Generated models and designs are stored in the OracleAS InterConnect metadata repository, which is part of a hub. At runtime, the metadata repository is the source of instructions enabling message exchange to occur. Runtime management, which is handled through Oracle Enterprise Manager, includes such management tasks as:

- Starting and stopping components
- Monitoring message flow
- Performing problem detection
- Handling error management

OracleAS InterConnect Adapters and Messages

OracleAS InterConnect Adapters provide connectivity via a bridge, the protocol/application-specific portion of the adapter. The adapters transform and route messages between an application and the hub. Data is transformed from application views to common views and from common views to application views, as defined in the metadata repository. Figure 15-3 shows the architecture of an adapter.

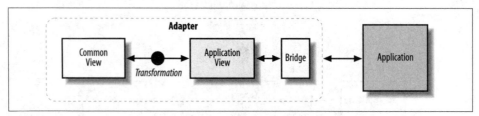

Figure 15-3. OracleAS InterConnect Adapter architecture

A number of prepackaged OracleAS InterConnect adapters are available, including:

Technology Adapters
> These adapters are used in cases where endpoints don't have APIs. They include Oracle database, Oracle AQ, MQSeries, HTTP/S, SMTP, FTP, and CICS.

Packaged Application Adapters
> These adapters are used to integrate JD Edwards, PeopleSoft, SAP, and Siebel applications.

Adapter SDK

The SDK enables the creation of adapters for applications and protocols that aren't supported by other adapters. The kit is a collection of Java JAR and Javadoc files.

Messages are commonly communicated using database adapters, Oracle AQ, or XML messaging, or through the Data Definition Description Language (D3L). All OracleAS InterConnect messages are guaranteed to be delivered exactly once in the order sent. Messages can be load-balanced across multiple adapters using Real Application Clusters (RAC), a clustered Oracle database configuration. Routing of messages can be implemented using business rules based on message content.

> Interfaces to Oracle's E-Business Suite of Applications are typically via database access to the Oracle Applications interface tables or through an XML gateway (as XML is supported in several of the technology adapters). Interfaces can be created to Oracle's CRM application via SOAP and to Oracle's Supply Chain applications via the Supply Chain Trading Connector (SCTC).

OracleAS InterConnect supports two distinct models:

Publish and subscribe

With this model, applications may be subscribers. These subscribers receive messages whenever they are published by specific applications. When this model is used, the publishing application doesn't expect a reply.

Request/reply

Alternatively, an application may publish a message and expect a reply either in synchronous mode (the message can't be received until the reply is sent) or asynchronous mode (the reply is sent after message reception).

Both publish and subscribe and request/reply messaging can behave in a point-to-point manner if the sending application calls out which specific application should receive a message.

Values in one application can be mapped to equivalent values in another application by defining domain value maps using *i*Studio. Keys for corresponding entities in two different applications can also be correlated using *i*Studio.

*i*Studio Interface

The interface in the *i*Studio modeling and design tool consists of two navigation trees for design and deployment, as well as five main menus.

Here are the navigation trees:

Design Navigation Tree
> Groups objects as Common Views, Applications, Workflow, and Enabling Infrastructure

Deploy Navigation Tree
> Groups objects as Applications or Workflow

The menus include:

File Menu
> Handles creating and opening existing projects and workspaces, project reloading, object creation and migration, export of PL/SQL stubs, and metadata push to adapters

Edit Menu
> Handles editing, copying, deleting, versioning, or loading objects, renaming applications, adding or removing applications from domain value maps or cross-reference tables, and deploying events to or editing Workflow configurations

Procedure Menu
> Handles invoking or implementing procedures via wizards

Event Menu
> Handles publishing or subscribing to events via wizards

Help Menu
> Handles access to the *iStudio User's Guide*

Figure 15-4 shows a typical view of the *iStudio* interface and the Design Navigation Tree.

Oracle Workflow for Java

The Oracle Workflow for Java (OW4J) engine can be used with OracleAS InterConnect to enable business process definition, automation, and integration. Oracle Workflow for Java enables execution of a sequence of events in a specific order. You can view the progress of processes through these sequences via either monitors or notification methods (for example, JMS messages and email). The following components are part of OW4J:

Workflow Builder
> Provides a graphical business process-modeling tool

Workflow Engine
> Manages business process execution and exception handling

Business Event System
> Provides a Java API for propagating events

Process Monitor
> Used to view and administer events

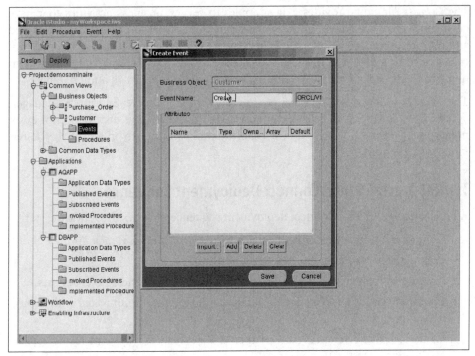

Figure 15-4. Typical iStudio interface

Directory Service

Enables OracleAS Single Sign-On, synchronization with the Oracle Internet Directory, and integration with LDAP

Workflow Manager

Monitors system metrics and processes, and configures and monitors notification mailers

Business process models are typically created using the JDeveloper OW4J Modeler as the *Workflow Builder*. Business processes might be either short or long. Very short business processes are served by in-memory workflows. Long-lived tasks may extend to weeks and beyond.

Version numbers are automatically assigned to workflow tasks, thus enabling different versions of activities.

Models of these processes can be built to include logic for looping, branching into parallel flows and rendezvous, decomposing into subflows, branching into subtasks, and others. Escalation processes can be created and then executed after periods of inactivity based on predefined rules. Notification routing can also be set up to handle typical occurrences such as delegation of responsibility or rerouting during absence of a participant.

The *Process Monitor* provides a Java applet to review business activities that have been completed, are active, or are yet to be initiated. Decision makers are identified and their responses are shown. Administrators can intervene to explore stopped processes or to skip or retry processes. It is possible to review the time and cost of business processes by exploring workflow processing data stored in an audit database.

The *Workflow Manager* interface is exposed through Oracle Enterprise Manager. Work items and event messages can be viewed (including the distribution of event messages by status). This interface enables administrators to more quickly determine business bottlenecks.

Typical OracleAS InterConnect Deployment Sequence

A typical OracleAS InterConnect deployment sequence includes the following steps:

1. Configure a source triggering mechanism (such as through Oracle AQ).
2. Create a new project in *i*Studio.
3. Create common view business objects in *i*Studio and business object events.
4. Create an *i*Studio application in which an adapter communicates with a business application.
5. Create a cross-reference table mapping keys between systems using *i*Studio applications.
6. Create published events in *i*Studio that map application views to common views, perform transformations, and publish new events to subscribers.
7. Subscribe applications to events in *i*Studio.
8. Create content-based routing in *i*Studio if required (e.g., routing based on message or message header contents via Oracle Workflow with appropriate applied business logic).
9. Create an Oracle Workflow process bundle in *i*Studio if business logic is to be applied (including a bundle name, business process, and publish-and-subscribe activities), and then deploy it.
10. Create objects in Oracle Workflow for modeling, and then model business logic.
11. Deploy application queues in *i*Studio, and test the integration prior to final production deployment.

Oracle Application Server ProcessConnect

The linkage of business data or systems leveraged in a corporate business activity is known as Business Process Integration (BPI). OracleAS ProcessConnect is designed to enable BPI through a single middleware service. Integration can extend beyond internal business processes to suppliers, partners, and customers. The Oracle BAM and BPO capabilities described earlier in this chapter are designed to leverage either OracleAS InterConnect or the newer OracleAS ProcessConnect.

 Oracle Corporation expects that OracleAS ProcessConnect will increasingly be used in situations in which OracleAS InterConnect with Oracle Workflow was previously the only choice and where adherence to a Java connector standard is desirable.

In building integrated business processes, the following OracleAS ProcessConnect concepts are especially important:

Profiles
> Contain identification and contact information

Parties
> Contain organizations within a profile (typically applications or trading partners) that participate in B2B exchanges

Agreements
> Contain specific collaborations, roles, and communications options describing how two parties will interact

Events
> Contain internal definitions of business data that come from or are sent to a party, including header information on the party from which the event is coming, information on the party to which to send the event, event instance creation time, instance life cycle state, event type definition, and body elements

In BPI implementations, message exchange and data flow (defined as data passed as an event) must be in the correct sequence. Translations and transformations must be recognizable, and data must be validated. Roles define how data flow events are executed. Figure 15-5 shows a typical OracleAS ProcessConnect flow with adapter interactions.

Data in the form of messages is received from a party as an Oracle *record*. When OracleAS ProcessConnect receives this record, it creates two events:

Native event
> Provides an internal representation of the business data

Application event
> Provides a translation of native event content in a format that can be interpreted by the OracleAS ProcessConnect

To enable better scalability, a business event can establish a common structure and vocabulary between parties. As transformations then take place to and from common business events, the number of transformations required is greatly reduced because all parties can use the business event as a starting point. This efficiency becomes pronounced when four or more parties exist.

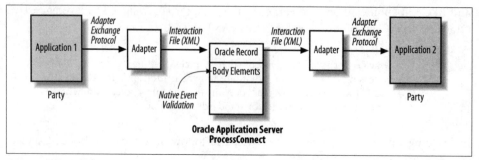

Figure 15-5. OracleAS ProcessConnect adapter interactions

OracleAS ProcessConnect integration projects generally use either an adapter-centric methodology or a business process-centric methodology for development:

Adapter-centric
   With this methodology, you model capabilities of parties, adapters, and delivery channels before creating roles or business processes.

Business process-centric
   This methodology starts with roles and business process modeling.

In general, Oracle suggests that you choose the methodology that creates the more complex portion of the model first. We describe the OracleAS ProcessConnect modeling tool in the next section and then delineate typical steps taken in development using each methodology.

Using OracleAS ProcessConnect

The following OracleAS ProcessConnect components are used to build, deploy, and maintain a business process integration infrastructure:

Modeling tool
   An easy-to-use, web-based business-process modeling tool designed to support the complete life cycle management of BPI, from modeling to deployment to monitoring and optimization

Metadata Repository
   An OracleAS ProcessConnect metamodel schema in the OracleAS Infrastructure database

OC4J ProcessConnect
   An OracleAS ProcessConnect component that instantiates the modeling tool and is used by the modeling tool to read and write integration definitions in the metadata repository

Adapter Framework (AF)

A J2EE connector architecture framework engine that enables Java applications to read the business process definitions from the runtime metadata repository to adapters and vice versa

Integration Manager (IM)

An event-driven business process execution engine that interfaces to AF

The modeling tool provides a modeling interface to design business processes and to enable business event modeling for common content. The profile section of the tool enables endpoint modeling (*endpoints* are defined as the physical addresses of trading partners), agreement definitions, and trading partner management. Wizards guide you through end-to-end basic integration, adding end-to-end basic event flows and other event flows, and creating spokes. Version control of integration objects is supported through an update facility.

Parties (e.g., applications or trading partners) are included in the integration through the use of adapters. The adapters can be defined using an adapter exchange protocol for specific tasks or can call specific actionable files. There are three types of OracleAS ProcessConnect adapters:

Technology adapters

HTTP, SMTP, FTP, Oracle database, Oracle AQ, JMS, and Web Services

Packaged application adapters

JD Edwards, PeopleSoft, SAP, and Siebel

Legacy adapters

CICS, IMS/DB, IMS/TM, and Tuxedo

Unlike the older OracleAS InterConnect adapters, OracleAS ProcessConnect adapters are built to the J2EE Connector Architecture 1.0 specification with extensions to support introspection. Figure 15-6 shows how to select an adapter for use with a specific application (or party) through the modeling tool.

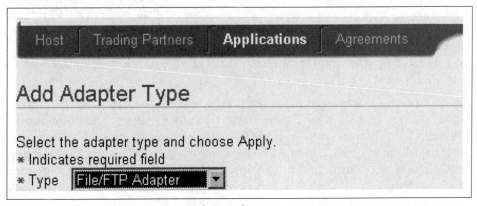

Figure 15-6. OracleAS ProcessConnect adapter selection

Oracle's E-Business Suite of Applications can be integrated using Database Adapter connectivity to Oracle Applications interface tables, AQ Adapter connectivity with linkage to the Application Business Event System, or Web Service Adapter connectivity in which J2EE-based modules are deployed as Servlets or Business Components for Java.

A deployment section in the modeling tool provides final validation of process integration definitions (e.g., processes and profiles). Once validated, the tool can deploy the configuration from the design-time repository to a runtime repository.

The deployment engine supports numerous standards, including:

- B2B standards (RosettaNet and AS2)
- EDI standards (X.12, UN/EDIFACT)
- Web Services
- SOAP
- WSDL
- UDDI
- Internet transports (HTTP/S, SMTP, FTP/S)
- Packaging standards (SOAP 1.1, SMIME 3.0)
- Security standards (LDAP, X.509)
- Trading partner management (CPP/CPA, TPAML)

 RosettaNet, created by a group of technology companies, defines XML-based e-business standards for the exchange of business documents including transport, routing, packaging, security, signals, and trading partner agreements.

All actions in the modeling tool are captured in a metadata repository via OC4J ProcessConnect. The repository stores definition models, the results from monitoring of runtime processes, and administrative actions. An export/import utility enables movement of integration model objects from one repository to another, which is a typical procedure when moving from development to production. The object definitions are exported in XML.

Business processes are triggered in reaction to events. Such event triggers might include a state change in a business document, multiple business event communications, certain integration event behavior, or certain event stages such as initiation, progress, and completion. Events are created through the modeling tool or by import of XML schemas. Event services supported include event validation, translation (from one format to another), transformation (e.g., semantics such as one-to-many), mapping where events are similar, and correlation.

The Integration Diagram viewer shows a high-level view of the entire process integration. Pictured in such a view or diagram (see Figure 15-7 as an example) is the business process, other roles ("spokes"), all the endpoint parties participating in the process at every spoke, and agreements in place between endpoints (trading partners) and processes. From this view, you can drill down to a specific event flow diagram.

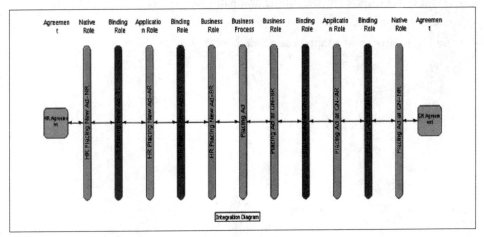

Figure 15-7. OracleAS ProcessConnect Integration Diagram

When run concurrently, events and activities must use different business processes. Real-time monitoring of business events and activities takes place in a reports section of the tool. The administrative section can be linked to Oracle Enterprise Manager for configuration and management tasks.

Typical Deployment Sequences

As we noted earlier, the approaches that Oracle recommends for business process integration using OracleAS ProcessConnect vary depending on the complexity of the business processes. Oracle typically suggests an adapter-centric approach in situations in which business processes are relatively simple, there are a small number of parties, and endpoint details are known.

The adapter-centric approach typically involves using the modeling tool in the following sequence:

1. Create applications, and add adapter details for each party.
2. Create native and application events, and select translators for each party.
3. Create roles, transformations, business events, and business processes for each party.
4. Create agreements between parties.
5. Create, deploy, test, and validate the configuration before production.

When more complex business processes are involved, BPI developers use a business process-centric approach. This approach includes the following steps, in this order:

1. Manually create a business process and business event.
2. Create native and application events and select translators for each party.
3. Use the create spoke wizard in the modeling tool.
4. Create the parties.
5. Add translators and adapters as needed.

Additional Resources

In this concise volume, we've attempted to give you a firm grounding in all the basic concepts you need to understand Oracle Application Server 10g and begin to use it effectively. We hope we've accomplished this goal.

At the same time, we realize that there is more to using a complex product such as Oracle Application Server than simply understanding how and why it works the way it does. Although you can't use Oracle Application Server without a firm grasp of the foundations of the product, you still need details if you're actually going to implement a successful system.

This appendix lists two types of additional sources of information for the topics covered in this book—relevant web sites, which act as a constantly changing resource for a variety of information, and a chapter-by-chapter list of relevant books, articles, and Oracle documentation.

For the chapter-by-chapter list, the sources fall into two basic categories: Oracle documentation (both manuals and white papers) and third-party sources. Typically, the Oracle documentation provides the type of hands-on information you will need regarding syntax and keywords, and the third-party sources cover the topics in a more general and problem-solving way. We've listed the third-party sources first and ended each listing with the relevant Oracle documentation. Please keep in mind that Oracle Application Server isn't nearly as established or popular a product as the Oracle database, so there aren't as many sources of third-party information for the product at this time.

Most Oracle documentation is available at the Oracle Technology Network web site (*http://www.otn.oracle.com*). Because the locations of specific documents are likely to change over time, we haven't provided specific URLs for all documents. To find a particular document, your best bet is to go to the OTN web site and use the Search option to see if it is available there.

Web Sites

Oracle Corporation—http://www.oracle.com
> The home of the company. Contains the latest information and marketing, as well as some good technical and packaging information.

Oracle Technology Network—http://otn.oracle.com
> The focal point of Oracle Corporation's attempt to reach a wider audience of developers. You can find tons of stuff at the OTN, including low-cost developer versions or free downloads of most Oracle software and lots of information and discussion forums. You can also sign up for specific technology tracks here. The home page for information on Oracle Application Server is *http://www.oracle.com/appserver/books/*.

International Oracle Users Group (IOUG)—http://www.ioug.org
> The International Oracle Users Group web site. Includes information on meetings, links to Oracle resources, a technical repository, discussion forums, and special interest groups.

Apache— http://apache.org
> The Apache site. Contains the Apache Web Server, XML Parser implementations, XSLT implementations, XML-RPC and SOAP Web Service implementations, and much, much more.

OASIS—http://www.uddi.org
> The web site for the Universal Description, Discovery, and Integration standards consortium. Contains information on the UDDI protocol—a major building block for Web Services—and related standards.

O'Reilly Media—http://www.oreilly.com
> The O'Reilly Media web site. Contains information about good books on all kinds of web-related technologies, Oracle technologies, and other technologies. See also *http://safari.oreilly.com* for online books and *http://oreillynet.com* for a variety of specific technology sites (e.g., Apache, Java, XML).

The Server Side—http:// www.theserverside.com
> The Enterprise Java community web site. Although this site is typically focused on other products, you can pick up a tip or two about Oracle Application Server and Java programming here.

World Wide Web Consortium—http://w3c.org
> The web site for the original web standards, including HTTP, HTML, DOM, and CSS, and the locale for ongoing web standardization activity.

Books and Oracle Documentation

The following books and Oracle documentation provide additional information for each chapter in this book.

Chapter 1, Introducing Oracle Application Server

Bakken, David E. *Encyclopedia of Distributed Computing (Middleware entry)*, Kluwer Academic Press.

Byous, Jon, *Java Technology: An Early History*. Sun Microsystems. *http://java.sun.com/features/1998/05/birthday.html*.

Garmany, John and Donald Burleson, *Oracle Application Server 10g Administration Handbook*, McGraw-Hill Osborne Media.

Greenwald, Rick, Robert Stackowiak, and Jonathan Stern, *Oracle Essentials: Oracle Database 10g*. O'Reilly Media, Inc.

MiddleAware, *http://www.middleware.net* (contains the history of Tuxedo and other middleware components)

Oracle Application Server 10g Concepts, Oracle Corporation.

Oracle Application Server 10g: Grid Computing, An Oracle White Paper, Oracle Corporation.

Oracle Application Server 10g: New Features Overview, A Technical White Paper, Oracle Corporation.

Oracle9i Application Server Release 2 New Features, An Oracle White Paper, Oracle Corporation.

Oracle9iAS Infrastructure, An Oracle Technical White Paper, Oracle Corporation.

Oracle Application Server 10g FAQ, Oracle Corporation. *http://otn.oracle.com/products/ias/htdocs/as10gfaq.html*.

Chapter 2, Architecture

Aliminati, Janga, *9iAS Enterprise Architecture: Architecture Design and Creating Multiple Portals, Wireless, UltraSearch and SSO Tiers*, Oracle Corporation.

Oracle Application Server 10g Advanced Topologies for Enterprise Deployment (9.0.4), Oracle Corporation.

Oracle Application Server 10g Concepts 10g (9.0.4), Oracle Corporation.

Oracle Application Server 10g High Availability Guide 10g (9.0.4), Oracle Corporation.

Oracle Application Server Containers for J2EE Services Guide 10g (9.0.4), Oracle Corporation.

Oracle Application Server Web Cache Administrator's Guide 10g (9.0.4), Oracle Corporation.

Oracle HTTP Server Administrator's Guide 10g (9.0.4), Oracle Corporation.

Chapter 3, Systems Management

Application Service Level Management, Oracle Data Sheet, Oracle Corporation, 2003, *http://otn.oracle.com/products/oem/pdf/DATASHEET_ADSP_0_4.pdf*.

Managing the Oracle Application Server with Oracle Enterprise Manager 10g, An Oracle White Paper, Oracle Corporation.

Oracle9i Application Server: Backup and Recovery, An Oracle White Paper, Oracle Corporation.

Oracle Application Server 10g Administrator's Guide, Oracle Corporation.

Oracle Application Server 10g Concepts 10g (9.0.4), Oracle Corporation.

Oracle Application Server Management: Managing the Application Server with Oracle Enterprise Manager 10g, Oracle Data Sheet, Oracle Corporation.

Oracle Enterprise Manager Advanced Configuration, Oracle Corporation.

Oracle Enterprise Manager Concepts, Oracle Corporation.

Oracle Enterprise Manager EM2Go, Feature Overview, Oracle Corporation.

Oracle Enterprise Manager Grid Control Installation and Basic Configuration, Oracle Corporation.

Chapter 4, Security and Identity Management

Oracle Application Server 10g Security, Oracle Corporation. *http://otn.oracle.com/products/id_mgmt/osso/htdocs/oracleas_security_10g_fov.html*.

Oracle Application Server 10g Security Guide, Oracle Corporation.

Oracle9i Application Server Architecting for Security, Oracle Corporation.

Oracle Application Server Certificate Authority 10g. An Oracle White Paper, Oracle Corporation. *http://otn.oracle.com/products/id_mgmt/oca/pdf/oracleas_certificate_authority_10g_wp.pdf*.

Oracle Identity Management Concepts and Architecture. An Oracle White Paper, Oracle Corporation. *http://otn.oracle.com/products/id_mgmt/pdf/OracleAS_IDmanagement_10g_TWP.pdf*.

Oracle Internet Directory, Technical White Paper, Oracle Corporation. *http://otn.oracle.com/products/oid/htdocs/oidwp9iAS2.pdf*.

Oracle Internet Directory Features Overview, Oracle Corporation. *http://otn.oracle.com/products/oid/htdocs/oid_overview/oidfov9iASv2.html*.

Oracle Internet Directory: User Provisioning Integration, Oracle Corporation. *http://otn.oracle.com/products/ias/daily/jan29.html*.

Pepper, Jason, *Worried about Security and Scalability? Not with Oracle9iAS Portal Release 2*, Oracle Corporation.

Chapter 5, Oracle HTTP Server

Bowen, Rich, *Apache Administrator's Handbook*, Sams Publishing.

Oracle HTTP Server Administrator's Guide 10g (9.0.4), Oracle Corporation.

Overview of Oracle HTTP Server Components, Oracle Corporation. *http://otn.oracle.com/products/ias/ohs/htdocs/OHS-904-TWP.pdf*.

Young, Geoffrey and Paul Linder and Randy Kobes, *mod_perl Developer's Cookbook*, Sams Publishing.

Chapter 6, Oracle Application Server Containers for J2EE

Oracle Application Server 10g Multimedia Tag Library for JSP User's Guide and Reference 10g (9.0.4), Oracle Corporation.

Oracle Application Server Containers for J2EE Enterprise JavaBeans Developer's Guide 10g (9.0.4), Oracle Corporation.

Oracle Application Server Containers for J2EE JSP Tag Libraries and Utilities Reference 10g (9.0.4), Oracle Corporation.

Oracle Application Server Containers for J2EE Security Guide 10g (9.0.4), Oracle Corporation.

Oracle Application Server Containers for J2EE Servlet Developer's Guide 10g (9.0.4), Oracle Corporation.

Oracle Application Server Containers for J2EE Services Guide 10g (9.0.4), Oracle Corporation.

Oracle Application Server Containers for J2EE Support for JavaServer Pages Developer's Guide 10g (9.0.4), Oracle Corporation.

Oracle Application Server Containers for J2EE User's Guide 10g (9.0.4), Oracle Corporation.

Chapter 7, Caching

Oracle Application Server Containers for J2EE JSP Tag Libraries and Utilities Reference 10g (9.0.4), Oracle Corporation.

Oracle Application Server Containers for J2EE Services Guide 10g (9.0.4), Oracle Corporation.

Chapter 8, Java Development

Bales, Donald, *Java Programming with Oracle JDBC*, O'Reilly.

Bales, Donald, *JDBC Pocket Reference*, O'Reilly.

Bergsten, Hans, *JavaServer Pages*, O'Reilly.

Hunter, Jason and William Crawford, *Java Servlet Programming*, O'Reilly.

Monson-Haefel, Richard, *Enterprise JavaBeans*, O'Reilly.

Monson-Haefel, Richard and David A. Chappell, *Java Message Service*, O'Reilly.

Oaks, Scott, *Java Security*, O'Reilly.

Oracle Application Server TopLink Application Developer's Guide 10g (9.0.4), Oracle Corporation.

Oracle Application Server TopLink Getting Started Guide 10g (9.0.4), Oracle Corporation.

Oracle Application Server TopLink Mapping Workbench User's Guide 10g (9.0.4), Oracle Corporation.

Oracle Business Components for Java Developing Business Components 10g (9.0.4), Oracle Corporation.

Chapter 9, Oracle Development

Callan, Steve, "Installation Cookbook: Installing Oracle Application Server 10g Forms and Report Services," *Database Journal. http://www.databasejournal.com/features/oracle/article.php/3322591*.

Enterprise Data Publishing with Oracle Reports: Any Data, Any Format, Anywhere, Oracle Corporation.

Oracle9iAS Reports Services Scalability, An Oracle White Paper, Oracle Corporation.

Oracle Application Server 10g Performance Guide 10g (9.0.4), Oracle Corporation.

Oracle Application Server Forms Services Deployment Guide 10g (9.0.4), Oracle Corporation.

Oracle Application Server Reports Services Publishing Reports to The Web 10g (9.0.4), Oracle Corporation.

Oracle Reports 10g New Features, An Oracle White Paper, Oracle Corporation.

Chapter 10, XML Development

Harold, Elliot Rusty and W. Scott Means, *XML in a Nutshell*, O'Reilly.

Oracle Application Developer's Guide—XML 10g (9.0.4), Oracle Corporation.

Oracle XML Reference 10g (9.0.4), Oracle Corporation.

Chapter 11, Web Services

Chappell, David A., and Tyler Jewell, *Java Web Services*, O'Reilly.

Cerami, Ethan, *Web Services Essentials*, O'Reilly.

St. Laurent, Simon, Joe Johnston, and Edd Dumbill, *Programming Web Services with XML-RPC*, O'Reilly.

Snell, James, Doug Tidwell, and Pavel Kulchenko, *Programming Web Services with SOAP*, O'Reilly.

Oracle Application Server Web Services Developer's Guide 10g (9.0.4), Oracle Corporation.

Chapter 12, Business Intelligence Components

Enterprise Data Publishing with Oracle Reports: Any Data, Any Format, Anywhere, Oracle Corporation.

Leveraging Oracle Database Features with Oracle Reports: Business Intelligence, Oracle Reports Technical Note, Oracle Corporation.

Leveraging Oracle Database Features with Oracle Reports: Virtual Private Database, Oracle Reports Technical Note, Oracle Corporation.

Oracle9i Application Server: Business Intelligence Technical Overview, An Oracle White Paper, Oracle Corporation.

Oracle9iAS Discoverer: Best Practices for Release 1.0.2.2, An Oracle White Paper, Oracle Corporation.

Oracle9iAS Discoverer Integration with Oracle9iAS Portal, An Oracle White Paper, Oracle Corporation.

Oracle9iAS Discoverer Version 4.1 Capacity Planning Guide, An Oracle White Paper, Oracle Corporation.

Oracle9iAS Reports Services Scalability, An Oracle White Paper, Oracle Corporation.

Oracle Application Server 10g Concepts (Chapter 5), Oracle Corporation.

Oracle Application Server Discoverer 10g, An Oracle White Paper, Oracle Corporation.

Oracle Application Server Discoverer Plus Tutorial 10g, Oracle Corporation.

Oracle Application Server Discoverer Plus User's Guide 10g, Oracle Corporation.

Oracle Application Server Reports Services, Publishing Reports to the Web, Oracle Corporation.

Oracle Discoverer Administrator, Administration Guide 10g, Oracle Corporation.

Oracle Discoverer EUL Command Line for Java, An Oracle White Paper, Oracle Corporation.

Oracle Reports 10g New Features, An Oracle White Paper, Oracle Corporation.

Chapter 13, Oracle Application Server Portal

Getting Started With Oracle Application Server Portal, Oracle Corporation.

Greenwald, Rick and Milbery, Jim, *Oracle9iAS Portal Bible*, John Wiley & Sons.

Oracle Application Server Portal Configuration Guide 10g (9.0.4), Oracle Corporation.

Oracle Application Server Portal User's Guide 10g (9.0.4), Oracle Corporation.

Chapter 14, Oracle Application Server Wireless

Oracle9iAS Wireless: Creating a Mobilized Business, An Oracle White Paper, Oracle Corporation.

Oracle Application Server 10g Concepts (Chapter 4), Oracle Corporation.

Oracle Application Server Wireless Administrator's Guide 10g, Oracle Corporation.

Oracle Application Server Wireless: Complete Mobile Platform, An Oracle Technical White Paper, Oracle Corporation.

Oracle Application Server Wireless Developer's Guide 10g, Oracle Corporation.

Oracle Application Server Wireless: Messaging Services, An Oracle Technical White Paper, Oracle Corporation.

Chapter 15, Integration Components

Introducing Oracle Workflow for Java, Oracle Workflow Team, Oracle Corporation.

Oracle Application Server 10g Concepts (Chapter 6), Oracle Corporation.

Oracle Application Server 10g InterConnect, An Oracle Technical White Paper, Oracle Corporation.

Oracle Application Server 10g ProcessConnect, An Oracle White Paper, Oracle Corporation.

Oracle Application Server InterConnect User's Guide 10g, Oracle Corporation.

Oracle Application Server Integration Product Overview, An Oracle Technical White Paper, Oracle Corporation.

Oracle Application Server ProcessConnect User's Guide 10g, Oracle Corporation.

Oracle Workflow Administrator's Guide, Oracle Corporation.

Oracle Workflow User's Guide, Oracle Corporation.

Oracle Workflow with J2EE Components, An Oracle Technical White Paper, Oracle Corporation.

Index

We'd like to hear your suggestions for improving our indexes. Send email to *index@oreilly.com*.

APIs (application programming interfaces)
  Java, 118
  Oracle Application Server, 127
  Reports Services API, 140
applets, 120
application adapters, 222
application components, Oracle Application
    Server, 9
application deployment, 85–86
  J2EE, 85
  OC4J, 86
Application Development Framework
    (ADF), 126
application event (OracleAS
    ProcessConnect), 227
application scope (cached objects), 115
Application Server Configuration
    Management Pack, 48
Application Server Control, 14, 22, 39–42
  accessing, username and password, 50
  administering J2EE, 42
  administering OC4J application
      clusters, 42
  configuring Forms Services, 134
  home page, 40
  management stack, 41
  managing ports, 41
  security management activities, 63
  viewing and managing log
      information, 41
  viewing Log Repository error logs, 190
Application Server Diagnostics Pack, 48
application servers, history of, 2
Application Servers, Oracle
  application components, 9
  applications, 35–37
    business intelligence, 36
    OracleAS Portal, 35
    OracleAS Wireless, 36
  components, additional, 11
  core components, 8
  description of editions, 7
  download site for software, xiv
  Enterprise Edition, 7
  family of products, 6
  functionality, 1
  managing, 14
  Oracle Application Server 10g, 1
    grid computing, 5
  Oracle Enterprise Manager, mobile
      version (EM2Go), 15

Standard Edition, 7
  XML, use by components, 157
Application Service Level Management
    (ASLM), 39
  Application Server Diagnostics Pack, 48
application service level management (ASLM)
  tools available to Grid Control, 46
Application Service Level Management
    (ASLM), Oracle Enterprise
    Manager, 108
application views, 221
  transformations, 222
application.xml file, 85
AQ (Advanced Queueing), Oracle, 81
ASLM (see Application Service Level
    Management)
asynchronous messaging, 81
attributes (OracleAS Portal objects), 197
authentication
  Java Authentication and Authorization
      Service (see JAAS)
  multilevel, OracleAS Single Sign-On, 59
  Oracle Application Server, 51, 55
  Web Services, 173
authorization
  Java Authentication and Authorization
      Service (see JAAS)
  Oracle Application Server services, 55
  Web Services, 173
availability
  of an application server, 31–35
  of web-based applications, 46

B

B2B (business-to-business)
    collaboration, 219
backup and recovery, 48–50
  backups, types of, 49
  complete backup of Oracle Application
      Server environment, 49
  using Oracle Application Server backups
      for recovery, 50
Backup and Recovery Tool, OracleAS, 50
BAM (Business Activity Monitoring), 220
BC4J (Oracle Business Components for
    Java), 7
bean-managed persistence (BMP), 75
  mapping EJBs to relational
      databases, 126
bean-managed transactions (BMT), 75, 80
Beans wizard (Oracle JDeveloper), 10

BEEP (Blocks Extensible Exchange Protocol), 162
BI Beans (Business Intelligence JavaBeans), 175, 185
BI (see business intelligence components)
BIG-IP hardware load balancer (F5 Networks), 29
bind-params attribute (XSQL Pages tags), 156
block names (Java objects in Web Object Cache), 114
  implicit and explicit, 115
block naming policy, 115
Blocks Extensible Exchange Protocol (BEEP), 162
BMP (see bean-managed persistence)
books about Oracle Application Server, 234
BPI (Business Process Integration), 226
BPO (Business Process Optimization), 220
browsers, 3
  OracleAS Discoverer Viewer, 181
  (see also web browsers)
bursting reports, 140, 178
Business Activity Monitoring (BAM), 220
Business Components for Java, Oracle Application Server, 126
business entities
  modeled by EJB entity beans, 75
  registration in UDDI, 57
Business Intelligence and Forms installation, 25
business intelligence components, 36, 174–190
  data mining, 187
  listing of, 175
  managing, 189
  partnerships among tool vendors, 184
  reporting, 176–179
    query and analysis, 179–184
  resource reference for, 239
business intelligence, database schemas for, 185
Business Intelligence JavaBeans (BI Beans), 175, 185
business logic
  enabled through JavaBeans and Enterprise JavaBeans (EJBs), 6
  modeled by EJB session beans, 75
business objects, 221
Business Objects, query and analysis tool, 184
Business Process Integration (BPI), 226

Business Process Optimization (BPO), 220
business process-centric methodology (OracleAS ProcessConnect), 228
  deployment sequence, 232
business processes
  integration of, OracleAS ProcessConnect, 14
  modeling of, Oracle Workflow, 13
  models of, 225
  triggered by events, 230
business rules and data layer, web applications, 121–123
business-to-business (B2B) collaboration, 219

C

C/C++
  mod_fastcgi module and, 68
  OracleAS support for web-based applications in, 145
  XML class generator for C++, 150
cache cluster, 96
cache hierarchies, 97
cache key policy (caching rules), 103
cache key (Reports Cache), 139
CacheAccess class, 109
  put( ) method, 112
cache.conf file (mod_plsql), 69
CacheEventListener interface, 112
CacheLoader class, 109
  custom, creating, 112
caching, 89–117
  cacheability rules, indicating compression in, 105
  cacheability/invalidation rules, 102
  cubic cache, OracleAS Discoverer, 183
  of data sources, support by OC4J, 80
  Java Object Cache, 84, 89, 108–113
    basic principles, 108
    how it works, 109
    initialization, 112
    invalidating cached objects, 113
    management of, 113
  OracleAS Portal pages, 206
  Reports Cache, 137, 139
    clustered Reports Servers, 141
  resource reference, 237
  Web Object Cache, 89, 113–117
    basic principles, 114
    invalidating cached objects, 116
    organization, 115
    repository management, 116

D

D3L (Data Definition Description
    Language), 223
DADs (database access descriptors), 69
dads.conf file (mod_plsql), 69
data access technologies, OracleAS 10g, 6
data and business rules layer (web
    applications), 121–123
data component portlets, 200
Data Definition Description Language
    (D3L), 223
Data Definition Language (DDL), 122, 155
Data Feeder (OracleAS Wireless), 217
Data Form wizard (Oracle JDeveloper), 10
Data Manipulation Language (DML), 122
data mining, 174, 187
    developing applications with JDeveloper
        and DM4J, 175
    OracleAS Personalization, 188
data protection, 55
data sources
    OC4J, types of, 79
    Oracle Reports, 176
data warehouses
    Oracle Warehouse Builder Common
        Warehouse Metamodel, 184
    Oracle Warehouse Builder (OWB), 175
    OWB and, 185–187
database access descriptors (DADs), 69
database availability concepts, 33
Database Providers (OracleAS Portal), 199
database repositories, 21
database stored procedures
    as RPCs, 159
databases
    management tools, Oracle Enterprise
        Manager, 14
    Oracle
        advanced query optimization, 174
        XML functionality, 149
    RAC (Real Application Clusters) as, 34
Data-Direct (type 4) JDBC drivers, 79
DataSource object (JDBC), 79
data-sources.xml file, 79
datatypes, common, 222
DBAccessBean, 151
DCM (Distributed Configuration
    Management), 20, 23, 41
    backups of, 49
DDL (Data Definition Language), 155
Delegated Administration Services,
    Oracle, 21, 58

delegation model (for privileges), 63
deleting from a database using an XML
    document, 154
demilitarized zones (see DMZs)
deployment
    applications, 85–86
        J2EE deployment, 85
        OC4J deployment, 86
        OC4J development, 86
    common OracleAS Web Cache
        topologies, 94
    secure, Oracle Application Server, 61–63
        delegation of privileges, 63
        DMZ deployment, 61
        Oracle Enterprise Manager, 63
deployment descriptors
    application.xml file, 85
    ejb-jar.xml files, 85
    EJBs, 76
    J2EE, OC4J counterparts, 86
    servlet (web.xml files), 85
Deployment wizard (Oracle JDeveloper), 10
destinations for reports, 178
development
    Java, 118–128
        development tools, 124–127
        Oracle Application Server APIs and tag
            libraries, 127
        resource reference, 238
        web applications, 119–124
    OC4J, using as development
        environment, 86
    Oracle
        Forms Services, 131–135
        Reports Services, 135–142
        resource reference for, 238
    OracleAS Wireless, 212–214
        tools for, 212–214
    XML, 143–158
        Oracle XML parsers, 150
        resource reference, 238
        XML Transviewer Beans, 151
        XSU (XML SQL Utility), 151–155
diagnostics pack for Oracle Application
    Server, 48
directives, Apache Web Server, 67
Directory Provisioning Integration Service,
    Oracle, 21, 58
directory services (see Oracle Internet
    Directory)
Discoverer (see OracleAS Discoverer)

high availability for application
servers, 31–35
infrastructure failover, 32–35
provided by OracleAS Web Cache, 91
HTML
browser client based on (Discoverer
Viewer), 12
in JavaServer Pages, 74
Oracle Enterprise Manager, 14
produced by servlets to provide web
content, 74
transforming to XHTML with
PDKIS, 157
use with PL/SQL programs, 131
web applications, presentation layer, 120
HTML <form> tag, hardcoding servlet URL
in, 123
HTML pages
caching static pages, 98
dynamic, caching, 99
HTTP
caching of web content transmitted
over, 89
replicating HTTP session objects, 26
use by Web Services, 159, 162
(see also Oracle HTTP Server)
HTTP validators, 102
HTTPRequest object (Java servlets), 84
HTTPS for Client Connections (Oracle
HTTPS), 82
HTTPS, support by OracleAS Web
Cache, 91
HttpServletRequest object, 114
Hypertext Markup Language (see HTML)

I

identity management, 55
IDEs (Integrated Development
Environments)
Oracle JDeveloper, 124
OracleAS InterConnect, 13
third-party support for Oracle Application
Server, 127
IIS (Internet Information Server),
Microsoft, 70
implicit block names, 115
implicit invalidation (cached objects), 113
include fragments, 100
incremental backups, 49
infrastructure, Oracle Application
Server, 20–24
backups of, 48

failover solutions, 32–35
Identity Management, 21
Metadata Repository, 21
inline fragments, 100
InputStream class, 111
inquiry Web Service (UDDI), 170
INSERT statement (SQL), 154
inserting data into database with XML
document, 154
installation, Oracle Universal Installer, 59
installation types, Oracle Application
Server, 24
Integrated Development Environments (see
IDEs)
integration components, Oracle Application
Server, 219–232
OracleAS InterConnect, 220–224
OracleAS ProcessConnect, 226
OW4J (Oracle Workflow for Java, 224
resource reference for, 240
Integration Manager (IM) (OracleAS
ProcessConnect), 229
InterConnect (see OracleAS InterConnect)
interfaces
programming interfaces, Web Object
Cache, 114
(see also APIs; GUIs)
"Internet database" (Oracle8i), 4
Internet Directory (see Oracle Internet
Directory)
Internet, three-tier architecture, 3
interprocess communication (IPC), use by
OracleAS Web Cache, 93
intrusion detection, 55
Oracle HTTP Server, logging of
authentication attempts, 56
invalidating cached objects, 101
invalidation messages, 103
Java Object Cache, 113
performance and, 104
rules for, 102
Web Object Cache, 116
islands, 26, 87
iStudio, 220
components created in, 221
defining domain value maps, 223
menus, 224
navigation trees, 223
items (OracleAS Portal pages), 194
end user manipulation of, 203
types and attributes, 197

About the Authors

Rick Greenwald has been active in the world of computer software for nearly two decades, including stints with Data General, Cognos, and Gupta. He is currently an analyst with Oracle Corporation. He has published a dozen books and countless articles on a variety of technical topics, and has spoken at conferences and training sessions across six continents. In addition to *Oracle Application Server 10g Essentials*, Rick's books include *Oracle Essentials: Oracle Database 10g* (principal author with Robert Stackowiak and Jonathan Stern, O'Reilly), *Oracle in a Nutshell* (principal author with David C. Kreines, O'Reilly); *Oracle9iAS Portal Bible* (principal author with Jim Milbery, John Wiley & Sons); and *Administering Exchange Server* (principal author with Walter Glenn, Microsoft Press).

Robert Stackowiak is Senior Director of Business Intelligence in Oracle Corporation's Technology Business Unit. He works with Oracle's largest customers in North America, providing insight into the company's products and data warehousing strategy. In addition, he frequently assists Oracle Corporate in developing product strategy and training. Prior to joining Oracle in 1996, Robert was the Decision Support Segment Manager in IBM's RISC System/6000 Division. There, he met with IBM's largest customers throughout North America who were implementing RS/6000s and the IBM RS/6000 SP. He also previously worked as a Senior Field Analyst at Harris Computer Systems and as Chief of Programming at the St. Paul District of the U.S. Army Corps of Engineers. In addition to *Oracle Application Server 10g Essentials,* Robert is the coauthor of *Oracle Essentials: Oracle Database 10g*. Articles written by Robert have appeared in publications including *The Journal of Data Warehousing, Database Trends and Applications, Informix Tech Notes*, and *AIXcellence Magazine*.

Donald Bales is a computer applications consultant specializing in the analysis, design, and programming of distributed systems, systems integration, and data warehousing. Donald has more than 18 years of experience with Oracle as both a developer and a database administrator and more than 8 years of experience with Java. He is currently working on the migration and internationalization of medical and industrial hygiene systems to a web environment for a major energy company. In addition to *Oracle Application Server 10g Essentials*, Donald's books include *Java Programming with Oracle JDBC* (O'Reilly) and *JDBC Pocket Reference* (O'Reilly).

Colophon

Our look is the result of reader comments, our own experimentation, and feedback from distribution channels. Distinctive covers complement our distinctive approach to technical topics, breathing personality and life into potentially dry subjects.

The animal on the cover of *Oracle Application Server 10g Essentials* is a praying mantis. These large, predatory insects are widely scattered throughout the world;

some of the approximately 1,500 species are endangered. They have highly special-ized prehensile legs, with elongated front segments that allow them greater reach. Their long neck-like thorax enables them to swivel their heads completely to the rear, making them the only insects who can look directly behind themselves.

The word "mantid" is Greek for "prophet" or "seer." The insects were so named because the position in which they hold their legs while at rest or preparing to attack their prey gives them the appearance of folding their arms in prayer. In African art, the praying mantis is often depicted as a god or spirit.

Mantises lie in wait and then quickly pounce on their prey, giving them no time to flee. It is not uncommon for a mantis to hold onto its prey with one leg while going after another with the second. They eat almost anything—insects, small reptiles, small birds, and other mantids. Females often eat their mates during copulation; once the process has begun, she bites off his head. The male's copulatory activity isn't curtailed by this, and in some species is stimulated, because it's controlled by a ganglion center completely distinct from that controlling the head. By eating her mate, the female ingests extra protein to nourish her eggs.

A praying mantis will lay 1,000 to 2,000 eggs, protected in foamy, papery capsules that hold 100 to 200 eggs each. The eggs are laid in the fall and hatch in the spring. Young mantises immediately begin hunting and disperse themselves over a wide area, presumably to avoid fratricide.

Mary Anne Weeks Mayo was the production editor and proofreader, and Audrey Doyle was the copyeditor for *Oracle Application Server 10g Essentials*. Matt Hutch-inson and Claire Cloutier provided quality control. Mary Agner provided production assistance. Ellen Troutman Zaig wrote the index.

Ellie Volckhausen designed the cover of this book, based on a series design by Edie Freedman. The cover image is a 19th-century engraving from the Dover Pictorial Archive. Emma Colby produced the cover layout with QuarkXPress 6.1 using Adobe's ITC Garamond font.

Melanie Wang designed the interior layout, based on a series design by David Futato. This book was converted by Julie Hawks to FrameMaker 5.5.6 with a format conversion tool created by Erik Ray, Jason McIntosh, Neil Walls, and Mike Sierra that uses Perl and XML technologies. The text font is Linotype Birka; the heading font is Adobe Myriad Condensed; and the code font is LucasFont's TheSans Mono Condensed. The illustrations that appear in the book were produced by Robert Romano and Jessamyn Read using Macromedia FreeHand 9 and Adobe Photoshop 6. The tip and warning icons were drawn by Christopher Bing. This colophon was written by Clairemarie Fisher O'Leary.

Related Titles Available from O'Reilly

Oracle PL/SQL

Learning Oracle PL/SQL

Oracle PL/SQL Best Practices

Oracle PL/SQL Developer's Workbook

Oracle PL/SQL Language Pocket Reference, *3rd Edition*

Oracle PL/SQL Programming, *3nd Edition*

Oracle Books for DBAs

Oracle DBA Checklists Pocket Reference

Oracle RMAN Pocket Reference

Unix for Oracle DBAs Pocket Reference

Oracle SQL and SQL Plus

Mastering Oracle SQL

Oracle SQL Plus: The Definitive Guide

Oracle SQL Tuning Pocket Reference

Oracle SQL*Plus Pocket Reference, *2nd Edition*

Oracle SQL: The Essential Reference

Oracle

Building Oracle XML Applications

Java Programming with Oracle JDBC

Oracle Essentials: Oracle Database 10g, *3rd Edition*

Oracle in a Nutshell

Perl for Oracle DBAs

TOAD Pocket Reference

O'REILLY®

Our books are available at most retail and online bookstores.
To order direct: 1-800-998-9938 • *order@oreilly.com* • *www.oreilly.com*
Online editions of most O'Reilly titles are available by subscription at *safari.oreilly.com*

Keep in touch with O'Reilly

1. Download examples from our books

To find example files for a book, go to:

www.oreilly.com/catalog

select the book, and follow the "Examples" link.

2. Register your O'Reilly books

Register your book at *register.oreilly.com*

Why register your books?
Once you've registered your O'Reilly books you can:

- Win O'Reilly books, T-shirts or discount coupons in our monthly drawing.
- Get special offers available only to registered O'Reilly customers.
- Get catalogs announcing new books (US and UK only).
- Get email notification of new editions of the O'Reilly books you own.

3. Join our email lists

Sign up to get topic-specific email announcements of new books and conferences, special offers, and O'Reilly Network technology newsletters at:

elists.oreilly.com

It's easy to customize your free elists subscription so you'll get exactly the O'Reilly news you want.

4. Get the latest news, tips, and tools

www.oreilly.com

- "Top 100 Sites on the Web"—PC Magazine
- CIO Magazine's Web Business 50 Awards

Our web site contains a library of comprehensive product information (including book excerpts and tables of contents), downloadable software, background articles, interviews with technology leaders, links to relevant sites, book cover art, and more.

5. Work for O'Reilly

Check out our web site for current employment opportunities:

jobs.oreilly.com

6. Contact us

O'Reilly & Associates
1005 Gravenstein Hwy North
Sebastopol, CA 95472 USA

TEL: 707-827-7000 or 800-998-9938
(6am to 5pm PST)

FAX: 707-829-0104

order@oreilly.com
For answers to problems regarding your order or our products. To place a book order online, visit:

www.oreilly.com/order_new

catalog@oreilly.com
To request a copy of our latest catalog.

booktech@oreilly.com
For book content technical questions or corrections.

corporate@oreilly.com
For educational, library, government, and corporate sales.

proposals@oreilly.com
To submit new book proposals to our editors and product managers.

international@oreilly.com
For information about our international distributors or translation queries. For a list of our distributors outside of North America check out:

international.oreilly.com/distributors.html

adoption@oreilly.com
For information about academic use of O'Reilly books, visit:

academic.oreilly.com

O'REILLY®

Our books are available at most retail and online bookstores.
To order direct: 1-800-998-9938 • *order@oreilly.com* • *www.oreilly.com*
Online editions of most O'Reilly titles are available by subscription at *safari.oreilly.com*